P9-COP-084

DOWNTOWN CORE
Pages 36–57
Street Finder maps 3 & 4

**SOUTH LOOP AND
NEAR SOUTH SIDE**
Pages 78–97
Street Finder maps 3–6

SOUTH SIDE
Pages 98–109
Street Finder maps 7 & 8

NORTH SIDE

DOWNTOWN
CORE

SOUTH
LOOP AND
NEAR
SOUTH SIDE

SOUTH SIDE

EYEWITNESS *Travel Guides*

CHICAGO

DK EYEWITNESS *TRAVEL GUIDES*

CHICAGO

Main contributors:
LORRAINE JOHNSON AND JOHN RYAN

DORLING KINDERSLEY, INC.
**LONDON • NEW YORK • SYDNEY • DELHI
PARIS • MUNICH • JOHANNESBURG**
www.dk.com

DORLING KINDERSLEY PUBLISHING, INC.

www.dk.com

Produced by International Book Productions,
Part of Denise Schon Books Inc.
Toronto, Canada

PROJECT EDITOR AND ART DIRECTOR Barbara Hopkinson
EDITOR Judy Phillips
DESIGNERS Dietmar Kokemohr, Stella Powelczyk
EDITORIAL AND MAP ASSISTANCE Terri Rothman
PICTURE RESEARCH
Karen Taylor Permissions and Photo Research

MAIN CONTRIBUTORS
Lorraine Johnson, John Ryan

PHOTOGRAPHER
Andrew Leyerle

ILLUSTRATOR
William Band

Reproduced by Colourscan, Singapore
Printed and bound by L. Rex Printing Company Limited, China

First American edition, 2001
2 4 6 8 10 9 7 5 3 1

Published in the United States by
Dorling Kindersley, Inc.,
95 Madison Avenue, New York, NY 10016

Copyright 2001 © Dorling Kindersley Limited, London

Library of Congress Cataloging-in-Publication Data
Chicago.
　p. cm. -- (DK eyewitness travel guides)
Includes index.
ISBN 0-7894-7080-2 (alk. paper)
　1. Chicago (Ill.)--Guidebooks. I. Eyewitness travel
guides.

F548.18. C395 2001
917.73'110444--dc21

00-053106

Nuclear Energy by Henry Moore at
University of Chicago *(see p100)*

CONTENTS

HOW TO USE THIS GUIDE 6

Twisted Columns by Ricardo Bofill,
R.R. Donnelley Building *(see p55)*

The ornate lobby of the Palmer House Hilton *(see p134)*

Painted-glass window in St. James
Episcopal Cathedral *(see p67)*

Raptor perched on a tree branch
in Washington Park *(see p104)*

Street-by-street map of South Loop *(see pp80–81)*

How to Use this Guide

This Dorling Kindersley travel guide helps you get the most from your stay in Chicago. *Introducing Chicago* locates the city geographically, sets modern Chicago in its historical context, and describes events through the entire year. *Chicago at a Glance* highlights the city's top attractions. The main sightseeing section of the book is *Chicago Area by Area*. It describes the city sights, with photographs, maps, and drawings. It also offers suggestions for day trips outside the city center. *Beyond Chicago* delves into destinations in the region ideal either for day trips or longer sojourns, such as weekend getaways. Restaurant and hotel recommendations, as well as specially selected information about shops and entertainment, are found in *Travelers' Needs*. The *Survival Guide* gives practical information on everyday needs, from using Chicago's medical system and public transportation to the telephone system.

FINDING YOUR WAY AROUND THE SIGHTSEEING SECTION

Each of the sightseeing areas in Chicago is color-coded for easy reference. Each chapter opens with a description of the area and a list of sights to be covered, located by numbers on an area map. This is followed by a Street-by-Street map, illustrating an interesting part of the area. Finding your way around the chapter is made simple by the numbering system used throughout. Sights outside Chicago have a regional map.

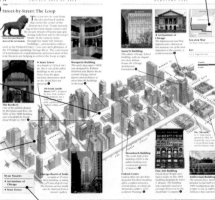

Each area has color-coded thumb tabs.

1 Area Map
For easy reference, the sights in each area are numbered and plotted on a map of the area. The map also shows CTA and Metra stations and major parking areas, as well as indicating the area covered by the Street-by-Street map. The sights are also shown on the Chicago Street Finder on pages 184–97.

Locator map

A locator map shows where you are in relation to other areas in the city center.

A suggested route takes in some of the most interesting streets in the area.

2 Street-by-Street Map
This gives a bird's-eye view of the most important part of each sightseeing area. The numbering of the sights ties in with the area map and the fuller descriptions on the pages that follow.

The list of star sights recommends the places that no visitor should miss.

CHICAGO AREA MAP

The colored areas shown on this map *(see inside front cover)* are the four main sightseeing areas – each covered by a full chapter in *Chicago Area by Area (see pp34–109)*. The four areas are highlighted on other maps throughout the book. In *Chicago at a Glance (see pp18–29)*, for example, they help locate the top sights.

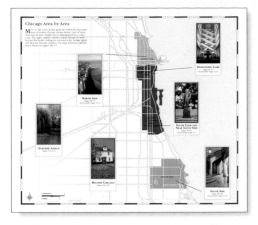

Numbers refer to each sight's position on the area map and its place in the chapter.

Practical information provides all you need to know to visit each sight, including a map reference to the *Chicago Street Finder (see pp184–97)*.

3 Detailed information
All the important sights in Chicago are described individually. They are listed in order, following the numbering on the area map. Practical information such as address, telephone number, and opening hours is provided for each sight. The key to the symbols used is on the back flap.

The visitors' checklist provides all the practical information needed to plan your visit.

Façades of important buildings are often shown to illustrate their architectural style, and to help you recognize them quickly.

4 Chicago's major sights
These are given two or more full pages in the sightseeing area where they are found. Museums and galleries have color-coded floor plans to help you find important exhibits.

Stars indicate the features no visitor should miss.

INTRODUCING CHICAGO

Putting Chicago on the Map

CHICAGO, A CITY of almost 3 million people, covers 228 sq miles (591 sq km) of the US's Midwest. Situated at the southwest edge of Lake Michigan, the world's fifth-largest freshwater body, Chicago claims 29 miles (47 km) of lakefront. Two airports handle international and internal flights. There are also interstate highways and rail links serving both the East and West Coasts and other parts of the country, and Canada.

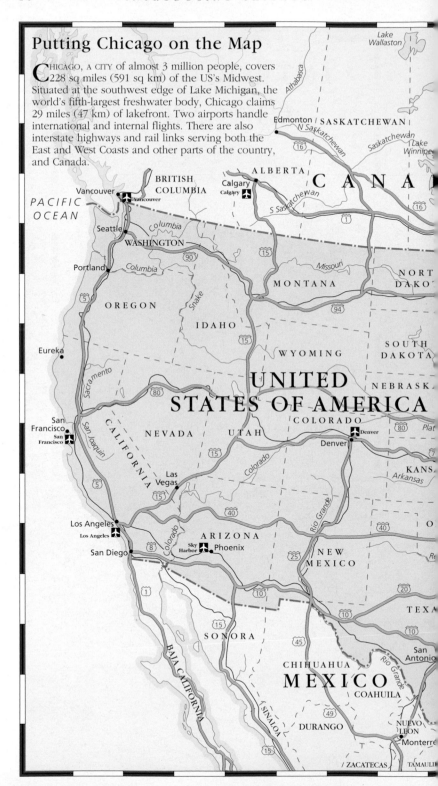

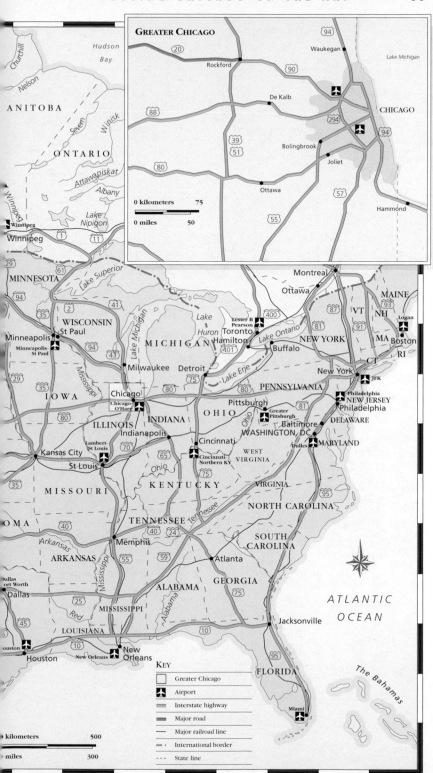

THE HISTORY OF CHICAGO

HE THIRD LARGEST CITY in the US is world famous for magnificent and innovative architecture, its colorful and turbulent political history and significance as a national transportation hub, the now-vanished stockyards, as well as its educational institutes and vibrant cultural venues.

The French missionary Jacques Marquette and French-Canadian explorer Louis Jolliet were the first Europeans to record a visit to this spot at the foot of Lake Michigan, in 1673. The peaceful, friendly local Potawatomi Indians called the low-lying swampy area "Checaugou," which likely means "wild onion" or "skunk cabbage." Jolliet and Marquette used this Indian name on the maps they drew, which were then used by later explorers.

French-Canadian explorer Louis Jolliet

More than 100 years passed before the first permanent settlement was established in 1779 by Jean Baptiste Point du Sable, an African-American trader from the Caribbean. Du Sable and his Indian wife built a house on the north bank near the mouth of the Chicago River.

A treaty negotiated with local Indian tribes in 1795 gave US citizens access to most of Ohio and a 6-sq-mile (15.5-sq-km) area of land where the Chicago River emptied into Lake Michigan – now the heart of Chicago's downtown.

In 1803, the US Army built Fort Dearborn along the river to protect settlers from the Indians, the British, and the French. Fort Dearborn was destroyed during the War of 1812 between the US and Britain; soldiers and their families were slaughtered by the Indians, allies of the British, as they fled the fort. Although the fort was rebuilt in 1816 and Illinois became a state in 1818, the area remained Indian territory until it was ceded in 1933 and the Natives relocated to reservations by the federal government. That same year, Chicago became a village.

EARLY CHICAGO

With the land open for development, the rivers gained importance as shipping routes. In 1837, Chicago, its population now over 4,000, received city status. The expansion of the lake ports, completion of the Illinois and Michigan Canal connecting the Great Lakes with the Mississippi River, and arrival of the railroads spurred rapid growth. Public schools were established in 1840, and by 1847 the new city had two daily newspapers. From 1855 to 1858, Chicago literally pulled itself out of the mud, jacking up its downtown buildings and filling in the swamp muck with soil *(see p57)*.

TIMELINE

1650	1700	1750	1800	1850
1673 Explorers Jacques Marquette and Louis Jolliet arrive at "Checaugou"	**1779** First settlement in Chicago established by trader Jean Baptiste Point du Sable		**1803** Fort Dearborn built	**1848** Illinois & Michigan Canal completed *(see pp118–19)*
1682 Frenchman La Salle explores area and establishes forts		*Jean Baptiste Point du Sable*	**1825** Erie Canal opens	**1858** Chicago becomes US's chief railroad hub
		1783 British cede land that is now Chicago to the newly established US government	**1837** Chicago incorporates as a city	**1847** *Chicago Tribune* newspaper founded

A Potawatomi chief

◁ **A contemporary lithograph depicting the Great Chicago Fire of 1871**

Chicago's proximity to both the Mississippi River and the Great Lakes confirmed it as the nation's transportation hub. By 1860, 15 railroad companies had terminals here. Christmas Day 1865 saw the opening of the gigantic Union Stock Yards, the city's largest employer for decades. (It eventually closed in 1971.) Meatpacking laws, along with the Food and Drug Administration, were created after Upton Sinclair's stirring 1906 book, *The Jungle,* revealed the poor conditions of such stockyards.

Detail of cow (1879) on the archway to Union Stock Yards

Although meat processing remained Chicago's major industry, positioning the city as the US's primary supplier, the grain-handling and manufacturing industries were also strong in 19th-century Chicago.

THE GREAT FIRE

The Great Chicago Fire of 1871 burned for 36 hours, October 8 to 10, destroying most of the buildings in downtown Chicago, all of which were made of wood. At least 300 people died, and about 100,000 – one-third of the population – were left homeless. A cow, belonging to a certain Mrs. O'Leary, was blamed for kicking over a lantern and starting the fire. Although an inquiry confirmed that the blaze started in the O'Leary shed, the cause of the fire was not determined.

An 1874 bylaw prohibited the building of wooden structures downtown. Consequently, Chicago architect William Le Baron Jenney *(see pp24–5)* designed the Home Insurance Building (1884), a nine-story structure supported by a steel skeleton, regarded by many to be the first skyscraper. Jenney's design paved the way for the canyons of tall buildings found in city centers today.

SOCIAL UNREST, SOCIAL REFORM

As Chicago's downtown rebuilt and the city continued to expand – to 500,000 inhabitants by 1880 – social divisions grew. In the 1873 Bread Riot, police trapped thousands of protesting hungry workers under a bridge, clubbing many to death. Four years later, during the 1877 national railroad strike, Chicago police fired on demonstrators, killing 30. On May 4, 1886, workers rallied at Haymarket Square to protest the police killing of two laborers demanding the shortening of the workday to eight hours. A bomb exploded in the midst of the police officers, starting a riot that

The aftermath of the Great Fire, as seen from Chicago Harbor

Protesters clash with police in the 1873 Bread Riot

Christopher Columbus' journey to the Americas with the 1893 World's Columbian Exposition, held in Jackson Park *(see p105)*. Over 25 million visitors came to it, the largest fair yet to be held in the Americas. Despite a deep national economic depression, the city built a fabulous fairground, dubbed the "White City" because of its Neo-Classical white marble buildings. It was to have a huge impact on US architecture. Most of the buildings burned down or were vandalized after the fair.

eventually killed seven officers. The ensuing trial, in which eight men were charged with murder and four subsequently executed, is considered one of the worst miscarriages of justice in the US.

Into this social tumult stepped Jane Addams *(see p29)* and Ellen Gates Starr. In 1889, they founded Hull-House to help settle immigrants *(see p116)*. It would soon become a leader in US social welfare and reform.

PROGRESS, AND THE 1893 WORLD'S COLUMBIAN EXPOSITION

Downtown, other initiatives were underway. The Art Institute of Chicago *(see pp46–9)* was founded in 1879, the Chicago Symphony Orchestra *(see p162)* in 1889, and the University of Chicago *(see pp100–101)* in 1891. The elevated tramway opened in 1892, its circle around the commercial core giving the downtown the nickname "The Loop."

Chicago celebrated the 400th anniversary of

Guidebook for the 1893 World's Columbian Fair

GROWTH AND GROWING PAINS

By 1890, Chicago's population climbed past one million. Awareness of public health issues led to concern that the city discharged, directly or indirectly, most of its waste into the Chicago River, and from there into Lake Michigan, the source of drinking water. In 1900, the Chicago Sanitary and Ship Canal opened, the direction of the Chicago River reversed so that the river flowed away from the lake rather than into it *(see p57)*.

A 1903 Chicago disaster affected both urban design and bylaws nationwide. More than 600 people died when a fire tragically destroyed the Iroquois Theater on December 30 *(see p51)*. Investigators blamed the fatalities on the doors. Many opened inward: impossible to open with a frantic crowd pressed against them. Most US cities now require that doors of public buildings open outward.

By 1914, waves of immigrants from Europe

Speakeasy directions written in chalk

had arrived in Chicago. Industrialization now brought another wave: African Americans from the South, seeking work after being displaced from farm work by the cotton gin and other new machinery. Chicago's Black population skyrocketed, from about 14,000 in 1910 to almost 110,000 by the early 1920s. Previous arrivals did not always welcome the new migrants. A 1919 race riot that started at a segregated South Side beach raged for several days, leaving 38 dead and at least 500 injured.

Speakeasies, illicit social clubs offering liquor despite the prohibition of alcohol, flourished in the 1920s and made way for the bootlegging gangster. The most famous gangster – and the one most closely linked to Chicago in the public mind – was Al Capone, who arrived in 1920 from New York. Capone is legendary for his bloody gang war. In the notorious 1929 St. Valentine's Day Massacre, seven mobsters from a rival gang were killed execution-style by mobsters loyal to Capone.

Almost as famous were Elliot Ness and his FBI team, who collected the evidence of income-tax evasion that put Capone in prison in 1931, where he died 16 years later.

Chicago Milestones: 1920s–60s

The Chicago Municipal Airport (now Midway Airport) opened in 1927. From 1945 to 1958, it was the world's busiest airport, before being replaced by O'Hare, which was equipped to handle the new jetliners and is today one of the world's busiest airports.

The old airport brought visitors to the 1933–4 World's Fair. Showcasing innovative uses of electricity, the fair attracted 39 million people. Another kind of energy came to the fore when, in 1942, physicist Enrico Fermi from the University of Chicago conducted the world's first controlled atomic reaction (*see p100*).

After World War II, the city's economy boomed, its population peaking at 3.6 million. New arrivals included musicians from the Mississippi Delta and by 1950, they were recording a new form of blues.

Physicist Enrico Fermi

The 1950s saw many milestones: Carl Sandburg won the Pulitzer Prize for Poetry in 1951; and Ray Kroc's first McDonald's opened in 1955 in Des Plaines, just outside Chicago.

Chicago's O'Hare Airport, one of the world's busiest

TIMELINE

1920	1930	1940	1950	1960
1928 Chicago River straightened to allow for expansion of downtown	**1933** Chicago hosts Century of Progress World's Fair	**1942** First controlled atomic chain reaction, at University of Chicago	**1953** Hugh Hefner publishes first issue of *Playboy* magazine	Lut brings m
1920 Mobster Al Capone arrives	**1929** St. Valentine's Day Massacre	**1931** Elliot Ness succeeds in convicting Al Capone	**1943** Chicago's first subway opens	**1955** Richard J. Daley elected mayor **1959** White Sox win American League baseball pennant

Elliot Ness

Richard J. Daley, mayor of Chicago for 21 years

TURBULENT POLITICS

In 1955, Chicago elected Democrat Richard J. Daley as mayor, a position he held until his fatal heart attack in 1976. In 1966, Martin Luther King Jr. brought the civil rights movement to Chicago, challenging Daley's Whites-only political machine and the segregation of the Black population. Daley's administration survived the West Side riots, prompted by the assassination of King in Memphis, and the disastrous confrontations between police and demonstrators outside the Democratic National Convention, both in 1968. Daley was equally well known for his commitment to a clean city, in keeping with his motto "Keep Chicago beautiful."

Daley's successors include Jane Byrne, Chicago's first female mayor (1979–83), and Harold Washington, Chicago's first Black mayor (1983–7), called "the people's mayor" because he was considered to be in touch with the grassroots. Washington made significant structural changes in city operations before dying of a heart attack at his desk, shortly after his re-election as mayor in 1987.

In 1989, Chicagoans elected Richard M. Daley, son of former mayor Richard J. Daley, as mayor.

CHICAGO TODAY

In 1990, Chicago's title of "Second City" became an honorific, as the population of Los Angeles surpassed that of Chicago and became the largest in the US after New York. But Chicagoans continue to glory in the city's triumphs. It remains the US's largest transportation center and the financial capital of the Midwest. Chicago Board of Trade, founded in 1848, continues to be the most important grain market in the nation. Sears Tower *(see p40)* recaptured the title of World's Tallest Building in two of four categories in 1997. The Chicago Bulls won six NBA championships. The 1999 Cows on Parade, a public-art project of 300 fiberglass cows decorated by Chicago artists, delighted locals and visitors alike.

Chicago has had its share of recent disasters. In 1992, the Chicago River poured into a hole pierced in an abandoned tunnel in the Loop. Water filled downtown basements, threatening to sink the city center below the level of the original swampland.

As a mature city, Chicago offers superb public art and architecture, and natural, cultural, and gastronomical delights. The city's dynamism is sure to linger in the memories of its visitors for decades to come.

One of the herd in the wildly popular Cows on Parade project

	1971 Union Stock Yards close		1979 Jane Byrne elected mayor of Chicago	1983 Harold Washington elected mayor of Chicago	1990 Chicago drops in ranking to third-largest US city	2001 Millennium Park opens *(see p53)*
1970			1980		1990	2000

tin Jr. nts to go

1973 Sears Tower *(see p40)* opens as tallest building in world

Sears Tower

emocratic National tion riots

1986 Refurbished Chicago Theatre reopens *(see p54)*

1992 Chicago River leaks into abandoned freight tunnel, threatening to collapse downtown

CHICAGO AT A GLANCE

MORE THAN 100 places of interest are described in the *Area by Area* and *Beyond Chicago* sections of this book. They range from the Gothic-style Rockefeller Memorial Chapel *(see p102)* to the Post-Modern James R. Thompson Center *(see p56)*, from the offbeat neighborhood of Wicker Park *(see p114)* to tranquil Washington Park *(see p104)*. To help make the most of your stay, the following ten pages are a time-saving guide to the best Chicago has to offer. The guide highlights the city's best museums and architecture, as well as the people and cultures that have given Chicago its unique character over the years. Below are the top ten tourist attractions that no visitor to Chicago should miss.

CHICAGO'S TOP TEN   TOURIST ATTRACTIONS

Museum of Science and Industry
See pp106–109

John G. Shedd Aquarium
See pp96–7

Magnificent Mile
See pp60–61

Sears Tower
See p40

Navy Pier
See p65

Art Institute of Chicago
See pp46–9

Oak Park
See pp114–15

Lincoln Park Zoo
See pp112–13

Adler Planetarium and Astronomy Museum
See pp92–3

Field Museum
See pp86–9

◁ **View of Chicago's River North district from Franklin Bridge**

Chicago's Best: Museums

C HICAGO HAS some of the world's finest museums, and the buildings in which they are housed are often works of art themselves. The Art Institute of Chicago, world-renowned for its Impressionist and Post-Impressionist paintings, and Museum Campus – consisting of the Field Museum, Adler Planetarium, and Shedd Aquarium – are prominent on any visitor's itinerary. There are many smaller museums, too, celebrating Chicago's heritage and giving insight into the people and events that have left their mark on the city.

Chicago Historical Society
This museum traces Chicago's rich history, beginning with its first explorers and settlers, through the development of the city, to major events in modern-day Chicago (see p74).

North Side

Downtown Core

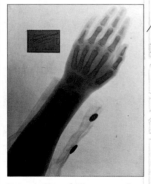

International Museum of Surgical Science
The history of medicine and surgery, from blood-letting to X-rays, is brought to life at this fascinating museum (see p75).

Museum of Broadcast Communication
Visitors role-play as news anchorpeople at this unique museum showcasing radio and TV (see p53).

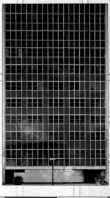

Spertus Museum
An outstanding collection of art and artifacts reflecting 5,000 years of Jewish culture and ritual is exhibited in this museum's thematic displays (see p84).

| 0 kilometers | 2 |
| 0 miles | 1 |

Museum of Contemporary Art
Cutting-edge modern works by European and American artists such as sculptor Alexander Calder are featured in permanent and rotating exhibits (see p65).

Art Institute of Chicago
One of the largest holdings of Impressionist and Post-Impressionist paintings outside France can be found here (see pp46–9).

Field Museum
An encyclopedic collection of objects relating to the earth's natural and cultural history are explored in vivid displays at this museum (see pp86–9).

Adler Planetarium and Astronomy Museum
One of the world's foremost planetariums, the Adler has a webcam atop its dome – offering a superb view of Chicago – and over 2,000 astronomical artifacts (see pp92–3).

Smart Museum
The specialties within the wide-ranging collection of this compact museum are antiquities and Old Masters (see p103).

South Loop and Near South Side

Museum of Science and Industry
Many of the technological inventions and scientific discoveries that have changed our world are on display at this very popular museum, a leader in interactive exhibits (see pp106–9).

South Side

Chicago's Best: Architecture

CHICAGO'S DOWNTOWN SKYLINE is characterized by high-rises, both modern and historic, while a range of residential architecture styles, such as Queen Anne and Prairie, are found in the city's neighborhoods. After the 1871 fire *(see p14)* and subsequent ban on wood as a building material, the use of terracotta and cast-iron – both fire resistant and durable – became prevalent. Terra-cotta was also an excellent material for decorative carving and so sheaths many of the city's steel-frame buildings. A detailed overview of Chicago's architecture is found on pages 24–5.

North St

Downtown Core

Crilly Court

The Crilly Court row houses (see p71), with their turrets and bays, are one of the finest examples of Queen Anne style in the city.

CRILLY COURT
PRIVATE

Newberry Library

Henry Ives Cobb, master of the Richardsonian Romanesque style, designed the library in 1890–93 (see p67). Its heavy stone walls and recessed, arched windows are typical of this style, popular in the second half of the 19th century.

333 Wacker Drive

A Post-Modern structure designed by the architect firm Kohn Pedersen Fox, this building (see pp56–7) was met with critical acclaim and local approval when constructed in 1983.

0 kilometers   2

0 miles   1

Harold Washington Library Center

This Post-Modern giant (see p82) alludes to Chicago's many historic buildings through its varied architectural features.

John Hancock Center
The towering glass walls and horizontal beams of the John Hancock Center (see p64) are characteristic of the International Style.

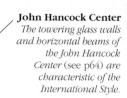

Gage Group
These three buildings reflect different approaches to the Chicago School: two, designed by Holabird and Roche, have minimal exterior decoration; the third, by Louis Sullivan, has a more ornate façade.

Water Tower
The Gothic Revival-style castellated tower is one of the city's best-loved landmarks (see p63).

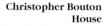

Field Museum
Designed in white marble by Daniel H. Burnham, this monumental Neo-Classical building (1921) features a long colonnaded façade with Greek-style caryatids (see pp86–9).

South Loop, and Near South Side

Christopher Bouton House
This villa-like residence, with its tall windows and dominant cornice, was built in 1873 in the Italianate style popular in 19th-century Chicago.

Robie House
Built 1906–1909, this house is considered by many to be Frank Lloyd Wright's Prairie School masterpiece (see pp102–103).

South Side

Exploring Chicago's Architecture

Carving on the Rookery

CHICAGO IS WORLD FAMOUS as a center of architectural innovation, a city where new building techniques have been developed and where architects have pushed the boundaries of creative expression. This reputation had its beginnings in the defining event of Chicago's history – the tragic fire of 1871. With a blank slate on which to build, architects rose to the challenge, transforming devastation into opportunity and reshaping the city. It was in Chicago that the world's first skyscraper was built, and here that Frank Lloyd Wright developed his distinctive Prairie School of architecture.

GOTHIC REVIVAL

POPULAR IN the 1830s and 1840s, Gothic Revival was inspired by the medieval architecture of Europe, particularly of England. Steeply pitched roofs, pointed arches, turrets, and buttresses are typical features. One of Chicago's best examples of this style is the **Water Tower** (1869). Interest in Gothic continued through the 19th century and is reflected in many of the city's most impressive buildings, such as the **Fourth Presbyterian Church** (1914) and those of the **University of Chicago**.

ITALIANATE STYLE

The elegant Drake Hotel, built in the popular Italianate style

POPULAR FROM the mid- to late 1800s, the Italianate design style is based on the historic architecture of Italy: the villas of northern Italy and the palaces of the Italian Renaissance. Characteristic features include asymmetrical balancing, low-pitched roofs, projecting eaves, and ornate door and window designs, the windows often grouped into arcades. Two notable examples are the **Samuel M. Nickerson House** (1883) and the **Drake Hotel** (1920).

RICHARDSONIAN ROMANESQUE

RICHARDSONIAN Romanesque, or Romanesque Revival, was popularized in the US in the latter half of the 19th century by Bostonian Henry Hobson Richardson (1838–86). His architectural legacy is represented in Chicago by the severe yet subtly ornamented **Glessner House** (1887). Typical features of this style are heavy rough-cut stone, round arches, and deeply recessed windows. Richardson's influence can be seen in the work of Henry Ives Cobb, particularly Cobb's design of **Newberry Library** (1890–93) and the former home of the Chicago Historical Society *(see p74)* at Dearborn and Ontario streets.

QUEEN ANNE

MAINLY USED in residential architecture, Queen Anne style was highly influential in Chicago from the mid- to late 1800s. The name does not reflect a historical period but was coined by English architect Richard Shaw. Queen Anne homes are built on a human scale. A mix of Classical, Tudor, and Colonial elements lead to a hybrid look. Victorian detailing, such as curlicue cutouts on the trim, is often prominent. **Crilly Court** (1885) and the **Olsen-Hansen Row Houses** (1886) are fine examples of Queen Anne style. There are also many Queen Anne houses to be found in the **Pullman Historic District**.

Crilly Court, the name of Crilly's son carved above the door

CHICAGO SCHOOL

NAMED AFTER the city in which it developed, the commercial style of the Chicago School led to both an engineering and aesthetic revolution in architecture. William Le Baron Jenney created the first skyscraper when he designed the nine-story Home Insurance Building (1884; demolished 1929), using skeletal steel

BALLOON FRAME

Balloon-frame construction was first developed in Chicago by Augustine D. Taylor, in 1833 (though some credit George Washington Snow's 1932 Chicago warehouse as the first such construction). The name refers to the ease of construction: it was as simple as inflating a balloon, although critics said it referred to the ease with which the wind would blow away such structures. Raising a balloon-frame house required simply joining machine-cut lumber with machine-made nails, rather than interlocking time-consuming joints. Various interior and exterior surfaces could then be applied. Chicago's early balloon-frame houses fed the flames of the 1871 fire, but some built after the fire still exist in Old Town *(see pp70–71)*.

frames rather than the conventional height-limiting, masonry load-bearing walls.

Jenney trained many of Chicago's celebrated architects, including Louis Sullivan, William Holabird, Daniel Burnham, and Martin Roche, whose architect firm designed several Chicago School buildings, such as the **Rookery** (1885–8) and the **Reliance Building** (1890–95). The new window style of these buildings, made possible by Jenney's structural innovation, became known as Chicago windows. Each consists of a large central glass pane, flanked by two slender windows that open.

Reliance Building, Chicago School

NEO-CLASSICAL OR BEAUX-ARTS

Neo-classical, or Beaux-Arts, style became popular in Chicago once it was chosen as the design style for the 1893 World's Fair. Based on classical Greek and Roman architecture, with its columns, pilasters, and pediments, these buildings are often monumental in scale. Many of Chicago's most notable cultural institutions, such as the **Chicago Cultural Center** (1893–7), are housed in Neo-Classical buildings.

PRAIRIE SCHOOL

In the first two decades of the 20th century, Frank Lloyd Wright developed a truly indigenous American architectural style. Reflecting the sweeping lines of the Midwestern landscape, Prairie style is characterized by low horizontal lines, projecting eaves, and rectangular windows. It is used mostly in residential architecture.

Oak Park is a treasure-trove of Wright-designed houses. Notable Wright buildings elsewhere in Chicago are **Robie House** (1906–1909) and **Charnley-Persky House** (1891–2).

Prairie School is considered a part of the Chicago School.

INTERNATIONAL STYLE

The international style developed primarily at Germany's Bauhaus School. Luminary Ludwig Mies van der Rohe immigrated to Chicago in 1938, after the Nazis closed the Bauhaus, and his ideas took root in the US. Simple, severe geometry and large expanses of glass are typical elements. One of the best places to see examples of Mies' "less is more" philosophy is at the **Illinois Institute of Technology** campus. Another landmark Mies' building is the austere but beautifully proportioned **IBM Building** (1971).

Chicago firm Skidmore, Owings and Merrill, architects of the **John Hancock Center** (1969) and **Sears Tower** (1974), is world famous for its International-style designs.

The Post-Modern Harold Washington Library Center *(see p82)*

POST-MODERN

Post-modern architecture developed in the 1970s primarily in response to – and as a rejection of – the formal ideals of the International style. It is an eclectic style without strict rules or unified credo, although playful references to architectural styles of the past are typical features of Post-Modern structures.

The building at **333 West Wacker Drive** (1983), designed by the firm Kohn Pedersen Fox, and the **James R. Thompson Center** (1985), designed by architect Helmut Jahn, are notable examples of Post-Modern design.

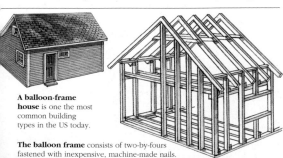

A balloon-frame house is one the most common building types in the US today.

The balloon frame consists of two-by-fours fastened with inexpensive, machine-made nails.

Multicultural Chicago

Chinatown street signs

CHICAGO PRIDES ITSELF on being one of the most ethnically diverse cities in the US. In the 1840s, the Irish, fleeing their country's potato famine, arrived in droves in the young city of Chicago. Since then, successive waves of immigrants from countries around the world have shaped the city's many neighborhoods. These varied ethnic communities continue to celebrate their cultures at various festivals that are held throughout the year *(see pp30–33)*.

Spanish sign welcoming visitors to Pilsen, once a Czech community

THE IRISH

Irish police officers joining the St. Patrick's Day celebrations

THE FIRST IRISH immigrants to Chicago worked as laborers, helping build the Illinois and Michigan Canal *(see p118)* in the mid-1800s. By 1870, the Irish represented over 13 percent of the city's population. Settled mostly in the South Side industrial town of Bridgeport, they soon became a powerful force in city politics. Over the years, there have been eight Irish mayors.

An Irish tradition not to be missed is a foaming glass of Guinness beer at one of the city's many Irish pubs.

THE WESTERN EUROPEANS

GERMANS WERE some of the earliest immigrants to Chicago. Settling primarily in the North Side neighborhood of Old Town, by the 1870s they were Chicago's largest ethnic group. Today, the core of Germantown is Old Town's Lincoln Square, teeming with delicatessens and dance halls.

Swedes established, also in the mid-1800s, a small community just north of the Chicago River. They later moved to Clark Street and Foster Avenue, an area now known as Andersonville. The community, with its many delicatessens and shops, retains its original character. Midsommarfest is celebrated here each June.

Prosperous Italians arrived in Chicago in the 1860s. By 1900, they were joined by poorer Italian farmers, many of whom settled between Van Buren and 12th Streets. Today, Taylor Street, between Madison and Halsted Streets, on Chicago's West Side, is the nucleus of Little Italy.

Greek immigration was spurred by the 1871 fire, when laborers came to help rebuild the city. By 1927, 10,000 shops, mainly selling fresh produce and flowers, were operated by Greeks. A short stretch of Greek restaurants is along South Halsted Street near Van Buren Street, on the West Side.

South Side neighborhoods such as Hyde Park and Kenwood *(see pp104–105)* were populated with wealthy German Jews. Over 125 Jewish congregations

Jim's Original, a local favorite since 1939 for Maxwell Street-style Polish sausage

worshiped in the city by the late 1920s, with the Jewish population and synagogues spread throughout the city, much like today.

THE EASTERN EUROPEANS

THE POLITICAL UNREST in Czechoslovakia in 1848 led to the first wave of Czech immigrants to the US, many settling in the Midwest. By the 1870s, Chicago had a Little Prague along DeKoven Street on the West Side. Over the next few decades, a thriving Czech community developed nearby, along Blue Island Avenue from 16th Street to Cermak Road (then known as 22nd Street). Named Pilsen, after the west Czechoslovakian city Plzeň, the neighborhood today is predominantly Hispanic. Remnants of the Czech community, however, can be seen in buildings such as Thalia Hall *(see p116)*.

The Polish community, the largest outside Warsaw, is the largest White ethnic group in Chicago after the Hispanics. Poles began arriving in large numbers in the 1870s. By the turn of the century, the Polish Downtown had been established at Division Street and Milwaukee Avenue.

Ukrainians arrived in Chicago during the early 1900s, settling Ukrainian Village, an area bounded by Division Street and Chicago, Damen, and Western Avenues, northwest of the Loop. Two interesting museums in the community celebrate Ukrainian culture.

The Lithuanian community, centered at Western Avenue and Marquette Road, southwest of Hyde Park, also has a strong presence in Chicago, as does the smaller Latvian community, west of Lakeview.

Eastern European Jews settled the West Side's Maxwell Street at Halsted Street from the 1880s until the 1910s. Community life focused around the Maxwell Street Market *(see p157)*, once the world's largest flea market.

THE AFRICAN AMERICANS

Jazz legend Nat "King" Cole, son of a Chicago Baptist minister

DESPITE CHICAGO'S first settler being mulatto *(see p13)*, racist laws significantly affected African-American settlement in the early 1800s. By 1850, Chicago was a destination for fugitive slaves from the South. In the 1890s, a thin strip of the South Side, bounded by Van Buren and 31st Streets, State Street and Lake Michigan, became known as the Black Belt, with about half of the city's Black population living here.

The early 1900s saw another wave of settlement in the Black Belt: the "Great Migration" of Blacks from the South looking for factory work. Over the next decade, a lively jazz and blues scene developed in the area.

In the 1940s and 1950s, the Chicago Housing Authority replaced South Side tenements with public-housing projects, which soon became notorious for crime. But by the 1960s and 1970s, Chicago

also had several middle-class Black communities, such as Park Manor, as well as racially integrated areas, such as Hyde Park. The Black Metropolis Historic District (35th Street and Indiana Avenue) was created in 1984 to commemorate the vibrant Black Belt community of the early 1900s. Today, African Americans represent approximately 40 percent of Chicago's population.

THE HISPANIC AMERICANS

THE FIRST FLOOD of Mexican immigrants was early in the 20th century, as laborers came to Chicago to help build the city's railroad. A second wave came after World War II, again as laborers. This time they were accompanied by Puerto Ricans. Cubans, fleeing from the 1959 revolution, joined Chicago's Hispanic community. Today, the Hispanic Americans – more than 20 percent of the city's population – continue to have an enormous impact on the cultural fabric of Chicago.

In the two southwest neighborhoods of Pilsen *(see p116)* and Little Village (south of Cermak Road between

Menu and graffiti on the wall of Mi Barrio Taqueria, in Pilsen

Western Avenue and Pulaski Road), the colorful streets are alive with Latin music, and inviting aromas waft from the numerous eateries.

THE ASIANS

IN 1870 THERE WERE but two Chinese immigrants in Chicago. By the turn of the century, a Chinese community was growing in the South Side vice district of Custom

Colorful Vietnamese and Chinese signs on bustling Argyle Street

House Levee. That Chinatown dissolved in the early 1900s once the vice lords left. Chinese immigrants, faced with anti-Chinese sentiment reflected in excessive rent increases, found themselves forced to the fringes of the district. They settled at 22nd (now Cermak Road) and Wentworth Streets, an area that is now the heart of Chicago's Chinese community *(see p94)*. There is also a new Chinatown on the North Side, marked by a pagoda at the Argyle CTA station entrance.

Chicago's Asian population swelled considerably in the 1980s with the arrival of Vietnamese, Cambodian, and Thai political refugees, as well as Filipino, Indian, Korean, and Japanese immigrants. Many settled in pockets on the North Side, where various Asian communities have developed, such as the Vietnamese neighborhood of Little Hanoi at Argyle Street and Broadway.

THE MELTING POT

OTHER CULTURES are represented in Chicago but are not as distinctly defined. Chicago's American Indian population of approximately 17,000, concentrated in Uptown, north of Lakeview, is the highest of any US city after San Francisco and Los Angeles. Chicagoans of Middle Eastern origin are scattered throughout the city.

Remarkable Residents

CHICAGO HAS ALWAYS BEEN a city at the forefront. It has nourished leaders in diverse fields, from music to industry, from architecture to sports. Some have been drawn to Chicago from other parts of the US and abroad; others were born and bred in Chicago and continue to call it home. All have left their mark on the city and, indeed, on the world. As the city where the skyscraper was developed, in the late 1800s, Chicago has long been a center for architectural innovation, with many of North America's influential architects based here for at least part of their careers. Having nurtured outstanding musicians since the 1910s, the city is also famous for its jazz and blues.

Blues legend Muddy Waters playing his electric guitar

Frank Lloyd Wright, one of the world's most influential architects

ARCHITECTS

CHICAGO architects have literally shaped the city. Daniel Burnham (1846–1912) was one of Chicago's most successful architects. His partnership with John Well-born Root (1850–91) led to buildings such as the Rookery (see p40), a stunning early skyscraper. His later partnership with Charles Atwood (1849–95) resulted in the groundbreaking Reliance Building (see p50).

Burnham was in charge of designing the 1893 World's Fair. However, it is for the 1909 Plan of Chicago he coauthored that he is best known. This document of civic planning became the vision for Chicago, proposing a series of riverfront public spaces and the widening of major roads to make the downtown easily accessible.

Louis Sullivan (1856–1924) has been called the first truly American architect. Celebrated for his organic style of ornamentation, as seen on the windows of Carson Pirie Scott (see p50), Sullivan declared that form follows function. Indeed, the detailing allowed the architect artistic license while drawing in passers-by.

Sullivan nurtured a young draftsman with whom he worked, Frank Lloyd Wright (1867–1959). Over the next 70 years, Wright played a significant role in modern architecture, fathering the Prairie School (see p25) and designing such masterpieces as Robie House (see pp102–103).

Ludwig Mies van der Rohe (1886–1969) moved to Chicago in 1937. The impact of his International style (see p25) was profound.

MUSICIANS

AN INNOVATOR of American music, Louis Armstrong (1901–1971) lived in Chicago from 1922 to 1929. Here he launched a revolution with his trumpet playing, popularizing the new art of jazz.

If Armstrong was the king of jazz, Benny Goodman (1909–1986) was the king of swing. His Russian parents settled in Chicago's West Side, where Goodman joined the Hull-House (see p116) youth band. Later, he led the US's first racially integrated band, inviting Black pianist Teddy Wilson to join his orchestra. Jelly Roll Morton (1890–1941), the great pianist from New Orleans, came to Chicago in 1922. Morton claimed to have invented jazz. Muddy Waters (1915–83) didn't claim to have invented blues, but he did take credit for bringing the sound of the Mississippi Delta to Chicago, where his use of electric guitar was seminal.

Nat "King" Cole (1919–65) began his career playing the organ at his father's church. Cole, with his unique and velvety vocals, broke several color barriers in the 1950s. He was the first African American to have a radio show, and later, a weekly TV show.

ACTORS AND COMEDIANS

PAUL SILLS and Bernie Sahlins opened Chicago's renowned improvisational comedy spot Second City in 1959. Many comics, including Gilda Radner (1946–89), Mike Nichols, Elaine May, Dan Aykroyd, and Joan Rivers, got their start here. Comic genius Jack Benny (1894–1974) and *Saturday Night Live* star John Belushi (1949–82) both lived in Chicago suburbs.

Several Chicago-based actors, including John Cusack and John Malkovich, have

Chicago's Oprah Winfrey, a national TV personality

gone on to international fame. One of the city's best-known TV personalities is talk-show host Oprah Winfrey *(see p161),* watched by nearly 15 million Americans each weekday morning. It was in Chicago that the TV talk show was born, in 1949, with NBC's *Garroway at Large.*

ATHLETES

SPORTS TEAMS in Chicago are not known for their winning streaks, but they do boast a number of superstars. Chicago Bulls basketball player Michael Jordan is perhaps most famous, known as much for his product endorsements as for his basketball scoring.

Hockey legend Bobby Hull, as the star of the 1961 Chicago Blackhawks team, helped bring the Stanley Cup to the city – the team's only cup win in more than half a century.

Johnny Weissmuller (1904–1984) may be best known as the star of 18 Tarzan movies; however, the boy who swam at Oak Street Beach *(see p77)* became the man who held every world freestyle swimming record of the 1920s.

Michael Jordan, the Chicago Bulls' No. 1 basketball player

WRITERS

CHICAGO'S MOST famous literary figure is Ernest Hemingway (1899–1960), who grew up in Oak Park *(see pp114–15).* He rejected the conservative mindset of

this Chicago suburb, saying it was full of "wide lawns and narrow minds."

Theodore Dreiser (1871–1945), considered the father of American literary naturalism, wrote about Chicago, his home city, in his masterpiece *Sister Carrie.*

African-American novelist Richard Wright (1908–1960) moved to Chicago at age 19, though he wrote his best-selling novel *Native Son,* about a man raised in a Chicago slum, in New York.

Illinois-native poet Carl Sandburg (1878–1967) moved to Chicago in 1912, where he worked as a literary critic. His 1914 poem "Chicago" describes it as the "City of the Big Shoulders." Poet Gwendolyn Brooks (b.1917) has lived in Chicago her whole life, writing exclusively about it. She was, in 1950, the first African American to win a Pulitzer Prize, for *Annie Allen,* her collection exploring the Black experience in Chicago.

Renowned poet Carl Sandburg

GANGSTERS AND CRIMINALS

THE CITY'S REPUTATION for lawlessness was secured in the 1920s with the rise of the US's infamous crime lord, Al Capone (1899–1947). Prohibition set the stage for mob warfare as gangsters monopolized the lucrative market of banned alcohol. More than 300 gang-related murders occurred in the 1920s, including the Capone-orchestrated St. Valentine's Day Massacre *(see p16).*

Bank robber John Dillinger's daring made him a folk hero of sorts. When he was killed by the FBI outside Lincoln Park's Biograph Theatre in 1934, onlookers dipped handkerchiefs in his blood for morbid mementos.

A bank robber as folk hero, John Dillinger

ENTREPRENEURS AND INDUSTRIALISTS

YOUNG Chicago attracted many enterprisers. Cyrus Hall McCormick (1809–1884) transformed wheat farming with his invention of the Virginia reaper. In 1848, he concentrated his farm-implement empire in Chicago. He died the richest man in Illinois.

Charles Wacker, city planner

Real-estate developer Potter Palmer (1826–1902) built luxury hotels and is credited with creating the wealthy Gold Coast area *(see pp72–7).*

Marshall Field (1834–1906) built his fortune as a department store owner *(see pp50–51),* funding some of Chicago's most important institutes.

Brewer Charles H. Wacker (1856–1929), son of Frederick Wacker *(see p71),* helped shape the city as chair of the Chicago Plan Commission, overseers of the 1909 Plan of Chicago *(see p28).*

SOCIAL REFORMERS

AT THE TURN of the 20th century, Chicago was home to three of the most influential women in the US.

Black civil-rights activist Ida B. Wells (1862–1931) successfully sued a railroad company for racial discrimination. Her columns appeared in many of the nation's 200 Black papers during the 1890s *(see p95).*

Jane Addams (1860–1935) was involved with almost every US social movement of the early 20th century, winning a Nobel Peace Prize for her work. In 1889, she cofounded Hull-House *(see p116).*

Suffragist Frances Willard (1839–98) helped found the World's WCTU, the first international women's organization *(see Rest Cottage, p124).*

CHICAGO THROUGH THE YEAR

CHICAGO'S NICKNAME "Windy City" originally referred to its blustery politicians who lobbied to host the 1893 World's Columbian Exposition. Visitors will be struck by the appropriateness of the label. Chicago is a windy city whatever the season – although it ranks only 14th for wind velocity in the country.

Cyclist on Lincoln Park's lakefront path

Springtime in Chicago begins in late March. The city bursts into bloom after a long winter, living up to its official motto, *Urbs in Horto*, or "City in a garden." In summer, Chicago's beaches offer cooling breezes and the sun-warmed waters of Lake Michigan. These same waters keep the city temperate during autumn. In winter, they lead to "lake effect" storms: plenty of snow and chilling breezes. Intrepid locals bundle up and take advantage of winter attractions such as the WinterBreak festival. City Visitor Centers and the mayor's office *(see p161)* provide event information.

Irish reveler at Chicago's annual St. Patrick's Day Parade

SPRING

CHICAGOANS welcome the arrival of spring by jogging through Grant Park, enjoying Lincoln Park's magnificent flower displays, and cheering on the city's two baseball teams, the Chicago Cubs and the White Sox, whose seasons begin in April *(see pp162–3).*

MARCH

Pulaski Day Reception *(Mar 4),* Polish Museum of America, 984 N Milwaukee Ave. Celebrations in honor of Polish freedom fighter and later US Civil War hero Casimir Pulaski.

St. Patrick's Day Parade *(Sat before Mar 17),* the Loop. The Chicago River is dyed green in celebration.

South Side Irish Parade *(Sun before Mar 17),* Western Ave from 103rd to 114th Sts. One of the largest Irish parades outside Dublin.

Greek Independence Day Parade *(last Sun),* Halsted St from Randolph to Van Buren.

APRIL

Chicago Park District Spring Flower Show *(early Apr–mid-May),* Lincoln Park Conservatory. An exuberant display of colorful flowers.

International Vintage Poster Fair *(mid-Apr),* Navy Pier. Everything from Hollywood movie posters to reproductions of works by master artists are for sale at this three-day event.

MAY

Bike Chicago *(mid-May–mid-Jun),* city wide. Month-long celebration of cycling, with architecture bike tours, group bike rides, and workshops.

Great Chicago Places and Spaces *(mid- or late May),* 77 E Randolph St. Architecture in Chicago's downtown is celebrated through walking and lobby tours, special events, and exhibitions.

Wright Plus *(mid- or late May),* Oak Park *(p114).* Tour Frank Lloyd Wright-designed private residences and national historic landmarks in this annual housewalk.

SUMMER

CHICAGOANS THRONG to art fairs, neighborhood festivals, and outdoor concerts during the summer. A long-standing Chicago tradition is the free evening concerts – from opera to blues, from country to pop – at Grant Park's *(see pp84–5)* Petrillo Music Shell. Chicagoans and visitors alike take advantage of this opportunity for a picnic dinner in the park.

JUNE

Chicago Gospel Festival *(early Jun),* Grant Park. A two-day free event featuring gospel composers, singers, and musicians.

Chicago Blues Festival *(early Jun),* Grant Park. A three-day extravaganza of local blues musicians and southern artists.

Navy Pier, Chicago's amusement park for the entire family *(see p65)*

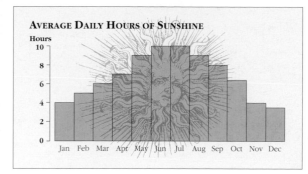

AVERAGE DAILY HOURS OF SUNSHINE

Sunshine
More than 50 days a year on average have clear skies, whereas 240 are overcast. Night descends early during the winter months, but the days can be brilliantly clear. December is the cloudiest month of the year, with an average of just four cloud-free days.

Printer's Row Book Fair
(early Jun), Dearborn Ave between Congress Pkwy and Polk St *(p82)*. Book dealers, and papermaking and bookbinding demonstrations.
Old Town Art Fair
(second weekend), 1800 W block of Lincoln Park W. Artists from around the world show and sell their work.
Wells Street Art Festival
(second weekend), Wells St between Division and North aves. Crafts and fine art on display and for sale.
Ravinia Music Festival
(mid-Jun–Labor Day), Ravinia Park. Dozens of performances in all musical styles *(p162)*.
18th Street Cultural Festival
(third weekend), 1617 W 18th St. Tastes, sights, and sounds of Hispanic culture.
Gay and Lesbian Pride Parade *(fourth Sun)*, Lincoln Park.

JULY

Taste of Chicago *(first week)*, Grant Park *(pp84–5)*. Concerts and cooking lessons accompany the cuisine of some of the city's finest restaurants.
Kwanzaa Summer Festival
(first Sat), 49 E 95th St. Musical entertainment, food, and activities for children of all ages.
Chicago Country Music Festival *(early Jul)*, Grant Park *(pp84–5)*.
Rock Around the Block
(mid-Jul), Lakeview *(p114)*. Annual weekend-long neighborhood festivities.
Chicago Folks and Roots Festival *(late Jul)*, Welles Park. An eclectic mix of musical styles from around the world.

La Fiesta del Sol *(Jul 29–31)*, Pilsen *(p116)*. Carnival rides, arts and crafts, local and visiting musicians, and Mexican cuisine are featured at this festival, one of Chicago's largest.
Jazzfest *(late Jul)*, South Shore Cultural Center, 7059 S Lake Shore Dr. Top jazz musicians perform.
Venetian Night *(late Jul)*, Monroe Harbor. Parade of boats and fireworks synchronized to music.
Chinatown Summer Fair
(late Jul or early Aug), Wentworth Ave between Cermak Rd and 24th St. Food, art, and dance.

AUGUST

Pullman Jazz, Blues and Gospel Fest *(early Aug)*, Gately Park *(p119)*.
Bud Billiken Day Parade
(second Sat), 39th and King Dr. One of the US's oldest African-American parades culminates with a picnic in Washington Park *(p104)*.
Chicago Carifete *(mid-Aug)*, Midway Plaisance *(p104)*. Music, dance, and food from the islands of the Caribbean.

Air maneuvers over the North Side as part of the Air and Water Show

Rock the River *(mid-Aug)*, Michigan Ave and Wacker Dr. River cruises, a fishing derby, and music in celebration of the Chicago River.
Chicago Air and Water Show *(late Aug)*, North Ave Beach. Planes and boats do stunts in the sky and water.
Bucktown Arts Fest *(late Aug)*, N Oakley Blvd *(p114)*. Local artists display their various works.
Viva! Chicago Latin Music Festival *(last weekend)*, Grant Park *(pp84–5)*.

Visitors sampling delicacies of dozens of restaurants at Taste of Chicago

AVERAGE MONTHLY RAINFALL

	MM										Inches
	300										12
	240										9
	180										6
	120										3
	60										
	0										0

Jan Feb Mar Apr May Jun Jul Aug Sep Oct Nov Dec

Precipitation
Chicago's average monthly precipitation is much the same throughout the year, with a modest peak in early summer. Summer storms are brief but dramatic, and provide relief from humidity. Winter brings blizzards.

▮ Rainfall
▯ Snowfall

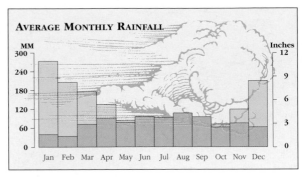

Pumpkins at a local farmers' market, a telltale sign of autumn

AUTUMN

AUTUMN IS an invigorating season in Chicago. September's comfortable weather provides an inviting backdrop to the numerous outdoor festivals held throughout the city.

Autumn is also the season when Chicagoans and visitors alike test their mettle and stamina during the internationally celebrated annual marathon.

Football season kicks off the first week of September with the Chicago Bears playing at Soldier Field. The city's many sports enthusiasts also flock to the United Center to see the Chicago Bulls play basketball and the Chicago Blackhawks play hockey (*see p163*).

In late autumn, the city gets a head start on the Christmas season, with many holiday traditions beginning immediately after Thanksgiving, in November.

SEPTEMBER

Chicago Jazz Festival (*Labor Day weekend*), Grant Park (*pp84–5*). Swing to the lively sounds of renowned jazz musicians and singers.
Around the Coyote (*second weekend*), Wicker Park (*p114*). Arts festival and gallery tours.
Celtic Fest Chicago (*mid-Sep*), Grant Park (*pp84–5*). A celebration of Celtic music.
Mexican Independence Day Parade (*mid-Sep*), Little Village. Floats, bands, and dancers join to celebrate Mexico's 1820 independence from Spain.
World Music Festival (*mid- to late Sep*), various locations. The eclectic sounds of world-beat music.
Art on Harrison (*third weekend*), Oak Park (*pp114–15*). Showcasing Oak Park's artists, galleries, and studios, with displays, demonstrations, and food.

OCTOBER

Haunted "L" Rides (*weekends*), Chicago Cultural Center (*p52*). Free Loop train tour with ghosts and goblins.
Mayor Daley's Kids and Kites Fest (*early Oct*), Lake Shore Dr and Montrose Ave.
Annual House Tour (*second weekend*), Pullman (*p119*). A rare opportunity to see inside this historic district's 19th-century houses.
Chicago Marathon (*second Sun*), downtown. One of the world's largest marathons, with thousands of participants, and spectators in the hundreds of thousands cheering runners along the 26.5-mile (43-km) course.
Oktoberfest (*mid-Oct*), Weed St from Dayton St to Halsted Ave. Celebrates German culture with food and beer gardens.
Pumpkin Plaza (*mid- to late Oct*), Daley Plaza. An outdoor haunted village kids will love.

NOVEMBER

Holiday Windows at Marshall Field's (*Nov–Dec*). Animated Christmas displays in the windows of the State Street store (*pp50–51*) are a Chicago tradition.
Christmas Around the World and Holidays of Light (*mid-Nov–Jan*), Museum of Science and Industry (*pp106–109*). Chicago's ethnic groups decorate trees in an "enchanted" forest and share holiday traditions.
Magnificent Mile Lights Festival (*third weekend*), Michigan Ave from the Chicago River to Oak St. Christmas lights are lit during this annual procession.

The Chicago Marathon, attracting athletes from around the world

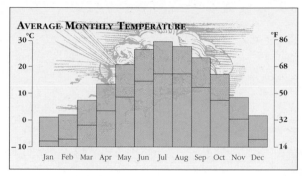

AVERAGE MONTHLY TEMPERATURE

Temperature
Spring in Chicago is generally mild. Most summer days are comfortably warm, but there may be some very hot and humid periods. Autumn is crisp, with unpredictable temperatures. Winter winds, rushing through the tunnels created by the city's tall buildings, are often bitingly cold.

Field's Jingle Elf Parade
(Thanksgiving Day), State St between Congress Pkwy and Randolph St. Santa Claus and his elves delight children.
Holiday Tree Lighting Ceremony *(day after Thanksgiving Day)*, Daley Plaza.
Christkindlmarket *(late Nov–Dec)*, Daley Plaza. Holiday shopping in a German marketplace, complete with an 80-ft (24 m) tree.

WINTER

THE CITY SPARKLES during winter with elaborate decorations, and buildings and trees festooned with seasonal green and red lights. The Merchandise Mart, on the north bank of the river, looks like a massive wrapped gift.

DECEMBER

Country Christmas
(throughout Dec), Galena *(pp128–9)*. Holiday traditions

and celebrations in the town's Victorian Historic District, including Santa visits, house-walks, and a Mistletoe Ball.
Caroling to the Animals *(first Sun)*, Lincoln Park Zoo *(pp112–13)*. Sing holiday favorites to the animals.
Chicago Park District Christmas Flower Show *(mid-Dec)*, Lincoln Park Conservatory. Colorful holiday poinsettia displays.
New Year's Eve *(Dec 31)*, Navy Pier *(p65)*. An evening of celebration with laser-lights and fireworks.

JANUARY

New Year's Day *(Jan 1)*, Navy Pier *(p65)*. Family activities and fireworks to start off the New Year.
WinterBreak *(Jan 1–Mar 31)*. More than 100 city-wide indoor and outdoor events, including the Magnificent Mile Crystal Carnival, with its giant ice sculptures, as well as theme weekends.

Illuminated Christmas tree in front of the Tribune Building

FEBRUARY

Chinese New Year Parade *(date varies)*, Wentworth Ave from Cermak Rd to 24th St. Festivities include colorful floats, traditional music and dancing, and food.

PUBLIC HOLIDAYS

New Year's Day (Jan 1)
Martin Luther King Day (3rd Mon in Jan)
President's Day (3rd Mon in Feb)
Pulaski Day (1st Mon in Mar)
Memorial Day (last Mon in May)
Independence Day (Jul 4)
Labor Day (1st Mon in Sep)
Columbus Day (2nd Mon in Oct)
Veterans Day (Nov 11)
Thanksgiving Day (4th Thu in Nov)
Christmas Day (Dec 25)

Ice skaters enjoying a bright winter day outdoors

CHICAGO
AREA BY AREA

Downtown Core

Bordered on the north and on the west by the Chicago River, on the east by Lake Michigan, and on the south by the Congress Parkway, the Downtown Core is Chicago's historic and financial center. The downtown's nucleus is the Loop, named for the elevated train tracks encircling it. Even though the area was completely destroyed by the Great Fire of 1871, a mere two decades later it had been rebuilt with pioneering skyscrapers, including the Marquette Building. Along with this architectural legacy, the area is home to such famous museums as the Art Institute of Chicago. State Street is home to landmark department stores.

Picasso sculpture at the Daley Center

Sights at a Glance

Historic Buildings
Auditorium Building 6
Carson Pirie Scott and Company 10
Chicago Theatre 17
Fine Arts Building 7
Marquette Building 3
Marshall Field and Company 12
Monadnock Building 5
Oriental Theater 13
Reliance Building 11
The Rookery 2
Santa Fe Building 8
35 East Wacker Drive 19

Modern Skyscrapers
Federal Center 4
James R. Thompson Center 21
R.R. Donnelley Building 20
Sears Tower 1
333 West Wacker Drive 22

Museums and Galleries
Art Institute of Chicago pp46–9 9
Chicago Cultural Center 14
Museum of Broadcast Communications 15

Bridges, Parks, and Streets
Michigan Avenue Bridge 18
Millennium Park 16
Wacker Drive 23

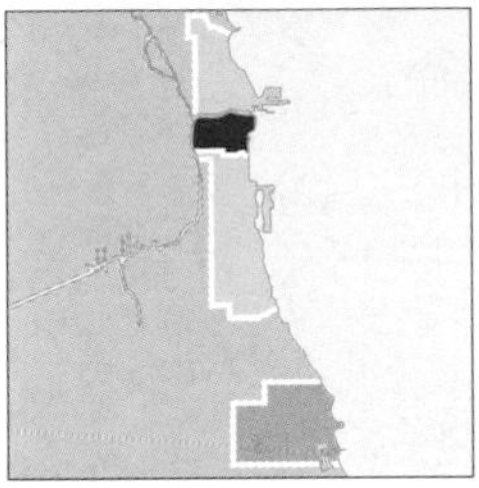

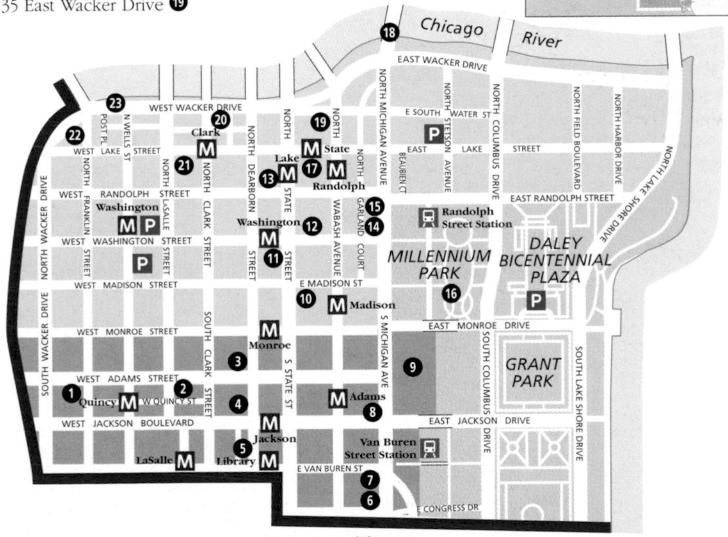

Key

[M] CTA train station
Street-by-Street map *See pp38–9*
Metra train station
[P] Parking

Getting There

The Downtown Core is easily explored on foot. Frequent CTA elevated trains circle the Loop. CTA buses also provide frequent service. Downtown routes include 20, 22, 36, and 56. Twelve Metra lines service Chicago's suburbs. Trains depart from one of five stations surrounding the Loop *(see pp180–83)*.

0 meters 500
0 yards 500

◁ **Atrium in Marshall Field's landmark department store**

Street-by-Street: The Loop

THE LOOP GETS ITS NAME from the elevated track system that circles the center of the Downtown Core. Trains screeching as they turn sharp corners and the steady stream of businesspeople during rush hour add to the Loop's bustle. In the canyon vistas through the many tall, historic buildings – and modern edifices such as the Federal Center – you can catch glimpses of the 19 bridges spanning Chicago River. The conversion of warehouses to condominiums and renovation of historic theaters are helping to enliven the Loop at night.

Stone lion guarding the doors of the Art Institute

The Rookery
One of the earliest designs by Burnham and Root, the lobby of this 1888 building was remodeled by Frank Lloyd Wright in 1907 ❷

★ Sears Tower
At a height of 1,454 ft (443 m), this is one of the tallest buildings in the world. Views from the glass-enclosed observation deck on the 103rd floor are stunning ❶

190 South LaSalle Street (1987), designed by New York architect Philip Johnson, has a white-marble lobby with a gold-leafed, vaulted ceiling.

Marquette Building
This early skyscraper (1895) was designed by William Holabird and Martin Roche, central Chicago School figures and architects of more than 80 buildings in the Loop ❸

STREET

CLARK

ADAMS

FRANKLIN

WACKER

STREET

DRIVE

STAR SIGHTS

★ **Art Institute of Chicago**

★ **Sears Tower**

Chicago Board of Trade
occupies a 45-story Art Deco building, a statue of Ceres atop its roof. The frenetic action inside can be observed from a viewers' gallery.

Santa Fe Building
This classic Chicago School building, with an elegant two-story atrium, houses the Chicago Architecture Foundation **8**

★ Art Institute of Chicago
The Impressionist and Post-Impressionist collection at this museum, one of the most important in the country, is world famous **9**

LOCATOR MAP
See Street Finder maps 3 & 4

KEY

- - - Suggested route

0 meters   100

0 yards   100

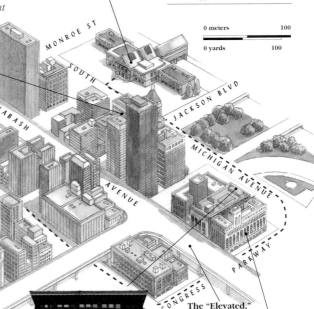

The "Elevated,"
or "L", train tracks opened in 1892. Its loop in the city's core is seven blocks long and five blocks wide.

Monadnock Building
The north half of this building (1891) is the tallest building ever constructed entirely of masonry **5**

Federal Center
Ludwig Mies van der Rohe designed this three-building office complex around a central plaza, which holds Alexander Calder's 1973 sculpture Flamingo **4**

Fine Arts Building
Frank Lloyd Wright once had a studio in this 1885 building designed by Solon S. Beman. The building was originally used as a carriage showroom by the Studebaker Company **7**

Auditorium Building
The seventh-floor, birch paneled recital hall in this 1889 multipurpose skyscraper is one of Adler and Sullivan's best interiors **6**

Sears Tower ➊

233 S Wacker Dr. **Map** 3 B2.
[📞] *875-9696.* [M] *Quincy.*
[🕐] *Mar–Sep: 9am–11pm daily;
Oct–Feb: 9am–10pm daily; last
adm 30 min before closing.*

IN JUNE 2000, Sears
Tower once again
became the world's
tallest building from
base to tip of antenna,
when a 22 ft (6.7 m)
extension was added to
one of the tower's two
broadcast antennas. It
had already regained
its title as the tallest
building in the world
in two of four
categories under
revised 1997
international
guidelines. Although
it no longer has the
tallest structural
height (Cesar Pelli's
Petronas Towers in
Kuala Lumpur has
that distinction,
which some say is
the most important),
it does have the
highest occupied
floor and also the
highest height to the
rooftop.

Sears Tower,
opened in
1974, was
designed by
Bruce Graham, a
partner at the Chicago
architectural firm of
Skidmore, Owings and
Merrill, with the assistance of
chief engineer Fazlur Khan.
Construction of the innovative
building took three years,
employing 1,600 people
during the peak period. More
than 110 concrete caissons
anchored in bedrock support
the tower's 222,500 tons.

Today, the tower contains
4.5 million sq ft (0.4 million
sq m) of office space, more
than 100 elevators. It also
contains approximately 43,000
ft (13,100 m) of telephone
cable, almost enough to
encircle the Earth twice.

The elevator to the Skydeck
travels at a stomach-churning
1,600 ft (490 m) per minute,
though the narrated history of

**The 110-story
tower** soars to
1,454 ft (443 m) – or
1,729 ft (527 m) if
the higher of the
two antennas is
included.

The tower top
sways 6 inches (15
cm) in strong wind.

**The glass-
enclosed,** 103rd-
floor Skydeck, the
world's third-highest
observation deck,
provides views of
the far shores of
Lake Michigan and
four states on
clear days.

**The 16,000
bronze-tinted
windows** are
cleaned by six
automatic machines
eight times a year.

Black aluminum
clads the frame-
work, which is
made from 76,000
tons of steel.

**Alexander
Calder's mobile
sculpture** *Universe*
(1974) is on display
in the lobby.

**View of the Sears Tower and
Skydeck, looking northeast**

The Rookery ➋

209 S LaSalle St. **Map** 3 C2. [📞] *553-
6150.* [M] *Quincy; Jackson (blue line).*
[🕐] *9am–8pm Mon–Fri; 9am–3pm
Sat.* [●] *major public hols.* [♿]

WHEN THE ROOKERY opened
in 1888, it was the tallest
building in the world. The 12-
story building, designed by
the influential firm Burnham
and Root in the Richardsonian
Romanesque style *(see p24)*,
has a dark red brick façade
with terra-cotta trim and a
rough granite base. The
building, now housing offices,
was constructed on a foundation of crisscrossing rails
– necessitated by the clay
soils unable to support the
weight of the massive
structure. While its thick
masonry walls are load
bearing, the iron framing
of the lower stories

the tower provides a very
welcome distraction from the
one-minute ride.

During the summer, there
are often lengthy lineups for
the Skydeck, but diversions
include a short movie on
Chicago and an exhibition
on the city's ten
most significant
buildings.

The Loop's glittering skyline as seen at sunset

allows for the use of large windows – a welcome innovation when artificial lighting technology was in its infancy.

Framing the main entrance is a monumental arch with geometric carvings, including eponymous rooks. Inside is a two-tiered court, remodeled in 1907 by Frank Lloyd Wright, who covered the original iron columns and staircases with white marble, inlaid with gold leaf. The central staircase, framed with Wright's signature urns, leads to a mezzanine enclosed by a domed skylight. A magnificent, cantilevered cast-iron staircase leads from the second floor to the top, and to views of the spectacular 11-story light-well.

Entrance to the Marquette Building

The Rookery's spectacular light court

Marquette Building ❸

140 S Dearborn St. **Map** 3 C2.
[422-5500. M *Monroe (blue line).*
○ *24 hrs daily.* &

Considered the premier remaining example of the Chicago School of architecture *(see pp24–5)*, the Marquette Building was designed by Holabird and Roche in 1895.

Commissioned by the owners of the Rookery, the architects faced the demanding task of equaling the Burnham and Root original sophisticated design of that building.

The grid of this early commercial 16-story high-rise's steel-frame skeleton is easily seen in the terra-cotta and brick exterior.

The building's groundbreaking expansive horizontal windows became known as Chicago windows *(see p25)*. They are one of the few remaining examples of this innovative window design.

Bronze bas-relief panels over the entrance doors, designed by Hermon Atkins MacNeil, illustrate Jesuit missionary Father Jacques Marquette's 1673–4 expedition to the area.

In the two-story lobby, mosaic panels of glass and mother-of-pearl designed by J.A. Holzer of Tiffany and Company depict scenes of the French exploration of Illinois. Sculpted heads inset above the elevators on the first and second floors pay tribute to the Native chiefs and early French explorers of the Chicago area *(see p13)*.

The building underwent restoration in 1980.

Federal Center ❹

219 S Dearborn St. **Map** 3 C2.
[353-3557. M *Jackson (blue line).*
○ *7am–6pm Mon–Fri.* ● *major public hols.* &

The three-building Federal Center complex, designed by Ludwig Mies van der Rohe and completed in 1974, expresses the pared-down functionalism of Mies' International style *(see p25)*. There is little ornamentation to distract from these austere curtain-wall structures made of glass and steel.

The 30-story Dirksen courtroom building stands on the east side of the complex; the 42-story Kluczynski office tower and one-story post office are to the west. The center is interesting for the expert arrangement of its buildings around the plaza and with each other.

The sterile plaza is graced with Alexander Calder's 53-ft (16-m) vermilion sculpture *Flamingo (see p44)*, which seems almost to be dancing – its steel organic form a surprising complement to the rigid geometry of the buildings.

The Monadnock Building's filigree wrought-iron staircase

Monadnock Building ❺

53 W Jackson Blvd. **Map** 3 C2.
M *Jackson (blue line).* ○ *7am–6pm Mon–Fri.* ● *public hols.* ♿

CONSTRUCTED in two parts two years apart (and by two different architectural firms), the interestingly bisected Monadnock Building looks both to the past and to the future. The northern half of this office building, designed by Burnham and Root, was built first, in 1891. Sixteen stories tall and with masonry load-bearing walls (the building method at the time), it is the tallest masonry building ever constructed. The southern section, on the other hand, designed by Holabird and Roche, has a steel skeleton sheathed in terra-cotta, an innovation that in the 1890s allowed skyscrapers to soar.

The building is named after one of New Hampshire's White Mountains. "Monadnock" is also a geological term for a mountain surrounded by a glacial plain – an appropriate name for this most solid of buildings, as its walls are 6 ft (2 m) thick at the base. The interior was restored in the 1980s: the mosaic floor is a replica; the white-marble ceiling and

ornate staircase are original. At the north entrance to the building and at the south elevator banks, you can see, under glass, part of the original marble floor. A corridor bordered by shops and restaurants runs the full length of the building, much like an interior street.

Auditorium Building ❻

430 S Michigan Ave. **Map** 4 D3.
C *341-3555.* **M** *Library.*
○ *7:30am–10:30pm Mon–Thu; 7:30am–6pm Fri; 8am–5pm Sat; 11am–4pm Sun (Sep–Apr only).*
● *major public hols.* ♿
📷 ***Building**: 341-3555; **Theater**: 431-2354. See **Entertainment** p162.*

DESIGNED BY Dankmar Adler and Louis Sullivan, their first major commission together, the Auditorium Building (1889), with its walls of smooth limestone typical of the Richardsonian Romanesque style *(see p24)* rising above the rough granite base, broke many records and achieved a number of firsts. Combining a 400-room hotel, a 17-story office tower, and a 4,300-seat theater, it was the tallest building in Chicago and the first building of its size to be electrically lighted and air-conditioned. Not surprisingly, it was also the most expensive, costing over $3 million to build. At 110,000 tons, it was the heaviest building in the world, and the most fireproof.

The building's crowning jewel is the lavish Auditorium Theatre, the

Roosevelt University admissions office in the Auditorium Building

first home of the Chicago Symphony Orchestra. After many years of neglect (World War II servicemen used the stage as a bowling alley), it was restored in the 1960s and is now a venue for performing arts events. Four elliptical arches span the width of the theater, which is ornamented with stenciling, stained glass, and gold-leaf plaster reliefs. Its excellent acoustics enable guests in the last row to hear an unamplified whisper on stage, six stories below.

The grand lobby, with its onyx walls and ornate staircase, contains an exhibition on the building's history. The tenth-floor library, originally the hotel's dining room, has a dramatic barrel-vaulted ceiling and superb lake views.

The building also houses Roosevelt University.

Stained-glass detailing in the Auditorium Building

Façade of the Auditorium Building, with cows from Chicago's public-art project in the foreground

White-marble lobby of the Santa Fe Building

Fine Arts Building ❼

410 S Michigan Ave. **Map** 4 D2.
☎ 427-7602. Ⓜ *Library.*
Ⓞ *7am–10pm Mon–Fri; 7am–9pm Sat; 10am–4pm Sun.* ⬤ *major public hols.* ♿

Although now closely associated with fine art and culture, the Fine Arts Building was originally commissioned by Studebaker Brothers Manufacturing to house a wagon carriage showroom. (The name "Studebaker" inscribed outside in stone is still visible above the first floor.)

Designed by Solon S. Beman and completed in 1885, the building, with its columns, rough stone, and arched entranceway and windows, is typical of the Romanesque style.

When the Studebaker Company moved to a new location, Beman was commissioned to renovate the building as a cultural center. The façade of the eighth floor was removed and replaced with a three-story addition. Inside, studios, shops, and offices were added, and the building quickly became a hub of artistic activity. The literary magazines *Dial, Poetry,* and *Little Review* were published here; the Little Theater staged dramas; and painters, sculptors, and architects (including Frank

Lloyd Wright, *see p28*) had their studios on the tenth floor. In 1892, resident artists, including Frederic Clay Bartlett and Ralph Clarkson, formed a group called the Little Room and produced eight murals, which still can be seen on the walls of the tenth floor.

Today, the building, which has been given national historic landmark status, has a slightly frayed, run-down charm. Many arts-related enterprises remain in the building, including the Fine Arts Building Gallery in Suite 433, which showcases Chicago artists, with a new exhibition each month.

The sound of singers practicing scales can be heard echoing through the halls, and a ride in the old elevator (complete with elevator operator) is an experience not to be missed.

Santa Fe Building ❽

224 S Michigan Ave. **Map** 4 D2.
☎ 341-9461. Ⓜ *Adams.* Ⓞ *24 hrs daily.* ⬤ *major public hols.*

The Santa Fe Building gleams – inside with white marble, and outside with white-glazed terra-cotta. Designed by D.H. Burnham and Co. in 1904 and originally known as the Railway Exchange Building, it is now called the Santa Fe because of the rooftop sign, erected in the early 1900s by the Santa Fe Railroad.

Porthole windows line the top floor; terra-cotta reliefs of ancient goddesses decorate the vestibule. The atrium's balustraded mezzanine, marble staircase, and

Decorative elevator door in the Santa Fe Building

elevators with grillwork are all notable. Upper floors provide a view of the spectacular light court. The Chicago Architecture Foundation holds exhibitions on the first floor.

The Artist's Snack Shop on the ground floor of the Fine Arts Building

A Three-Hour Walk in the Downtown Core

DOZENS OF WORKS by world-renowned artists are on public display throughout Chicago's Downtown Core. This walk explores a selection from this huge outdoor art gallery and the buildings in the area, many of which are themselves works of art. The spectacular backdrop that the Loop's commanding architecture provides ensures excellent sights along the way.

South Michigan Avenue to South Dearborn Street

Start at the Adams CTA Station ① and walk east on Adams Street, turning right onto South Michigan Avenue and past the stately Art Institute of Chicago *(see p46–9)*. Lorado Taft's (1860–1936) *Fountain of the Great Lakes* (1913) ②, with its five female figures, is at the

View of buildings in the Loop looking east from Grant Park ③

south end of the main building. One block farther south is the main entrance of Grant Park ③, from where there is a good view of the buildings along Michigan Avenue, including the Santa Fe Building *(see p43)*. Walk

***The Four Seasons* by Marc Chagall** ⑥

west along Van Buren Street, turning right at State. Continue north, bearing left at Jackson, to the Frank Metcalf Federal Building and the sculpture *Lines in Four Directions* (1985) ④ by American minimalist Sol Lewitt (b.1928).

Dearborn Street to West Randolph Street

Cross Dearborn Street and enter the courtyard of the Federal Center *(see p41)* to see American sculptor Alexander Calder's (1898–1976) dramatic *Flamingo* (1974) ⑤. Retrace your steps to

Dearborn Street. Continue to walk north, passing the Marquette Building *(see p41)* on your left, to *The Four Seasons* (1974) ⑥ by Marc Chagall (1887–1985), at First National Plaza. This huge, four-sided mosaic consists of thousands of tiles in more than 250 colors that illustrate various

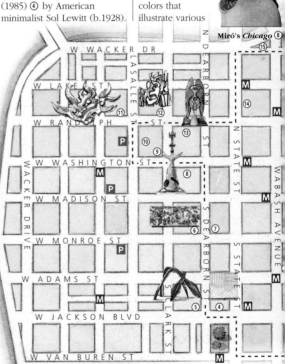

Miró's *Chicago* ⑧

Chicago scenes. Across the street is the groundbreaking Inland Steel Building ⑦. Steel pilings were driven 85 feet (26 m) down to the bedrock to support the building. Follow Dearborn Street to Washington, bearing left. On the left is Catalan artist Joan Miró's (1893–1983) *Chicago* (1981) ⑧, a surreal feminine figure made of plaster and bronze and studded with colorful ceramic tiles. County Building ⑨, with its 75-foot (23 m) Corinthian columns, can be seen at the corner of Washington and Clark. Continue along Washington Street, turning right onto LaSalle. Pass Chicago City Hall ⑩, the sister building of the County Building. On the northwest corner of Lasalle and Randolph is the Illinois State Office Building.

Lantern on No. 35 East Wacker Drive ⑮

On its exterior is *Freeform* (1993) ⑪, which Chicago sculptor Richard Hunt (b.1935) created to symbolize "a government supporting individual freedoms." Walk east on Randolph Street to the James R. Thompson Center *(see p56)* and French Art Brut artist Jean Dubuffet's (1901–1985) fiberglass sculpture *Monument with Standing Beast* (1984) ⑫. Its graffiti-like style is characteristic of the

(see p56)

Tips for Walkers

Starting point: *Adams CTA station, at the corner of Wabash Avenue and West Adams Street.*
Time: *Three hours.*
Getting there: *Take the brown, green, orange, or purple line CTA train to Adams Station.*
Stopping-off point: *Numerous cafés and restaurants can be found along the route, though many may be open only during weekday business hours. Sopraffina Marketcaffe, at 10 North Dearborn Street, serves Italian fare, from biscotti to pizza. West Egg Cafe, at 55 West Washington Street, offers breakfast and lunch at modest prices.*

State Street to East Randolph Street

One block east, on State Street, is the elegant Chicago Theatre ⑭ *(see p54)*. Turn right at Wacker Drive. At No. 35 ⑮ *(see p55)* is the former Jewelers Building, designed in 1926. Follow Wacker Drive east, turning right at Michigan Avenue, then left at Randolph Street to Prudential Plaza ⑯, consisting of two buildings. No. 1, a towering limestone and aluminum structure built in 1952, was the first sky-scraper to be built in the Loop since the 1930s. The design of No. 2, with its chevron top, suggests New York's Chrysler Building.

(see p54) … *(see p55)*

KEY

- - -	Suggested route
Ⓜ	CTA train station
Ⓡ	Metra train station
Ⓟ	Parking

0 meters 250
0 yards 250

artist's work. Just east, across the street in the Richard J. Daley Plaza, is the untitled sculpture by Pablo Picasso (1881–1973) ⑬. The piece created a stir when first erected, as Chicagoans debated its merits. Depending on where you stand, it is crowned with the head of a woman or of a hound dog.

The two buildings of Prudential Plaza, No. 1 on the far right ⑯

Façade of the Chicago Theater ⑭

Art Institute of Chicago ❾

Frieze on the west façade

THE EXTENSIVE COLLECTIONS at the Art Institute of Chicago represent nearly 5,000 years of human creativity through paintings, sculptures, textiles, photographs, cultural objects, and decorative artifacts from around the world.

The museum was founded by civic leaders and art collectors in 1879 as the Chicago Academy of Fine Arts, changing its name to the Art Institute of Chicago in 1882. Outgrowing two homes as wealthy patrons donated collections, it finally settled in a Neo-Classical structure built for the 1893 World's Fair. Today, the complex combines modern additions with the original structure designed by Shepley, Rutan and Coolidge.

Visitors admiring works in the 19th-century European gallery

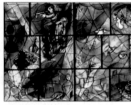 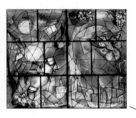

★ American Windows

Light from McKinlock Court streams through the azure stained glass designed by Marc Chagall, one of his last large-size works (1974–7), created in part as a tribute to the US bicentennial and to former Chicago mayor Richard J. Daley (see p17).

McKinlock Court

KEY TO FLOORPLAN

- ☐ Second floors
- ☐ First floors
- ☐ Lower levels
- ☐ Allerton Building
- ☐ Rice Building
- ☐ Rubloff Building
- ☐ School of the Art Institute

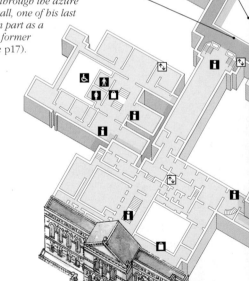

Main Entrance

STAR PAINTINGS

- ★ *American Windows* by Marc Chagall
- ★ *Old Man with a Gold Chain* by Rembrandt van Rijn
- ★ *A Sunday on La Grande Jatte–1884* by Georges Seurat

MUSEUM GUIDE

The lower levels of the Rubloff and Rice buildings house European decorative arts from 1600 to 1900. The Allerton's is geared toward children, but photography and the Miniature Rooms are also here. First-floor galleries range from ancient Egyptian artifacts to Asian collections. Second floors are devoted mostly to European works from the 15th to 20th centuries.

The Bath *(1891–2)*
American artist Mary Cassatt employed a raised vantage point and cropped figures in her work – artistic devices uncommon at the time. This painting is influenced by the realistic style prominent in Japanese prints.

Time Transfixed (1938), by René Magritte, is a juxtaposition of commonplace but unrelated items to create a surreal expression of reality.

Mother and Child, Pablo Picasso's 1921 painting, is exhibited along with a fragment that he removed from the final composition.

★ **A Sunday on La Grande Jatte–1884**
Post-Impressionist Georges Seurat composed this image of promenading Parisians using tiny dots of color.

Self-Portrait **by Vincent van Gogh**

The Assumption of the Virgin

★ **Old Man with a Gold Chain**
Rembrandt van Rijn's interest in the wisdom of age can be seen in this character study (c.1631).

American Gothic
Grant Wood's 1930 portrait of an Iowa farmer and his spinster daughter, initially criticized as satire, has become an American classic.

Exploring the Art Institute of Chicago

THE MUSEUM'S HOLDINGS span the globe as well as centuries, from 3rd-millennium BC Egyptian and Chinese artifacts to 20th-century American art. Almost every major artistic movement of the 19th and 20th centuries is represented. The museum's Early Modernism collection is particularly strong; its Impressionist and Post-Impressionist collection – one of the most significant in the world – is outstanding. Important Renaissance and Baroque paintings complement these exhibits.

Flower gardens in the grounds behind the Art Institute

Visitor to the European gallery appreciating works of old masters

ASIAN ART

SOME OF THE MUSEUM'S most exquisite pieces are in its distinguished Asian collection, which comprises 35,000 works of archeological and artistic significance.

The galleries of Chinese, Japanese, and Korean art include celebrated collections of ancient Chinese bronzes and jades, 19th-century Japanese woodblock prints, and early Korean ceramics.

The art from the Golden Age of the Tang dynasty (AD 618–907) is the prize of this exhibit, in particular, the magnificent brightly glazed earthenware funerary horses.

Indian, Himalayan, and Southeast Asian art dating from the 2nd to 19th centuries encompasses artifacts of the Hindu and Buddhist faiths. Among the gems here are the nearly life-sized 2nd- and 3rd-century bodhisattva sculptures from Gandhara (present-day Pakistan), and an elaborately carved 13th-century stone statute of Saraswati, the Hindu goddess of learning, from Southern India.

The Persian 16th-century illuminated manuscripts and miniature paintings are beautiful examples of that culture's precise and delicate art forms.

ARMS AND ARMOR

REMARKABLE WORKS of late medieval and Renaissance metal-craft are showcased in the George F. Harding Collection. One of the finest such collections in North America, it consists of 3,000 pieces of arms and armor. These include finely etched helmets, chain mail, equestrian equipment, historic weaponry, and decorated breastplates.

One of the earliest pieces in the collection is a breastplate from northern Italy. Dating from 1380, its original fabric covering is still intact. Also striking is a 1575 northern Italian armor, used for foot combat. Made of etched and gilded steel and brass, the suit is decorated with large medallions depicting allegorical figures.

DECORATIVE ARTS

FOR UNPARALLELED insight into the ever-changing taste of Western society, visit the decorative arts galleries. Their broad array embraces household items, including furniture and tableware, jewelry, and religious artifacts.

The impressive European collection contains 25,000 objects crafted from wood, metal, glass, ceramics, enamel, and ivory dating from 1100 to the present. It also includes sculpture from the medieval period to 1900.

The American collection includes an excellent selection of Arts and Crafts furniture, including a beautiful oak library table (1896) designed by Frank Lloyd Wright (see p28).

The fine European and American textile collection spans 15 centuries and

The grand staircase and foyer of the Art Institute

features vestments, tapestries, and embroideries. Highlights are a 19th-century William Morris-designed carpet and two rare fragments of Coptic cloth dating from between the 5th and 8th centuries.

Two of the quirkiest – and most renowned – collections are the Arthur Rubloff Paperweight Collection and the Thorne Miniature Rooms. The museum's holdings of more than 1,000 French, English, and American glass paperweights, popular in the mid-19th century, are one of the largest in the world.

The Thorne Miniature Rooms consist of 68 model rooms, painstakingly constructed to a scale of 1 inch (2.5 cm) to 1 foot (30 cm). The intricate European and American furnished interiors, ranging from the 16th to 20th centuries, are made with extraordinary technical precision.

The Gourmet (1901), painted by Pablo Picasso in his "Blue Period"

20TH-CENTURY ART

THE MUSEUM'S TROVE of more than 1,500 20th-century paintings and sculptures provides a comprehensive and provocative survey of the development of modern art. Representing every significant artistic movement in Europe and the US, the works are arranged in groupings that highlight stylistic affinities between varied artists.

The collection is divided into pre-1945 and post-1945 works. Particularly strong are

the examples of Cubism, the precursor of all abstract art forms; German Expressionism, the embodiment of the search for a strong emotional language in art; and Surrealism, the liberation of the irrational.

Post-World War II art is represented with works by such influential artists as Willem de Kooning and Jackson Pollock.

ARCHITECTURE

WHEN THE 1894 Chicago Stock Exchange (Adler and Sullivan) was demolished in 1972, its Trading Room was salvaged and reconstructed at the museum. Its ornate glory can still be seen in the room's stenciled ceiling and art-glass skylights. As memorable are the salvaged pieces from demolished Chicago buildings.

Special exhibits and a library with a comprehensive collection on Louis Sullivan complement the installations.

IMPRESSIONIST AND POST-IMPRESSIONIST ART

GIFTS FROM WEALTHY patrons such as Bertha Palmer *(see p77)* and Frederic Clay Bartlett, who astutely began collecting works by Monet, Degas, and Seurat in the late 19th century, led to the Art Institute becoming the first in the US to include a gallery of Post-Impressionist art. Today, it is one of the foremost centers of Impressionist and Post-Impressionist paintings outside France.

United only by their fiercely held belief in artistic experimentation, the French Impressionists were a diverse group who

The Basket of Apples (c.1895) by Paul Cézanne

exhibited together in the late 1800s. Dedicated to a new form of art – one that eschewed the constraints of the prevailing formal style – these artists attempted to capture the textures and moods of fleeting moments, or impressions. Their final exhibition was in 1886.

The artists who followed in the Impressionists' footsteps – labeled Post-Impressionists by English art critic Roger Fry – created works of art exploring evocative color relationships and rules of composition.

Highlights of the museum's holdings include the highly estimable Helen Birch Bartlett Memorial Collection, featuring Paul Cézanne's *The Basket of Apples* (c.1895) and Henri de Toulouse-Lautrec's *At the Moulin Rouge* (1895).

No better illustration of Impressionist and Post-Impressionist principles can be found than Claude Monet's six versions of a wheat field, which combines the basic doctrine of Impressionism – capturing nature's temporality – with the Post-Impressionist concern for reconstructing nature according to art's formal, expressive potential.

On the Seine at Bennecourt (1868) by Claude Monet

Carson Pirie Scott and Company ⑩

1 S State St. **Map** *3 C2.* 📞 *641-7000.* Ⓜ *Monroe; Washington (red line).* ⏱ *9:45am–7pm Mon–Wed, Fri; 9:45am–8pm Thu; 7:45am–6pm Sat; noon–5pm Sun.* ⬤ *Easter, Thanksgiving, Dec 25.* ♿ 🍽 📷 *See* **Shops and Markets** *p155.*

Iᴛ ɪs ᴀᴘᴘʀᴏᴘʀɪᴀᴛᴇ that such an architectural gem as the Carson Pirie Scott building, housing one of Chicago's oldest department stores, rests at Chicago's ground-zero address of State and Madison, the starting point for the city's street-numbering system.

The upper floors of the building are of white terra-cotta, but it is the ornamental metalwork on the first two floors that give this building, designed by Louis Sullivan in 1899, its distinctive character.

A particularly noteworthy feature of the store's exterior is the corner entrance pavilion, which extends 12 stories to the top of the building and has ornamental cast-iron motifs. Along with intricately entwined botanical and geometric forms, Sullivan's initials, L.H.S., can be seen above the corner entrance. While this is the showy heart of the building, it is worth walking east along Madison Street to view the metalwork and Chicago windows from a somewhat less busy vantage point.

The Reliance Building, precursor to the modern skyscraper

Reliance Building ⑪

32 N State St. **Map** *3 C1.* 📞 *782-1111.* Ⓜ *Washington (red line).* ⏱ *24 hrs daily.* ♿ 🅿 *See* **Where to Stay, Hotel Burnham** *p134.*

Tʜᴇ ʀᴇʟɪᴀɴᴄᴇ Building's two-stage construction (1890–95) was as unusual as were the structural-support techniques used. The leases for the upper floors of the original building on the site did not expire until 1894, so

when work on the new Reliance Building began in 1890, the upper floors of the old building were supported on jack screws and the lower stories demolished. The ground floors of the Reliance Building were completed and in 1894, when the leases expired, the upper floors were demolished and the steel framing for 13 more stories completed, in 15 days.

The new building, officially opened in March 1895, was considered revolutionary because of its steel frame and unusual two-story-column design, allowing for the masses of windows which give the building its modern look. The building's design was undertaken by John Root of Burnham and Root. Charles Atwood completed it upon Root's death in 1891.

The building was in serious disrepair in the mid-1990s, until the City of Chicago purchased it and began an exterior renovation, which involved the replacement of 2,000 pieces of terra-cotta. In 1998, a hotel company bought the building, undertaking a $27.5-million refurbishment before opening the Hotel Burnham in 1999. Root's original bronze and granite design of the first floor has been re-created and the 20-ft- (6-m-) high elevator lobby reconstructed using Italian marble, ornamental metal elevator grills, and elaborate mosaic floor tiles.

Marshall Field and Company ⑫

111 N State St. **Map** *4 D1.* 📞 *781-1000.* Ⓜ *Washington (red line).* ⏱ *9:45am–7pm Mon–Wed, Fri; 9:45am–8pm Thu; 9:45am–7pm Sat; 11am–6pm Sun.* ⬤ *Easter, Thanksgiving, Dec 25.* ♿ 📷 🅿 *See* **Shops and Markets** *p155.*

Nᴏ ᴏᴛʜᴇʀ retail establishment is, perhaps, as important to Chicago's cultural history as Marshall Field's department store. Originally a dry-goods shop begun by wealthy business-man Marshall Field (*see p77*), the store now occupies an

Ornamental metalwork above the entrance to Carson Pirie Scott

Christmas window display at Marshall Field's

entire city block. Built in five stages as the company grew, the original building, a Renaissance Revival-style design by Charles B. Atwood of D.H. Burnham, still stands at Washington and Wabash.

Field is credited with transforming State Street into the retail heart of Chicago in the early 1900s and for coining the commercial credo "Give the lady what she wants." When the store opened in 1907, it was considered the largest in the world, with 1,339,000 sq ft (124,400 sq m) of retail space, including the basement (such use was until then unheard of in US merchandising), 27,000 automatic fire sprinklers, 35,000 electric lights, 50 elevators, and 12 street-front entrances.

The store's most spectacular feature is its Tiffany mosaic dome, believed to be the largest piece of glass mosaic in the world. With more than 1.6 million pieces of iridescent glass covering 6,000 sq ft (557 sq m), it took 18 months and 50 artisans, supervised by designer Louis Comfort Tiffany, to complete.

Other interesting features of the store include the elegant Walnut Room restaurant and an exhibition tracing the store's history.

Oriental Theater ⓭

24 W Randolph St. **Map** 3 C1.
☎ 782-2004. Ⓜ *Washington (red line)*. ♿ ✉ *10:30am Sat; 11:30am Sun. See* **Entertainment** *pp162–3.*

THE ORIENTAL Theater occupies the site of one of the worst theater fires in US history: just weeks after opening in 1903, fire broke out in the Iroquois Theater, claiming more than 600 lives *(see p15)*. The theater was rebuilt and operated until

1925, when it was demolished. The Oriental, built on the site, opened in 1926. The 22-story building, with its 3,238-seat auditorium, was designed by renowned theater architects Cornelius W. and George L. Rapp.

The theater was used both as a movie palace and for live performances. Judy Garland, Jackie Gleason, and Bob Hope all performed here.

Inspired by the East Indian carnival-festival Durbar, the theater's interior is full of fantastic decorative elements, such as the elephant-head light fixtures in the foyer.

The Oriental is in what, for more than a century, was Chicago's bustling theater district: Randolph Street between Michigan Avenue and Wacker Drive. The Rice Theatre was the first to open in the area, in 1847 (since

Signs such as this mark the Loop's theatrical district

burned down). By the 1880s, more than 25 entertainment palaces were offering vaudeville, musicals, opera, and drama. Although few of the original theaters remain, the district is being revitalized, spurred by the restoration of the Oriental, which reopened as the Ford Center for the Performing Arts Oriental Theater. Restoration of the theater was completed in 1998 after a 17-year closure; 62,500 sq ft (5,800 sq m) of gold leaf were used in the theater's renovation.

Tiffany glass dome in Marshall Field's southern atrium

Grand staircase leading to the third-floor Preston Bradley Hall

Chicago Cultural Center ⑭

78 E Washington St. **Map** 4 D1.
📞 744-6630. Ⓜ *Randolph.*
🕐 *10am–7pm Mon–Wed;*
10am–9pm Thu; 10am–6pm Fri;
10am–5pm Sat; 11am–5pm Sun.
🚫 *Jan 1, Thanksgiving, Dec 25.* ♿
via Randolph St entrance. 🎫 *2pm*
Tue–Sat. 📷 🚻 ♿ *Weekly arts*
events; call 346-3278.

BUILT BETWEEN 1893 and
1897 as the city's main
library, the building was
dedicated in 1991 as the
Chicago Cultural Center to
showcase and celebrate the
performing, visual, and
literary arts.

Designed by the Boston
firm Shepley, Rutan and
Coolidge, this massive Neo-
Classical *(see p25)* edifice
features soaring arches of
white marble and classical
Greek columns. The 3-ft-
(1-m-) thick masonry walls,

clad with Bedford limestone,
rise 104 ft (32 m) above a
granite base. The elegant
building cost almost $2
million to construct.

There are two entrances to
the building. The north
entrance, at 77 East Randolph
Street, with Doric columns
and a massive portico, serves
the four-story north wing; the
deeply arched Romanesque
portal with bronze-framed
doors at the south entrance,
at 78 East Washington Street,
serves the five-story south
wing. The Garland Court
corridor connects the wings.

The interior of the building,
which includes a grand
Carrara marble staircase just
inside the Washington Street
entrance, is a monument to
elegant ornamentation. Inset
in the staircase are small
medallions made from a rare
Irish emerald marble. On the
underside of the staircase,
seen by looking up from each
landing, are intricate mosaics.

Two spectacular glass
domes complete the opulent
detailing. At the south end of
the building, on the third
floor in Preston Bradley Hall,
is a huge Tiffany dome. This
38-ft (11.5-m) jewel of
sparkling colored glass, stone,
and mother-of-pearl is valued
at $35 million. It is the largest
stained-glass Tiffany dome in
the world. At the north end of
the building, in the second-
floor G.A.R. Rotunda, is a
stained-glass dome in an
intricate Renaissance pattern.
It was created by the local
firm Healy and Millet. Both
domes were originally

Mosaic Tiffany dome in the G.A.R. Rotunda

skylights but have since
been sheathed with copper
and backlit to protect and
preserve the glass.

On the fourth floor is the
Sidney R. Yates Gallery, a
replica of an assembly hall
in Venice's 14th-century
Doge's Palace. Arched,
bronzed doorways are inlaid
with antique marble, and
the ceiling is coffered. The
stairway leading to the fifth
floor is modeled on the
Bridge of Sighs in Venice.

Although the building
itself rewards many hours of
architectural exploration,
allow enough time to view
the center's many exhibits
that reflect the city's rich
cultural heritage and
showcase local artists. The
Museum of Broadcast
Communications *(see p53)* is
on the first floor. Along the
western corridor on the
same floor is the Landmark
Chicago Gallery, displaying
photographs of the city's
architectural heritage.

The center also contains
two concert halls, two
theaters, a cabaret space,
and a dance studio. More
than 1,000 programs and
exhibitions are presented
annually; concerts, literary
readings, and cultural events
are held during the week.

One of several Visitor
Information Centers
operated by the Chicago
Office of Tourism is on the
first floor of the Chicago
Cultural Center, near the
Randolph Street entrance.

Façade of Chicago Cultural Center's Randolph Street entrance

Museum of Broadcast Communications ⓯

78 E Washington St. **Map** 4 D1. ☎ *629-6000.* [M] *Washington (red line).* 🕐 *10am–4:30pm Mon–Sat; noon–5pm Sun.* ● *major public hols.* ♿ ☕ 🛍

FOUNDED IN 1987 and housed in the Chicago Cultural Center *(see p52)*, the Museum of Broadcast Communications is one of only three broadcast museums in the US. Permanent displays and special exhibitions examine popular culture through the sights and sounds of TV and radio. A TV studio offers visitors the opportunity to anchor the "news" and take home a souvenir videotape. The Sportscaster Café shows replays of famous moments in sports history, and, in the Radio Hall of Fame, taped voices from radio's golden age, such as Jack Benny, Bing Crosby, and Red Skelton, can be heard throughout the room. Two current weekly radio programs (Chuck Schaden's nostalgic "Those Were the Days" and Bruce DuMont's political talk show "Beyond the Beltway") are broadcast from the museum; visitors can join the studio audience. Along with displays of vintage and contemporary TV sets and radios, the museum is also home to "the camera that changed America," the one used to televise the 1960 Kennedy/Nixon debate, which marked a turning point in the relationship between TV and politics.

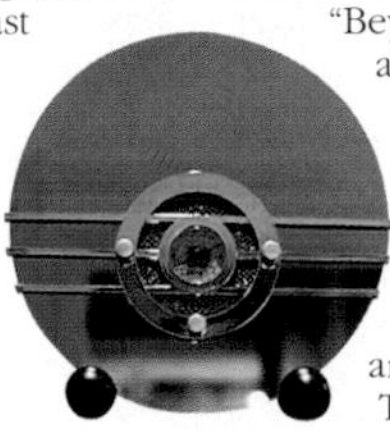

Antique mirror radio

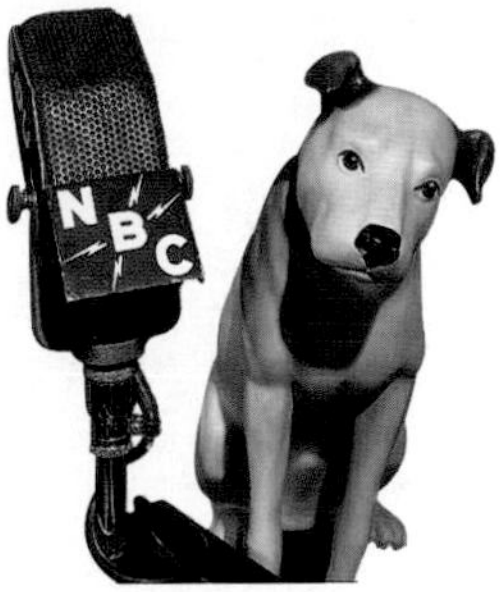

"His Master's Voice" dog and early NBC microphone

In the museum's research center, you can, for a small fee, hear from a collection of over 50,000 hours of radio programming, or view 15,000 TV broadcasts and 13,000 TV commercials. A gift shop sells postcards, books, reproductions of old advertisements, and broadcast memorabilia.

Millennium Park ⓰

Bounded by Randolph & Monroe Sts, Michigan Ave, & Columbus Dr. **Map** 4 D1. ☎ *588-0480.* [M] *Madison; Randolph.* ☕ [P] ***Concerts***.

A PROJECT TO CELEBRATE the 21st century, Millennium Park has provided year-round recreational opportunities since it opened in spring 2001. A northern expansion of Grant Park *(see pp84–5)*, it covers more than 1 million sq ft (93,000 sq m). This park-within-a-park transforms an unsightly rail yard into a cultural destination.

The showpiece of the park is the outdoor music pavilion, designed by internationally acclaimed architect Frank Gehry in association with the park's (and Sears Tower's) designers, Skidmore, Owings and Merrill. The pavilion accommodates up to 14,000 people and is the new home of the Grant Park Symphony summer concerts *(see p161)*.

The 1,500-seat music and dance theater was built 40 ft (12 m) below ground so as not to interfere with views through the park. Designed by Hammond Beeby Rupert Ainge, it features a glass pavilion with an indoor garden near its entrance.

The park's skating rink converts to an activity plaza in the summer, becoming a venue for Chicago's summer dance program *(see p160)*.

The restoration of the site's historic Peristyle – a semi-circle of columns that were torn down in the 1950s – provides a classical detail.

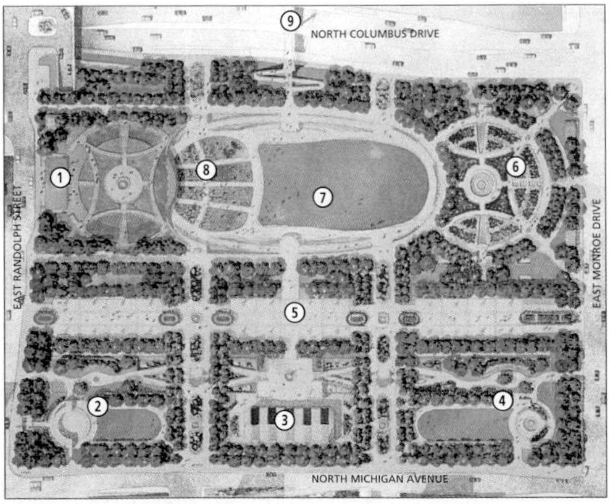

KEY TO MAIN SIGHTS

1. Music and Dance Theater Chicago Entrance
2. Peristyle – North Lawn
3. Ice Rink
4. South Lawn and Fountain
5. Millennium Terrace
6. Monroe Garden
7. Great Lawn
8. Music Pavilion
9. Pedestrian Bridge

Chicago Theatre ⑰

175 N State St. **Map** 4 D1. ☎ 443-
1130. Ⓜ *Washington (red line).*
◯ *10am–6pm Mon–Fri.*
See **Entertainment** *pp162–3.*

Slated for demolition in the
1980s but subsequently
saved, this grand 3,800-seat
theater has been restored to
its former glory. The oldest
surviving theater in Chicago,
it was designed by Rapp and
Rapp in 1921 and originally
operated as a vaudeville
movie palace. It now hosts
musicals and other live
performances.

Along with its
Beaux-Arts white
terra-cotta façade, the
theater has the last-
remaining cast-iron
building front in
Chicago. In 1902,
architects Hill and
Woltersdorf
remodeled the
west façade and
added another
floor. The elaborate
decoration of the
theater's marble-
columned entrance-
way, triumphal arch (inspired
by Paris' Arc de Triomphe),

**Chicago Theatre's
marquee and sign**

and palatial lobby reflect the
opulence of early theater
design. The six-story-high
"Chicago" sign above the
marquee has become a
glittering symbol of the city.

Michigan Avenue Bridge ⑱

Map 2 D5. Ⓜ *State.*

Linking the loop with the
Magnificent Mile, Michigan
Avenue Bridge, the first
double-deck bascule
bridge ever built, was
completed in 1920.
Spanning the Chicago
River, the bridge's two
leaves, each weighing
3,340 tons, open by
turning on enormous
trunnion bearings on
the riverbanks.

The bas-relief
sculptures, one on
each of the four
bridgehouses, com-
memorate important
events in Chicago's
history. A plaque on
the southwest corner
marks the site of Fort
Dearborn (1803–1812); brass
markers embedded in the

**Henry Hering's *Defence* depicting
the 1812 massacre, on bridgehouse**

concrete outline the shape of
the original fort.

At the bridge's north end, in
the 401 North Michigan
Avenue plaza, a plaque marks
the homestead of Jean
Baptiste Point du Sable,
Chicago's first permanent
non-American Indian resident.

Michigan Avenue Bridge is
one of 20 downtown bridges
spanning the Chicago River,
in a city that has the greatest
number of movable bridges
of any city in the world.

Visitors can also stroll along
nearby City-developed
Riverwalk, parallel to Wacker

The opulent interior of the restored Chicago Theatre

Drive from Wabash Avenue to Wells Street, stopping during the summer to enjoy any of the numerous café patios.

35 East Wacker Drive ⑲

Map 4 D1. 🄲 726-4260. Ⓜ Lake; State. 🄾 24 hrs daily. ♿

THIS SANDY-COLORED terra-cotta office building has been described as a "confection" – the dome at the top really does resemble a

Frieze on 35 East Wacker Drive

birthday cake! The building, designed by Thielbar and Fugard, opened in 1926. During Prohibition, the dome housed mobster Al Capone's notorious speakeasy, the Stratosphere Club.

The building once had private parking garages on each of the first 22 floors; jeweler tenants, concerned about security, drove into the elevator and were lifted up to their floors. The garages were converted into office space in the 1940s. A 1988 renovation restored the marble interior. Outside, a 6-ton clock with the gilded bronze figure of Father Time overhangs the Wacker Drive sidewalk.

35 East Wacker Drive, seen from across the Chicago River

Corberó's *Three Lawyers and a Judge* in the R.R. Donnelley Building

R.R. Donnelley Building ⑳

77 W Wacker Dr. **Map** 3 C1. 🄲 917-1177. Ⓜ Clark. 🄾 24 hrs daily. ♿

THE R.R. Donnelley Building (1992), a modern 50-story office tower over-looking the Chicago River, is one of the most recent skyscrapers to be built in the Downtown Core.

Designed by Chicago architect James DeStefano, with famed Catalan architect Ricardo Bofill as the design consultant, the building combines classical aesthetic with Chicago School (*see pp24–5*) functionality. The many classical references to ancient Greece and Rome include the four-pedimented roof, a contemporary take on a classically proportioned Greek temple. The building materials likewise conjure the classics: a grid of Portuguese white granite frames the exterior curtain wall of silver reflective glass.

The ground-floor marble lobby, with its 42-ft- (13-m-) high ceiling and huge, classical windows, is a monumental space housing two sculptural groupings: Ricardo Bofill's *Twisted Columns* (1992), a set of three Modernistic columns hand-carved from white Italian marble, and Catalan sculptor Xavier Corberó's *Three Lawyers and a Judge* (1992), rough-hewn basalt figures suggesting human forms.

At night, 540 high-intensity lamps dramatically illuminate the building in a lighting scheme designed by Pierre Arnaud, who also illuminated the Pyramids, the Parthenon, and the Louvre Museum.

View of buildings along water-front Wacker Drive, at twilight

The towering atrium in the James R. Thompson Center

James R. Thompson Center ㉑

100 W Randolph St. **Map** 3 C1.
C 814-6660. **M** Clark.
O 6:30am–6pm (atrium 8am–6pm)
Mon–Fri. **&** **■** Art exhibits.

Tʜᴇ ᴊᴀᴍᴇs R. Thompson Center (1985) is a refreshing change from the rectangular skyscrapers that make up Chicago's Downtown Core. Architect Helmut Jahn designed the center as a symbol of open democratic government, one with no barriers between it and the people. The all-glass walls and roof in this multishaped structure provide a monumental, dazzling – and some say, chaotic – transparency.

Originally called the State of Illinois Building, and often still referred to as such, the building was later renamed after the former Illinois governor who commissioned it. The tricolor (patriotic but often criticized salmon, silver, and blue) center is home to almost 70 government offices and numerous restaurants and shops. Performances and fairs are often held in the atrium.

The interior rotunda, at 17 stories and 160 ft (49 m) in diameter, is one of the largest enclosed spaces in the world. A cylindrical skylight soaring 75 ft (23 m) above the roofline caps the rotunda. The building's steel frame weighs almost 10,500 tons.

Exposed escalator and elevator machinery echo the building's no-barriers theme.

Elevators run up glass shafts to a viewing platform on the 16th floor. Here, visitors brave enough to look down will have a stunning view of the marble rosette in the granite concourse floor marking the building's center.

Throughout the building are 14 specially commissioned artworks showcasing Illinois artists, and selections from the building's permanent art collection are also on view. Ask for a directory at the information desk.

On the second floor is the Illinois Art Gallery, with visiting exhibitions, and the Illinois Artisans Shop, selling artworks and crafts.

Not on view to the public are eight ice banks – each 40 ft (12 m) long, 12 ft (3.5 m) wide, and 14 ft (4 m) tall – in the sub-basement. In summer, up to 400 tons of ice is frozen each night in these giant cubes, then used to cool the building.

Outside the building, at the Randolph Street entrance, sits Jean Dubuffet's 29-ft (9-m) lighthearted fiberglass sculpture *Monument with Standing Beast* (1984) *(see p44)*.

333 West Wacker Drive ㉒

Map 3 B1. **C** 443-8254.
M Washington (brown, orange, purple lines). **O** 7am–6:30pm
Mon–Fri. **&** **P**

Lᴏᴄᴀᴛᴇᴅ ᴀᴛ ᴀ ʙᴇɴᴅ in the Chicago River, this prominent Post-Modern, 36-story edifice echoes the curving form of its natural neighbor. Designed in 1983

The massive James R. Thompson Center, *Standing Beast* in foreground

by the architectural firm of Kohn Pedersen Fox, the office tower is sheathed with reflective, green-tinted glass that changes shade depending on the sun and water. Broad horizontal bands of brushed stainless steel run every 6 ft (2 m). Green marble and gray granite form the base of this elegant, wedge-shaped building, materials used again in the two-story lobby.

A cityscape reflected on 333 West Wacker Drive's convex surface

Wacker Drive ㉓

From N Wacker Dr to N Michigan Ave.
Map 3 C1. **M** *Clark.*

Wacker Drive's east-west segment offers one of the loveliest downtown walks of any US city. Running alongside the south bank of the main branch of the Chicago River and connecting to 17 of the city's bridges, this two-tiered street was the first of its kind in the world.

Named in honor of Charles Wacker, one of Chicago's civic planners *(see p71)*, the drive was built in 1926 to replace the run-down South Water Street Market.

The lower level is reserved for through traffic, but the upper level consists of a roadway, sidewalks, and a pleasant riverwalk, lined with public art.

Wacker Drive affords a splendid view across the river of impressive architecture, including the massive Merchandise Mart. Built by Marshall Field in 1931, it is, at

The fortresslike Merchandise Mart, best viewed from Wacker Drive

4.2 million sq ft (390,000 sq m), the world's largest commercial building.

State Street Bridge Gallery, in the bridge's mechanical room (open daily, no admission charge), offers visitors a rare opportunity to see the machinery at work behind this famous movable bridge. The gallery also displays local artwork.

At 75 East Wacker Drive is the city's thinnest skyscraper. This Gothic-style, 1928 building is clad in white terracotta.

The Chicago Architecture Foundation's river cruise tours, departing from Michigan Avenue Bridge at Wacker Drive, offer fantastic views of Chicago's towers.

CHICAGO'S RIVER

No other natural feature played as important a role in the early development of Chicago as did the Chicago River. For Native Americans and settlers alike, the river served as a trade route connecting the Great Lakes and the heart of the continent. By the mid-1800s, as shipping became a major economic activity in the area, the Chicago River was the main thoroughfare of a growing metropolis.

One unsanitary result of such growth was that the Chicago River also served as the city's sewer, a dumping ground for waste. The swampy conditions, with the surface of the land near to the level of standing water, made it impossible to construct an underground sewer system.

In the mid-1800s, a Boston engineer, Ellis Chesbrough, was hired to fix the problem. Chesbrough developed the country's first comprehensive sewer system – above ground. The streets, along with the buildings on them, were raised above the new system, sometimes by as much as 12 ft (3.5 m). The city's largest hotel at the time, the Tremont, was raised while still open for business, without breaking a pane of glass or cracking a plaster wall.

This new sewer system did not entirely eradicate the city's unsanitary conditions, however. In 1885, a devastating cholera and typhoid epidemic killed thousands of Chicagoans (12 percent of the population by some estimates) when sewage flowed into Lake Michigan, the city's source of drinking water.

In response to this tragedy, the city initiated the largest municipal project in the US at the time – the construction of the 28-mile- (45-km-) long Sanitary and Ship Canal. Built between Damen Avenue and the town of Lockport, the canal connected the Chicago River to the Des Plaines and Illinois Rivers and involved the digging out of more rocks, soil, and clay than was excavated for the Panama Canal. This massive project reversed the flow of the main and south branches of the river, which now drain away from Lake Michigan and into the Sanitary and Ship Canal.

Drawbridge spanning the Chicago River opening for water traffic

NORTH SIDE

JUST NORTH OF the Chicago River, Chicago's North Side encompasses several neighborhoods, most settled in the mid-1880s by Irish, German, and Swedish immigrants. Tragically, the 1871 fire razed the entire area. The communities

Ornate detailing on Present Bridge

rose from the ashes, and today the Magnificent Mile, Gold Coast, Streeterville, and River North are all upscale residential and shopping districts. Modest Old Town is an eclectic mix of residences, shops, and entertainment venues.

SIGHTS AT A GLANCE

Historic Buildings and Streets
Charnley-Persky House **29**
Crilly Court and Olsen-Hansen Row Houses **22**
Drake Hotel **9**
Edward P. Russell House **28**
1500 North Astor Street **27**
1550 North State Parkway **24**
Hotel Inter-Continental Chicago **3**
Menomonee Street **20**
Newberry Library **18**
Residence of the Roman Catholic Archbishop of Chicago **25**
Samuel M. Nickerson and Ransom R. Cable Houses **15**
Tribune Tower **2**
Wacker Houses **21**
Water Tower and Pumping Station **5**
Wrigley Building **1**

Modern Skyscrapers
John Hancock Center **7**
Marina City and IBM Building **13**

Churches and Cathedrals
Fourth Presbyterian Church **6**
Quigley Seminary and Chapel of St. James **17**
St. James Episcopal Cathedral **16**
St. Michael's Church **19**

Museums and Galleries
Chicago Children's Museum **12**

Chicago Historical Society **23**
International Museum of Surgical Science **26**
Museum of Contemporary Art **10**
River North Gallery District **14**
Terra Museum of American Art **4**

Shopping Streets
Oak Street **8**

Piers and Beaches
Navy Pier **11**
Oak Street Beach **30**

GETTING THERE
The Magnificent Mile is a short walk from the Loop. CTA stations Grand and Chicago are nearby, and buses 3, 145, 146, 147, and 151 run along Michigan Avenue to farther destinations. A free trolley circles Streeterville. CTA red line serves River North and the Gold Coast; Sedgwick station serves Old Town.

KEY
- Street-by-Street map
  See pp60–61
- **M** CTA train station
- **P** Parking

◁ **Aerial view of the Gold Coast, looking north to Lincoln Park**

Street-by-Street: The Magnificent Mile

T HE MAGNIFICENT MILE, a stretch of Michigan Avenue north of the
Chicago River, is Chicago's most fashionable street. Although
almost completely destroyed in the 1871 fire, by the early 1900s,
Michigan Avenue had become a major traffic artery. The 1920
opening of Michigan Avenue Bridge led to a retail boom. In 1947,
developer Arthur Rubloff, predicting that the street would be
Chicago's premier shopping district, dubbed it the Magnificent
Mile. His prediction came true and the name stuck. Exclusive
shops line the wide boulevard, while modern retail
complexes and mixed-use skyscrapers rub shoulders
with historic buildings.

★ John Hancock Center
*This tower offers spectacular
views from its open-air
skywalk on the 94th floor.
The ground-level plaza has
a fountain, cafés, and,
occasionally, live music* **7**

**Fourth Presbyterian
Church**
*Fourteen carved stone
angels, each holding a
musical instrument, adorn
the nave of this Gothic
Revival-style church, the
oldest structure on the
Magnificent Mile after the
Water Tower. A large fountain sparkles at the center of
its inner courtyard* **6**

City Place, a modern
candy-colored granite
building, houses shops
at street level, a hotel on
the middle floors, and
offices on the upper
floors.

KEY

- - - Suggested route

STAR SIGHTS

★ Hotel Inter-
   Continental
   Chicago

★ John Hancock
   Center

★ Terra Museum of
   American Art

★ Water Tower and
   Pumping Station

**★ Water Tower and
Pumping Station**
*These two historic
castellated structures, the
station housing a café and
information-packed visitors'
center, sit on an island in
the street – a relaxing,
shady retreat from busy
Michigan Avenue* **5**

Chicago Place *contains
specialty shops and an airy
food court with an excellent
view of Michigan Avenue.
Historical murals decorate
the building's lobby.*

★ **Terra Museum of American Art**
One of the major cultural attractions on the Magnificent Mile, this museum's highlight is its collection of American Impressionist paintings ❹

Water Tower Place
contains eight floors of upscale boutiques and numerous restaurants, as well as two major department stores.

★ **Hotel Inter-Continental Chicago**
An eclectic mix of detailing – from Mesopotamian-inspired carvings to knights in armor – vie for attention in this 1926 hotel ❸

Tribune Tower
Rock fragments from famous sites around the world, including St. Peter's Basilica in Rome, are embedded in the exterior of this Gothic-style tower ❷

Wrigley Building
This structure, one of Chicago's most beloved, boasts a giant four-sided clock and a quiet courtyard, which is open to the public. The building is particularly dazzling at night, when it is illuminated ❶

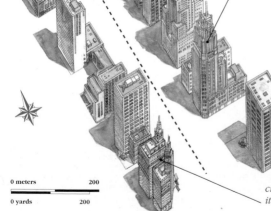

NORTH MICHIGAN AVENUE

0 meters 200
0 yards 200

View of the two-part Wrigley Building, to the left of Tribune Tower

Wrigley Building ❶

400–410 N Michigan Ave. **Map** 2
D5. **C** 923-8080. **M** Grand (red
line). **North lobby** ○ 24 hrs daily;
South lobby ○ 7am–6pm
Mon–Fri. **South building** ● public
hols. &

THE WRIGLEY BUILDING rests
on a historical site: it was
to here that Jesuit missionary
Jacques Marquette and
explorer Louis Joliet made
their first portage west of the
Great Lakes in the 1670s, and
here that La Salle planted the
flag of France (see p13).

Chewing-gum manufac-
turer William Wrigley, Jr.
commissioned the architectural firm Graham, Anderson,
Probst and White to design
the building. The 30-story
south tower was built in
1920, the 21-story north
tower in 1924. They are connected by three arcades. The
circular temple and cupola
rising above a massive four-
faced clock were inspired by
Seville's Giralda Tower.

Six shades of white enamel,
from gray to cream, were
baked onto the terra-cotta
cladding. Illuminated at
night, the building shimmers.

Tribune Tower ❷

435 N Michigan Ave. **Map** 2 D5.
C 222-3232. **M** Grand (red line).
○ 24 hrs daily. &

THE 36-STORY limestone
Tribune Tower is the
winning design of a 1922
international competition
sponsored by the Tribune
Company to celebrate the
75th anniversary of the
Chicago Tribune. Architects
were challenged to create the
most beautiful office building
in the world. From 263 sub-
missions, that of New York
firm Howells and Hood was
chosen. Their Gothic design,
reflected in the flying
buttresses of the crowning
tower, echoes France's
Rouen Cathedral.

The building's ornate three-
story arched entrance is
carved with figures from
Aesop's fables. Gargoyles,
such as the monkey symbol-
izing human folly (below the
south-side fourth-floor windows), embellish the façade.
More than 100 rock fragments
from famous sites, including
Beijing's Forbidden City and
London's Westminster Abbey,
are embedded in the exterior
walls, as is a 3.3-billion-year-
old piece of moon rock, collected by the Apollo 15 mission. A guide to the rocks is
available in the lobby.

Hotel Inter-Continental Chicago ❸

505 N Michigan Ave. **Map** 2 D5.
C 944-4100. **M** Grand (red line).
○ 24 hrs daily. & ♠ ♚ ⬜ ♟
P See **Where to Stay** p138.

ORIGINALLY the Shriners'
Medinah Athletic Club,
this magnificent building was
renovated at a cost of $130
million, reopening in 1990 as
the Hotel Inter-Continental
Chicago. Designed in 1929
by Walter W. Ahlschlager, it is
topped with a large onion-
shaped gilt dome.

Many of the building's
exterior and interior details
reflect the Shriners' interest
in all things Egyptian,
medieval, and Renaissance.
Ask the concierge for the free
self-guided tour audiotape,
which will explain the building's historic features.

Carved on the 2nd-floor
staircase to the Hall of Lions,
two lions guard the intricate
terra-cotta fountain. Inside
the King Arthur Foyer and
Court on the 3rd floor, colorful paintings on the ceiling
beams depict King Arthur's
life. On the 5th floor, classical Renaissance paintings
adorn the walls of the
Renaissance Room Foyer.
The Spanish Tea Court features a fountain lined with
Spanish Majolica tiles.

A gem is the 11th-floor
swimming pool, named after
the swimmer and actor
Johnny Weissmuller. It was
considered an engineering
feat in 1929 because it was
high above the ground floor.

The Johnny Weissmuller Pool at Hotel Inter-Continental Chicago

Terra Museum's marble exterior

Terra Museum of American Art ❹

664 N Michigan Ave. **Map** 2 D4.
C 664-3939. **M** Chicago (red line);
Grand (red line). ◯ 10am–8pm Tue;
10am–6pm Wed–Sat; noon–5pm
Sun. ● major hols. 🎟 (free Tue).
♿ 🚻 noon weekdays (except
Mon); 2pm weekends. 🎤 Lectures.

Amidst the Magnificent Mile's retail bustle is the Terra Museum of American Art. Daniel J. Terra, a former US ambassador-at-large for cultural affairs, founded the museum in 1980 in Evanston to display his extensive personal art collection.

The museum, now in its new five-story location, houses more than 800 American works, including paintings, prints, and sculptures from the 18th, 19th, and 20th centuries. Particularly noteworthy are the American Impressionist paintings by artists such as Theodore Robinson (1862–1948).

Other important artists represented include Mary Cassatt, Georgia O'Keeffe, Milton Avery, John Singer Sargent, and James A.M. Whistler. An early American masterpiece in the collection is Samuel F.B. Morse's *Gallery of the Louvre* (1831–3), purchased in 1982 for $3.2 million.

Water Tower and Pumping Station ❺

806 N Michigan Ave. **Map** 2 D4. **M**
Chicago (red line); Grand (red line).
Tower **C** 744-0808. ◯ 10am–
6:30pm Mon–Sat; 10am–5pm Sun.
● public hols. **Station** **C** 744-
2400. ◯ 7:30am–7pm daily. ●
Thanksgiving, Dec 25. ♿ station
only. 🚻 📷 🛈

Built just before the fire of 1871, the Water Tower (1869) and the Pumping Station (1866), housing Chicago's waterworks, were two of the few buildings in the city to survive the conflagration.

Designed by William W. Boyington, these structures look like Gothic castles. The 154-ft (47-m) tower consists of limestone blocks rising in five sections from a square base. The tower originally housed a standpipe that stabilized pressure of the water flowing in the mains. It is now home to a City Gallery, which specializes in photography. Lookingglass Theatre will make its new home here as well, in 2002.

In addition to housing a Visitor Information Center, the Pumping Station still fulfills its original purpose, pumping up to 250 million gallons (946 million liters) of water per day.

The Water Tower survived Chicago's Great Fire of 1871

Fourth Presbyterian Church ❻

866 N Michigan Ave. **Map** 2 D4.
C 787-4570. **M** Chicago (red line).
◯ 9am–5pm Mon–Fri; 8:30am–
9pm Sun. ✝ 8:30am, 11am,
6:30pm Sun. ♿ via 126 E Chestnut
St. **Concerts** 12:10pm Fri.

The 1871 fire destroyed the original Fourth Presbyterian Church the night it was dedicated. The new building (1914) was the first major structure built on Michigan Avenue after the fire.

Designed by Ralph Adams Cram, architect of New York's Cathedral of St. John the Divine, the church is Gothic Revival in style *(see p24)*. Its exposed buttresses, stone spire, and recessed main window all reflect the influences of medieval European churches.

The interior of the church is cathedral-like. The illuminated timber ceiling rises ten stories; the stained-glass windows are magnificent.

A covered walkway leads to a tranquil courtyard, surrounded by parish buildings, which was designed by Howard Van Doren Shaw.

The church's organ – a Chicago treasure – can be heard at weekly concerts.

The peaceful courtyard of the Fourth Presbyterian Church

John Hancock Center ❼

875 N Michigan Ave. **Map** 2 D4.
Observatory 751-3681. **M**
Chicago (red line). 9am–mid-
night daily. to observatory (children under 4 free).

Affectionately called
"Big John" by Chicago-
ans, John Hancock Center
stands out as a bold feature
of the Chicago skyline. The
100-story building has 18-
story-long steel braces crisscrossing the tapering obelisk
tower like stacked Xs.

The center's major attraction is the observatory on the
94th floor. Here, 1,000 ft (305
m) above the Magnificent
Mile, you can actually go outside, onto Chicago's only
open-air (screened) skywalk.
Designed by
architect
Bruce
Graham of
Skidmore,
Owings and
Merrill and
engineer
Fazlur R.
Khan, the
Hancock
Center
opened in
1969. It
houses
offices,
condo-
miniums,
and shops in
2.8 million
sq ft (0.26
million sq
m) of space.

**Open-air deck topping
the Hancock Center**

The elevator
ride to the top is touted as
the fastest in North America.
At 20 miles (32 km) per hour,
you reach the observatory in
just 40 seconds. On a clear
day, you can see for up to 80
miles (130 km). The view is
especially dazzling when
late-afternoon sun falls upon
the downtown buildings to
the south. A wall-to-wall
exhibition in the observatory
traces Chicago's history.

The Chicago Architecture
Foundation shop and tour
center is in the concourse.
The lower courtyard has
cafés, with patios in summer.

Entrance to the 1920s Drake Hotel

Oak Street ❽

Between Rush St & N Michigan Ave.
Map 2 D3. **M** Chicago (red line).
See **Shops and Markets** pp156–9.

Tree-lined Oak Street at
the north end of the
Magnificent Mile is home to
many upscale boutiques:
Giorgio Armani, Hermès,
Sonia Rykiel, and Gianni
Versace. The Daisy Shop
specializes in vintage couture
resale clothing. Wolford
Boutique sells European
hosiery and swimwear.

Along with its chic fashion
boutiques, Oak Street has
numerous art galleries, such
as Billy Hork Galleries,
which sells limited-edition
prints and vintage posters,
and Colletti Antique Poster
Gallery, specializing in original works from 1880 to 1940.
The Watermark offers sta-
tionery and unique gift-wrap-
ping: it seals gifts in a can.

The 20-story apartment
building (1929) at No. 40 was
designed by Ben Marshall,
architect of the Drake Hotel.

Drake Hotel ❾

140 E Walton Pl. **Map** 2 D3. 787-
2200. **M** Chicago (red line).
See **Where to Stay** p137.

The essence of luxury in the
heart of the Magnificent
Mile, the 537-room Drake
Hotel opened in 1920.
Designed by Marshall and
Fox in the Italian Renaissance
style (see p24), this 13-story
hotel is clad in limestone.

The lobby, paneled in
marble and oak, is graced
with grand chandeliers,
elegant red carpets, and a
magnificent fountain.

The elegant Palm Court, in
the lobby, offers traditional
afternoon tea and is also a
fashionable place for cocktails. The Cape Cod Room has
an extensive seafood menu.

Chicago jive-legend Buddy
Charles plays regularly at the
hotel's splendid piano bar, the
Coq d'Or. The piano bar is
famous for another reason,
too. When Prohibition ended
in 1933, it served the second
drink in Chicago.

Upscale boutiques lining Oak Street

The Museum of Contemporary Art's grand entrance

Museum of Contemporary Art ⑩

220 E Chicago Ave. *Map* 2 D4. 📞 280-2660. Ⓜ *Chicago (red line).* ◐ 10am–8pm Tue; 10am–5pm Wed–Sun. ⬤ *Jan 1, Thanksgiving, Dec 25.* 🎫 *(free Tue).* ♿ 🛍 🛒 💻 🔧 🅿

Founded in 1967, the Museum of Contemporary Art's mission is to preserve, interpret, and present contemporary art. Designed by Berlin architect Josef Paul Kleihues, the sleek building has four floors of naturally lit exhibition space. On display are selections from the museum's extensive collection of works by internationally acclaimed artists, including Andy Warhol, René Magritte, Cindy Sherman, and Alexander Calder. Don't miss Richard Long's *Chicago Mud Circle* (1996), an exuberant application of mud on the gallery wall. There are also temporary exhibitions.

Once a month, the museum hosts an evening of live music in its lovely Sculpture Garden.

Navy Pier ⑪

600 E Grand Ave. *Map* 2 F5. 📞 595-7437. 🚌 *29, 56, 65, 66, 120, 121.* ⬤ *Thanksgiving, Dec 25.* ♿ 🍴 🛒 📷 🅿 ℹ *Lake cruises.*

Navy Pier is a bustling recreational and cultural center. Designed by Charles S. Frost, the 3,000-ft- (915-m-) long and 400-ft- (120-m-) wide pier was the largest in

Tranquil fountains and palms at Navy Pier's Crystal Gardens

the world when built in 1916. More than 20,000 Oregon timber piles were used to support the buildings. Originally a municipal wharf,

the pier was used for naval training during World War II. After a four-year renovation, Navy Pier opened in its present incarnation in 1995.

Navy Pier Park has a 150-ft- (45-m-) Ferris wheel, (great views of the skyline); old-fashioned carousel; outdoor amphitheater; and IMAX 3D theater. The Smith Museum displays stained glass from Chicago's buildings.

Free trolleys run between Navy Pier and State Street.

Chicago Children's Museum ⑫

700 E Grand Ave. *Map* 2 F5. 📞 527-1000. 🚌 *29, 56, 65, 66.* ◐ 10am–5pm Tue–Sun; hol Mon. ⬤ *Thanksgiving, Dec 25.* 🎫 *(free 5–8pm Tue).* ♿ 🛒 🅿 *Special activities daily.*

Chicago Children's Museum, focusing on activating the intellectual and creative potential of children age 1 to 12, is an activity center for the whole family. All exhibits are hands-on. Kids can build a fort in the Under Construction exhibit, be part of a TV crew in the Info-Tech Arcade, or make a flying machine in the Invent-ing Lab. In the WaterWays, they can channel water with dams and locks.

The Dinosaur Expedition gallery has a reproduction of a huge *Suchomimus* skeleton. Kids can dig for bones in an excavation pit. Along with these educational exhibits, there are many opportunities for children to simply climb, slide, and jump around.

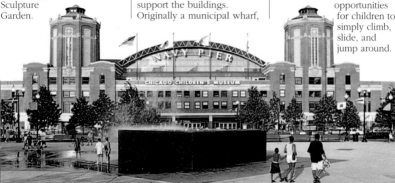

Chicago Children's Museum, at the main entrance to Navy Pier

Marina City and IBM Building ⑬

Marina City: 300 N State St.
Map 1 C5. **☎** 222-1111. **M** State.
◯ 24 hrs daily. **♿ 🏢 🅿**
IBM Building: 330 N Wabash Ave.
Map 2 D5. **☎** 923-8050. **M** State.
◯ 24 hrs daily. **♿**

THE TWO TOWERS of Marina City pay symbolic tribute to the Midwest's farming economy – they look like giant corncobs. Designed by Bertrand Goldberg Associates and opened in 1967, these twin circular towers function like a city within a city, with apartments, offices, shops, parking, a theater, marina, and even a bowling alley and skating rink.

To the east of Marina City, and in stark contrast to its organic form, rises the IBM Building, a sleek modern monument. Designed by Mies van der Rohe (see p28) with C.F. Murphy Associates and opened in 1971, the 52-story office tower has an exposed steel frame and dark bronze-tinted glass walls.

A small bust of Mies van der Rohe, who died before construction of the building was complete, is located in the lobby. In winter, the exterior plaza can be quite bleak and frigid. Strung ropes prevent people from being blown into the Chicago River.

Marina City's twin towers, flanked on the right by the IBM Building

Shops and galleries lining the streets of the River North Gallery District

River North Gallery District ⑭

Between N Wells & N Orleans Sts, from W Huron St to W Chicago Ave.
Map 1 B4. **M** Chicago (brown, purple lines). **☎** 649-0064.
See **Shops and Markets** pp156–9.

RIVER NORTH is home to some of Chicago's finest antique and home-furnishing shops. There are also more than 50 art galleries here – the largest concentration outside New York City.

West Superior Street is the center of the district. Galleries here and on adjoining streets offer a wide range of artwork by both international and local artisans. Unusual pieces by American folk artists, African-American art, glass sculpture, photography, and superb Arts and Crafts objects are just some of the treasures to be found. Most galleries are closed Sundays and Mondays.

Samuel M. Nickerson and Ransom R. Cable Houses ⑮

40 & 25 E Erie St. **Map** 2 D4. **M**
Chicago (red line); Grand (red line).
Nickerson House ☎ 640-1300.
◯ 9am–5pm Mon–Sat.
Cable House ● to public.

SAMUEL M. NICKERSON House offers a glimpse into the wealthy world of late-1800s Chicago high society. Commissioned by Nickerson, a

distillery owner and banker, this Italian Renaissance palazzo was designed in 1883 by Chicago church-architects Burling and Whitehouse. The mansion's owners, R.H. Love Galleries, restored the interior in the late 1980s.

It has 23 rooms on its three floors, each room seemingly more opulent than the next. More than 20 varieties of marble, along with onyx and alabaster, were used to build the main hall and great staircase. Even the ceiling is marble. The largest room is the first-floor Picture Gallery, illuminated by a domed, Tiffany leaded-glass skylight.

Across the street, the Ransom R. Cable House now quarters a securities and capital management corporation. Designed by Cobb and Frost, the 1886 Richardsonian Romanesque (see p24) mansion was built for the president of the Chicago, Rock Island and Pacific Railway Company. It features rough-hewn rusticated masonry, a triple-arched corner entrance, and a charming coach house.

Charming coach house belonging to the Ransom R. Cable House

St. James Episcopal Cathedral ⓰

65 E Huron St. **Map** 2 D4. 787-7360. M *Chicago (red line)*. ○ *for mass only.* **Cathedral** ♦ *9am, 11am Sun;* **Chapel** ♦ *12:10pm Mon–Fri; 5:30pm Wed; 9am Sat; 8am Sun.*   **Concerts**.

THE PARISHIONERS of St. James have worshiped at this site since 1857. After their original building was destroyed in the Great Fire of 1871 (only the 1867 bell tower survived), architects Clarke and Faulkner were hired to design a new building. The St. James Episcopal Cathedral, a Gothic Revival *(see p24)* structure of Joliet limestone, was completed in 1875.

Inside is a fine example of Victorian stencil work (1888), designed by Edward J. Neville Stent, a student of British designer William Morris. The stencils were restored in 1985 by the Chicago architects Holabird and Root.

The Chapel of St. Andrew is at the north end of the cathedral. Designed by Bertram G. Goodhue in 1913, it is said to be based on a private oratory in an ancient Scottish abbey. The painted-glass windows portray the figures of St. Paul, Mary Magdalene, and St. Francis.

The majestic altar and windows in the Chapel of St. James

Statue of Archbishop Quigley outside Quigley Seminary

Quigley Seminary and Chapel of St. James ⓱

831 N Rush St. **Map** 2 D4. 787-8625. M *Chicago (red line).* **Seminary** ● *to public.* **Chapel** ✓ *mandatory: noon, 2pm Tue, Thu–Sat.* **Concerts**.

THE QUIGLEY Seminary, a high-school-level seminary for the archdiocese of Chicago, was designed by Zachary T. Davis (architect of Wrigley Field) and Gustave E. Steinback. Completed in 1919, this Gothic monument has carved buttresses and spires.

Ten statues in the niches along the north wall represent saints, such as St. Cecilia, patron of music, and St. Elizabeth, patron of pregnant women. Adorning the spire of the library tower is a statue of St. George, his iron spear serving as the building's lightning rod. A statue of Archbishop James E. Quigley (1854–1915), known for his commitment to building Catholic schools in Chicago in the early 20th century, perches at the northwest corner of the grounds.

The school's Chapel of St. James was inspired by Paris' Gothic Sainte-Chapelle. The spectacular Rose Window, 28 ft (9 m) in diameter, depicts the life of the Virgin Mary. Smaller windows relate stories from the Bible. The pictorial scheme represents 245 events of scriptural and church history. More than 700,000 pieces of glass are set in limestone frames.

The magnificent 50-ft-(15-m-) tall limestone altar, adorned with sculptures, was hand-carved in France.

Newberry Library ⓲

60 W Walton St. **Map** 1 C3. 943-9090. M *Chicago (red line).* ○ *Hrs for lobby, book rooms, and exhibits vary; call ahead.* ● *public hols.* & ✓ *3pm Thu; 10:30am Sat.* **Exhibits, lectures, concerts**.

AT THE NORTH end of Washington Square Park, the city's oldest park, is the impressive Newberry Library. Founded in 1887 by Walter Newberry, a merchant and banker, this independent research library for the humanities – one of the best in the US – opened to the public in 1893. Henry Ives Cobb, master architect of the Richardsonian Romanesque style, was the designer.

Strengths of the collection include cartography, Native American history, and Renaissance studies. Rarities include a 1481 edition of Dante's *Divine Comedy* and first editions of Milton's *Paradise Regained* and the King James Version of the Bible.

Through the triple-arched entranceway, the lobby features a grand marble staircase, terrazzo flooring, galleries, and a bookstore.

Jeweled cover of the first edition of Milton's *Paradise Regained*

St. Michael's Church ⓭

447 W Eugenie St. **Map** 1 B1.
▮ 642-2498. Ⓜ *Sedgwick.*
◯ *8am–7pm daily.* ✝ *8am, 5:30pm
Mon, Wed, Thu, Fri; 8am, 6pm Tue,
Sat; 8am, 11am, 7pm Sun.* ♿
weekends or by arrangement. Ⓟ

THE ORIGINAL St. Michael's Church was a small brick building built in 1852. As St. Michael's small congregation expanded, it outgrew the building. The cornerstone for a new church was laid in 1866. Just three years later, the building's construction was complete.

Just two years later, the Great Fire of 1871 destroyed the roof and floors of the church. However, the thick, brick walls survived and remain to this day, incorporated into the 1872 Romanesque-style structure designed by architect August Wallbaum.

Angel in St. Michael's

The steeple, added to the bell tower in 1888, rises 290 ft (88.5 m) above the ground. The bell tower is adorned with a large four-faced clock with wooden hands. Each of the five bells in the tower weighs between 2,500 and 6,000 lbs (1,135 and 2,720 kg). By tradition, if you can hear the bells of St. Michael's, you are in Old Town.

Restoration of the church began in the 1990s. The first phase involved removing two tons of pigeon excrement from inside the bell tower.

The colorful, high-domed interior has stained glass, murals, and sculptures depicting the life of Christ. The carved high altar and its four subsidiary altars illustrate St. Michael, flanked by the archangels Gabriel and Raphael, triumphant over Lucifer.

A small monument on the grounds is dedicated to Catholic war veterans.

335 Menomonee Street, a wooden cottage typical of Old Town

Menomonee Street ⓴

From N Sedgwick St to Lincoln Park W. **Map** 1 B1. Ⓜ *Sedgwick.*

MENOMONEE STREET lies in the heart of Old Town Triangle Historic District (bounded by Cleveland Street and North and Lincoln Avenues), a delightful area of vintage cottages and Queen Anne-style *(see p24)* row houses settled in the mid-1800s by working-class German immigrants.

In the 1940s, community concern over the area's falling fortunes led to one of the city's earliest neighborhood revitalization efforts. Today, the Old Town Triangle's narrow tree-lined streets are home to picturesque houses and numerous interesting shops and restaurants.

Walk along Menomonee Street to view the residences that typify mid- to late-19th-century Old Town. Most of the original houses in the area were small cottages built using the method of balloon framing, so-called because such structures were reportedly as easy to construct as blowing up a balloon *(see p25)*. The lightweight wooden frames provided ample kindling when the 1871 fire swept through the area.

The whitish gray clapboard house at No. 350 is a rare surviving example of the fire-relief shanties the Chicago Relief and Aid Society built for people made homeless by the fire. These two-room

The high-domed interior and main altar of St. Michael's Church

structures, costing the City about $100 each, were transported on wagons to charred lots, providing fire victims with instant lodging.

The shanties were later replaced with permanent wooden cottages, constructed before an 1874 city ordinance prohibited the building of wooden structures. The high basements and raised front staircases typical of these cottages were designed to accommodate the above-ground sewage system *(see p57)*. The cottages at Nos. 325–45, although built after 1871, are typical of those in the neighborhood before the ravages of the Great Fire.

Wacker Houses ㉑

1836 & 1838 N Lincoln Park W. **Map** 1 B1. Ⓜ Sedgwick. ⚫ to public.

BOTH THE Charles H. Wacker House and the Frederick Wacker House, designed in the early 1870s by an unknown architect, are highly ornate examples of the Chicago cottage style.

Commissioned by Frederick Wacker, a Swiss-born brewer, No. 1836 was built as a coach house but served as the Wacker's temporary home until No. 1838, a wood-frame structure built just before the ban on wood as a building material, was completed.

Charles Wacker, Frederick's son and the city planner after whom Wacker Drive is named *(see p57)*, remodeled the

The elaborate Queen Anne-style Olsen-Hansen Row Houses

coach house after moving it to its present location beside the main family home.

No. 1838's elaborately carved trim is an excellent example of the handcrafted details on many houses in the Old Town neighborhood.

Crilly Court and Olsen-Hansen Row Houses ㉒

Crilly Court: north of W Eugenie St between N Wells St & N Park Ave; **Olsen-Hansen Row Houses**: 164–172 W Eugenie St. **Map** 1 C1. Ⓜ Sedgwick. ⚫ to public.

REPRESENTING TWO different approaches to Queen Anne-style row-house design are Crilly Court and the Olsen-Hansen Row Houses.

Crilly Court was created in 1885 by real-estate developer Daniel F. Crilly, when he bought a city block and cut a north-south street through it, which he named after himself. Over the next ten years, Crilly built a residential and retail development, creating what is now one of the quaintest streets in Chicago.

Two columns frame the entrance to the court. On the court's west side are two-story stone row houses. On the east side is a four-story apartment building, the names of Crilly's four children carved above the doors.

The renovation of the development in the 1940s, led by Crilly's son Edgar, included

closing off alleys behind the residences to create private courtyards and replacing wooden balconies with wrought-iron ones, giving the complex a New Orleans-like atmosphere. This redevelopment of Crilly Court initiated the renewal of the Lincoln Park neighborhood.

The Olsen-Hansen Row Houses, on West Eugenie Street, are more elaborate expressions of the Queen Anne style *(see p24)*. The row houses were designed by Norwegian-born architect Harald M. Hansen in 1886 for Adolph Olsen. Only 5 of the original 12 remain.

Turrets, various window styles, Victorian porches, irregular rooflines, and a mixture of building materials – ranging from red brick to rough stone – give each of the row houses a distinctive identity. Hansen himself lived here, at No. 164.

Frederick Wacker House, with its alpine-style overhanging porch

Daniel F. Crilly, developer of Chicago's handsome Crilly Court

Astor Street

For more than 100 years, Astor Street, named for fur tycoon and real-estate magnate John Jacob Astor, has been the heart of fashionable Gold Coast. Wealthy Chicagoans flocked to the area in the 1880s and built over the next 60 years the striking houses in myriad architectural styles that line the street, though interspersed today with more modern buildings. Just six blocks long, the charming Astor Street district, designated a Chicago landmark in 1975, is ideal for leisurely strolling.

STAR SIGHTS

* ★ **Charnley-Persky House**
* ★ **Edward P. Russell House**
* ★ **Residence of the Roman Catholic Archbishop of Chicago**

JOHN JACOB ASTOR

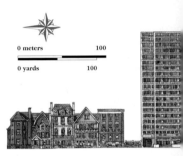

German-born John Jacob Astor (1763–1848) made his fortune in the fur trade. In 1808 he chartered the Chicago-based American Fur Company, creating a monopoly in the Great Lakes area. Astor's successful fur business helped fund later, highly profitable, real-estate ventures. When he died, he was the richest man in the US.

Astor Street East Side ‹

VISITORS' CHECKLIST

From North Ave to W Division St. **Map** 2 D1–D2. **M** *Clark/ Division.*

0 meters   100
0 yards   100

May House (No. 1443) is a granite Romanesque Revival-style mansion designed in 1891 by celebrated residential architect J.L. Silsbee, one of Frank Lloyd Wright's *(see p28)* first employers. The mansion's grand arched entranceway with ornate carving is one of its most striking features.

John L. Fortune House (No. 1451)

William D. Kerfoot
This real-estate business-man lived at No. 1425. The first Chicagoan to reopen for business in the Loop after the fire of 1871, he posted outside his hastily erected shanty a sign the day after the fire: "All gone but wife, children, and energy."

1400 Block North Astor Street
The buildings lining this handsome block of the Gold Coast reflect an eclectic mix of architectural styles, ranging from a Tudor Revival country-style house at No. 1451 to a Gothic-style chateau at No. 1449.

Astor Street West Side ‹

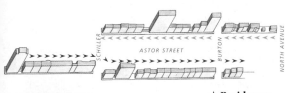

KEY

‹ ‹ ‹ ‹ ‹   East side walking south

› › › › ›   West side walking north

★ Edward P. Russell House

Carvings in a floral motif decorate the Art Deco façade and window metalwork of this 1929 Holabird and Root-designed townhouse (No. 1444) **28**

★ Residence of the Roman Catholic Archbishop of Chicago

Built in 1880 of red brick, this massive Queen Anne-style mansion is the oldest home in the area. Decorative exterior features include floral carvings and limestone trim **25**

Patterson-McCormick Mansion (No. 1500; *see p76)*

★ Charnley-Persky House

This superb house (No. 1365) is, appropriately, now the national headquarters of the Society of Architectural Historians. The building reflects the architectural styles of its two collaborators, Louis Sullivan and Frank Lloyd Wright, and is a masterpiece of Prairie School design (see p25) **29**

Astor Court

This Georgian-style mansion (No. 1355) was designed in 1914 by Howard Van Doren Shaw for William C. Goodman, who also commissioned Shaw to design the Goodman Theatre. An iron gate with decorative brass doorknobs opens to a courtyard. The building now contains luxury apartments.

Edwin J. Gardiner House (No. 1345)

Chicago Historical Society ㉓

1601 N Clark St. **Map** 1 C1.
🅲 642-4600. Ⓜ Clark/Division then
bus 22, 36. ⬤ 9:30am–4:30pm
Mon–Sat; noon–5pm Sun. ⬤ Jan 1,
Thanksgiving, Dec 25. 🏷 (free Mon)
◙ ♿ 🎫 (call for times). 🍽 🎁 🅿
Concerts, lectures.

FOUNDED IN 1856, the
Chicago Historical Society
(CHS) is the city's oldest
cultural institution. A major
museum and research center,
it boasts more than 20 million
objects, images, and
documents relating to the
history of Chicago and
Illinois. Permanent exhibits,
supplemented with temporary
exhibits, trace the early
recorded history of the
Chicago area, beginning with
the expeditions of 17th-
century French explorers such
as Father Jacques Marquette.

The first-floor Fort
Dearborn and Frontier
Chicago gallery includes early
portage maps and a wall built
of logs salvaged from the
second Fort Dearborn (see
p13). The Illinois Pioneer Life
gallery tells the settlers' story.
Visitors are introduced to
daily life on the Illinois
frontier through the re-creation
of a pioneer home and barn.
The Please Touch section,
where visitors are encouraged
to handle old farming tools,
exemplifies the hands-on
friendliness of the CHS.

Among the highlights of the
collection are the Chicago
history dioramas on the
second floor. Behind glass in
a darkened room, eight
miniature scenes show

**The original, Neo-Georgian
entrance to the Historical Society**

Chicago's rapid growth in the
18th and 19th centuries. The
dioramas begin with a
depiction of the signing of the
1795 Treaty of Greenville, in
which American Indians
ceded 25,000 sq miles (64,750
sq km) of land, including
6 sq miles (15 sq km) at the
mouth of the Chicago River.
In chronological order, the
dioramas illustrate significant
events, such as the Great Fire
of 1871 and the 1893 World's
Columbian Exposition, and
historic scenes, such as the
Chicago River during the Civil
War, and bustling LaSalle
Street in the mid-1860s.

American-history buffs
shouldn't miss the American
Wing, on the second floor,
which features 1 of only 23
surviving copies of the
Declaration of Independence
(the version printed in Philadelphia on July 4, 1776). As
well, there's a rare copy of
the American Constitution first
printed in a Philadelphia
newspaper, alongside the Bill
of Rights drafted in 1789.
Abraham Lincoln's deathbed
is also on display.

Along with the fascinating
exhibits, the building itself is
noteworthy, as it presents two
dramatic faces to the world –
one modern, one historic.
Both are imposing but
welcoming. The original Neo-
Georgian structure, designed
by Graham, Anderson, Probst
and White in 1932, is best
appreciated from Lincoln
Park. The 1988 addition faces
North Clark Street with a
three-story, glass-and-steel
atrium entrance. The most
dramatic feature is the curving
glass section at the south end,
containing a restaurant.

Contemporary sculptor
Sheila Klein's *Commemo-
rative Ground Ring*, a giant
ring with symbolic references
to landmarks of Chicago's
architectural heritage, such as
a Prairie-style roof and the
façade of the Wrigley
Building, stands at Clark
Street and North Avenue.

**1550 North State Parkway, once
the epitome of Gold Coast luxury**

1550 North State Parkway ㉔

Map 1 C1. Ⓜ Clark/Division then
bus 22, 36. ⬤ to public.

WHEN IT OPENED in 1912,
this apartment building
overlooking Lincoln Park
epitomized the luxury of the
Gold Coast. Designed by
Marshall and Fox (architects
of the Drake Hotel, see p64),
the 12-story Beaux-Arts (see
p25) structure is faced with
white terra-cotta.

Depiction of the 1871 Great Fire from the society's excellent collection

Originally, each of the floors comprised a separate apartment with 15 rooms (5 for servants) and 9,000 sq ft (835 sq m) of living space – more than four times the size of the average modest home. The luxurious apartments have since been subdivided.

The black grillwork of the iron balconies, bowed windows, and the large urns on top of the balustrade are all interesting features.

The imposing home of Chicago's Roman Catholic archbishop

Residence of the Roman Catholic Archbishop of Chicago 25

1555 N State Pkwy. **Map** 2 D1.
M Clark/Division. ● to public.

BUILT IN 1880 on the site of an early Catholic cemetery, the building is home to the archbishop of Chicago's Roman Catholic diocese. Archbishop Patrick A. Feehan was the first resident of this, the area's oldest home.

The two-and-a-half-story Queen Anne-style *(see p24)* mansion was designed by Alfred F. Pashley. Although not highly ornamented, its decorative features include Italianate windows and 19 chimneys rising from a peaked and gabled roofline, a landmark of the area.

The property surrounding the archbishop's residence was subdivided in the late 1800s by the Chicago Archdiocese and sold to Chicago's wealthy, who built their houses on the lots.

Today, the archbishop's residence has attractive landscaped grounds, complete with papal flag.

International Museum of Surgical Science 26

1524 N Lake Shore Dr. **Map** 1 D1.
C 642-6502. **M** Clark/Division then bus 22, 36. ● 10am–4pm Tue–Sat; 11am–5pm Sun. ● public hols. ● by donation. ● ● ●

THE INTERNATIONAL Museum of Surgical Science, with its cranial saws and bone crushers, is an unusual museum and well worth a visit. Where else in the world can one marvel at the variety, size, and intriguing shapes of gallstones and bladder stones?

Opened to the public in 1953, the museum is handsomely lodged in a historic (1917) four-story mansion designed by Howard Van Doren Shaw.

Fascinating exhibits from around the world trace the history of surgery and related sciences. Some of the earliest artifacts are 4,000-year-old Peruvian trepanning tools used to release evil spirits from the skull. Amazingly, some of the trepanned skulls on display show bony tissue growth,

Hope and Help, **by Edouard Chaissing, at museum entrance**

proof that patients survived the procedure.

Less grisly exhibits include a re-creation of a turn-of-the-20th-century apothecary, complete with medicine bottles, labels claiming to cure every ill. The Hall of Immortals showcases 12 larger-than-life sculptures of important figures in medical history, such as the earliest-known physician, Imhotep (c.2700 BC), and Marie Curie.

One of the most unusual exhibits is the 1935 Perfusion Pump created by Charles A. Lindbergh and Alexis Carrel, a device that enabled biologists to keep a human organ functioning once removed from the body. The scale model of a 1594 anatomical theater at the University of Padua, the extensive collection of early X-rays, a working iron lung, and a Chippendale convalescent wheelchair are also worth seeing.

The museum's library holds more than 5,000 books, including rare and antique volumes – some from as early as the 15th century. A fourth-floor art gallery displays medically related, contemporary artworks – just one more of the many surprises in this inimitable place.

Turn-of-the-20th-century apothecary shop, Museum of Surgical Science

Façade of 1500 North Astor Street, with its classical detailing

1500 North Astor Street **㉗**

Map 2 D1. **M** *Clark/Division then bus 22, 36.* ● *to public.*

THIS OPULENT four-story Italian Renaissance palazzo was built in 1893 for *Chicago Tribune* publisher Joseph Medill as a wedding gift for his daughter. Designed by McKim, Mead and White, it is built of orange Roman brick, with terra-cotta trim. The most impressive feature of this house, the largest on Astor Street, is the two-story front porch with Doric and Ionic columns.

Cyrus Hall McCormick II, son of the inventor of the Virginia reaper *(see p29)*, bought the mansion in the 1920s. He then commissioned an addition to be built at the north end, doubling the building's size. It now contains luxury condominiums.

Art Deco window on the exterior of Edward P. Russell House

Edward P. Russell House **㉘**

1444 N Astor St. **Map** 2 D2.
M *Clark/Division.* ● *to public.*

A UNIQUE, four-story townhouse, the Edward P. Russell House was designed in 1929 by the architect firm of Holabird and Root. Designed in the Art Deco style popular in the 1920s and 1930s, the house is, perhaps, the finest example of this architectural style in Chicago.

Graceful carvings in a floral motif decorate the building's smooth, white stone façade. These carvings are repeated in the metalwork on the windows. Although the shapes of the windows vary, they all unite to create a harmonious balance.

The stone on the townhouse's façade, which was quarried in Lens, France, is trimmed with polished granite. A subtle three-story bay of black metal embodies the grace and elegance of this truly refined, much-admired, building.

Charley-Persky House **㉙**

1365 N Astor St. **Map** 2 D2.
C *915-0105.* **M** *Clark/Division.* 📷 *mandatory.* ● *public hols.* 🈺 🈯

FRANK LLOYD WRIGHT called Charnley-Persky House (1891–2) "the first modern house in America." Two of America's most influential architects collaborated on the design: Wright *(see p28),* then a draftsman in the early stages of his career, and Louis Sullivan *(see p28),* known for his architectural detailing. They were commissioned by lumberman James Charnley and his wife Helen.

Charnley-Persky House is a pivotal work in the history of modern architecture. Its design embraces abstract forms, every interior view providing a perfectly balanced composition. The house's relatively simple façade of brick and limestone contrasts with the elaborate fronts of the exclusive Astor Street neighborhood.

An atrium reaching from the oak-paneled entry to a skylight two floors above is the interior's focal point. Dramatic arches frame the rooms on the first floor.

Along with the house's bold geometrical forms and organic abstractions are surprising details, such as windows in the closets. One of the most striking aspects of the house is the elegantly tapering wooden screen, on the second floor.

The elegant second-floor stairway screen at Charnley-Persky House

Oak Street Beach at dusk, looking southeast across Lake Michigan

Restored in 1988 by the architect firm of Skidmore, Owings and Merrill, the house now headquarters the Society of Architectural Historians. It was renamed in honor of Seymour Persky, who bought it for the society.

Oak Street Beach ③⓪

Between E Division & E Oak Sts, at N Lake Shore Dr. **Map** 2 D3.
M *Chicago (red line) then bus 36; Clark/Division.* 🚌 *145, 146, 147, 155.*

JUST STEPS from Chicago's Magnificent Mile is the fashionable Oak Street Beach, just one of the city's several beaches that together form a sandy chain along Chicago's lengthy lakefront.

As well as providing a great view of Lake Michigan, the Gold Coast, and towering North Side buildings such as the John Hancock Center and the Drake Hotel, Oak Street Beach presents a good opportunity to shed shopping bags and loafers and don swimsuit and sandals. Throngs of joggers, bicyclists, dog walkers, and in-line skaters make the broad expanse of Oak Street Beach a lively place to enjoy the sun and watch the waves. At the southern end of the beach is a promenade – a pleasant, if somewhat crowded, spot for strolling during the summer.

The din of cars heading along Lake Shore Drive is a constant reminder that the beach is in the city, but the sounds of squawking gulls provide noisy competition.

To reach the beach, use the pedestrian tunnels at Oak or Division Streets. There are washrooms at the beach, but the nearest changing rooms are at North Avenue Beach.

View of the Gold Coast skyline from Oak Street Beach

OLD MONEY

Chicago has a beautiful sound because Chicago means money – so the late actress Ruth Gordon reputedly said. By the turn of the century, 200 millionaires flourished in the city. One of the most prominent was dry-goods merchant and real-estate mogul Potter Palmer who, with his socialite wife Bertha Honoré, had an enormous impact on the city's social, cultural, and economic life.

Chicago's wealthy began to flock from the Prairie Avenue District to the Gold Coast after Palmer built, in 1882, an opulent home (since demolished) at present-day 1350 North Lake Shore Drive. Palmer quadrupled his investment when he subdivided and sold Gold Coast land he had astutely purchased before moving to the area.

Potter Palmer

Perhaps no feature of the Palmer mansion epitomized the family's wealth as much as did the doors: there were no outside handles, since the doors were always opened from inside – by the Palmer's servants.

Department-store owner Marshall Field *(see pp50–51)*, was less ostentatious in his display of wealth. Although he rode in a carriage to work, he always stopped short of his store to walk the last few blocks so people would not see his mode of transport. Likewise, he asked the architect of his $2-million, 25-room mansion not to include any frills. The influential Field provided major funding to the Field Museum *(see pp86–9)* and the 1893 World's Fair.

Marshall Field

SIGHTS AT A GLANCE

GETTING THERE
The South Loop is a short walk from the Downtown Core and is easily accessible from the Harrison and Roosevelt CTA stations, and via the State Street and Dearborn Street buses. The Near South Side, 3 miles (5 km) south of the city center, is best reached by car, taxi, or Michigan Avenue bus 3.

◁ T. Thomas Memorial, Grant Park

SOUTH LOOP
AND NEAR SOUTH SIDE

TWO OF CHICAGO'S neighborhoods have always been areas of diversity, with dereliction and gentrification coexisting side by side. South Loop developed as an industrial area in the late 1800s. But after World War II, manufacturers left and the area declined. Not until the 1970s did it again show signs of prosperity. The Near South Side also had cycles of boom and bust. After the 1871 fire, the city's elite created a wealthy enclave here that lasted until the early 1900s. Decay followed, as brothels and gambling houses formed the Levee vice district. In the 1940s, the Illinois Institute of Technology (IIT) transformed the area yet again. The contrasts remain striking. The oldest residence in the city, the Henry B. Clarke House, is minutes from the sleek IIT campus; the city's teeming Chinatown borders the historic Black Metropolis.

KEY

Street-by-Street map
See pp80–81

M CTA train station

Metra train station

P Parking

0 meters 500

0 yards 500

Street-by-Street: South Loop

Sculpted owl on the roof of Harold Washington Library

JUST SOUTH OF DOWNTOWN, the South Loop has changed dramatically in recent decades, from a run-down industrial area to a residential and retail neighborhood. With the 1970s conversion of the district's derelict warehouses to fashionable lofts, businesses sprang up as Chicagoans took advantage of the area's proximity to downtown. Today, the South Loop's diversity is evident in its industrial heritage, the green expanse of Grant Park, and the lively retail scene next door to several outstanding museums.

★ Harold Washington Library Center
Dominating the South Loop is the world's largest public library building, artwork displayed throughout ❶

★ Printing House Row Historic District
Many of this area's historic warehouses, built for the printing trade, have been converted into fashionable apartments, with numerous shops and cafés at street level ❷

The Transportation Building was one of the earliest buildings in Printers' Row to be converted to residential use and helped start the area's revival.

DEARBORN ST

CONGRESS PKWY

HARRISON STREET

CLARK STREET

LASALLE

POLK STREET

STREET

Details on the *Lakeside Press Building, at 731 S Plymouth Street, are typical of the rich decoration of buildings in this area.*

STAR SIGHTS

★ Harold Washington Library Center

★ Printing House Row Historic District

★ Spertus Museum

The Second Franklin Building *has handsome tilework illustrating the history of printing over its entranceway.*

Museum of Contemporary Photography
Focusing on American photography produced since 1959, the museum presents selections from its extensive collection and excellent temporary exhibitions **7**

★ Spertus Museum
This world-renowned collection of Judaic art highlights decorative objects and religious artifacts that span centuries of Jewish history **6**

LOCATOR MAP
See Street Finder maps 3 & 4

KEY

- - - Suggested route

South Michigan Avenue
Featuring a spectacular row of historic buildings, this is one of Chicago's grandest streets, an excellent place to window shop and from which to admire the varied architectural styles for which the city is famous **4**

Hilton Chicago
Decorated in the French Renaissance style, this 25-story building is one of Chicago's most opulent hotels and was the largest in the world when it opened in 1927 **5**

Buddy Guy's Legends
presents both big-name and local blues acts. Proprietor and blues legend Buddy Guy can often be found among the club's patrons.

Dearborn Station Galleria
Chicago's oldest surviving passenger train station building, an 1885 Richardsonian Romanesque design, has been converted into a shopping mall. Its square clock tower is a local landmark **3**

| 0 meters | 100 |
| 0 yards | 100 |

Harold Washington Library Center's ninth-floor Winter Garden

Chicago Public Library, Harold Washington Library Center ❶

400 S State St. **Map** 3 C2.
C 747-4300. **M** Library. ◯ call for hours. ● major hols. & call 747-4252. 𝕍 noon, 2pm daily. ▣
⬛ Exhibits, lectures, films.

THIS, THE LARGEST public library building in the world, was designed by Thomas Beeby – winner of a competition voted on by Chicagoans – and opened in 1991. It is named in honor of Chicago's first Black mayor.

Inspired by Greek and Roman structures – with five-story arched windows, vaulted ceilings, and decorative columns – the design also pays tribute to many of Chicago's historic buildings: the rusticated granite base recalls the Rookery (see p40), for example. Perched on each roof corner is a gigantic sculpted barn owl represent-ing wisdom; over the main entrance, a great horned owl with a 20-ft (6-m) wingspan grips a book in its talons.

The library holds close to 7 million books and periodi-cals on its 70 miles (110 km) of shelving. Artwork from almost every artistic medium is displayed throughout the building, including work by Cheyenne artist Heap of Birds. On the ninth floor are displays of artifacts relating to Chicago's history, two exhibit halls, and the Beyond Words Café.

Rowe Building on Dearborn Street, in the Printing House Row District

Printing House Row Historic District ❷

S Federal, S Dearborn, & S Plymouth Sts; between W Harrison & W Polk Sts. **Map** 3 C3.
M Harrison.

BY THE MID-1890s, Chicago was the printing capital of the US. The majority of this industry centered in a two-block area now known as Printing House Row Historic District. Nearby Dearborn Street railroad station (see p83) facilitated rapid industrial development in the neigh-borhood. However, by the 1970s, when the station closed, most of the printing companies had already moved out of the area.

Many of the massive, solid buildings erected to hold heavy printing machinery remain today. Their conver-sion into stylish condomini-ums and office lofts has led to the revitalization of the

Carved detail on façade of the historic Lakeside Press Building

neighborhood and an influx of commercial activity.

The landmark Pontiac Building (542 South Dear-born Street; 1891) is the old-est surviving Holabird and Roche (see p25) building in Chicago. Several other note-worthy buildings line South Dearborn Street. The 1883 Donohue Building (Nos. 701–721) has an impressive arched entranceway, Roman-esque Revival styling (see p24), and a birdcage elevator in the lobby. The Rowe Build-ing (No. 714, c.1882) houses the excellent Sandmeyer's Bookstore, specializing in local authors and travel liter-ature. The Second Franklin Building (No. 720) is signifi-cant for the ornamental tile-work gracing its façade. Above the entrance is a delightful terra-cotta mural of a medieval print shop.

Dearborn Station Galleria ❸

47 W Polk St. **Map** 3 C3.
🄲 554-4408. Ⓜ Harrison.
🄾 8am–8pm Mon–Fri; 8am–5pm
Sat. ● major hols. 🈲 🖳 🍴

Dearborn station, built in 1885, is the oldest surviving passenger railroad station building in Chicago, and is a monument to the historic importance of the nation's coast-to-coast rail system. By the turn of the century, more than 100 trains (from 25 different railroad companies) and 17,000 passengers passed through the station each day.

Designed by Cyrus L.W. Eidlitz, the station features masonry walls and terra-cotta arches in the Richardsonian Romanesque style *(see p24)*. A 1922 fire destroyed the roof, attic, and upper story. The clock tower was rebuilt and stands today as the striking terminus of Dearborn Street, visible from the northern Loop.

The station closed to rail traffic in 1971, its trains and platforms removed. In 1976, amid much controversy, the building's train shed was demolished. The building was converted in 1985 into a shopping mall and office complex, and many of its original features have since been restored.

Dearborn Station Galleria's high-ceilinged atrium

View along South Michigan Avenue looking north

South Michigan Avenue ❹

S Michigan Ave from E Madison St to E Balbo Ave. **Map** 4 C2–C3.
Ⓜ Madison.

South michigan avenue is the place to revel in the monumental solidity of late 19th- and early 20th-century architecture. This historic street has been described variously as a "cliff" and a "wall." Be warned: you may strain your neck gazing up to the tops of these massive structures. The longest span of pre-1920 buildings in Chicago, South Michigan Avenue contains numerous architectural styles, from the Gothic-inspired *(see p24)* Chicago Athletic Association Building (No. 12) to the Chicago School *(see pp24–5)* Gage Building (No. 18), one of three buildings making up the Gage Group. The Gage Building was designed by Holabird and Roche; Louis Sullivan designed the terra-cotta façade.

At Nos. 24 and 30 are striking examples of Chicago windows *(see p25)*, which allowed in plenty of light for the milliners once working here.

The School of the Art Institute of Chicago residence (No. 112) contains a frieze of the Greek god Zeus overseeing athletic games, a decorative detail that reflects the original 1908 purpose of the building as the home of the Illinois Athletic Club.

Hilton Chicago ❺

720 S Michigan Ave. **Map** 4 D3.
🄲 922-4400. Ⓜ Harrison. 🄾 24
hrs daily. ♿ 🈲 🍴 🅿 See **Where
to Stay** p139.

When it opened in 1927, this 25-story hotel had 3,000 rooms, a rooftop 18-hole miniature golf course, its own hospital, and a 1,200-seat theater. After the owner went bankrupt in the mid-1930s, the World War II Army Air Corps purchased the Holabird and Roche-designed redbrick building, converting the grand ballroom to a mess hall.

In 1945, Conrad Hilton acquired the building, reopening the hotel in 1951. Further renovations in the 1970s and 1980s secured the hotel's reputation for opulence. Its lofty centerpiece is the ballroom, a space decorated in the French Renaissance style, featuring mirrored doors and walls, arched windows, and huge crystal chandeliers. The hallway is equally ornate, with fluted columns, a marble stairway, and a cloud mural painted on the ceiling.

Marble fountain, lobby of the Hilton Chicago

Spertus Museum ❻

618 S Michigan Ave. **Map** 4 D3.
📞 322-1747. Ⓜ *Harrison.* ⭕
*10am–5pm Sun–Wed; 10am–8pm
Thu; 10am–3pm Fri.* ⬤ *major public
and Jewish hols.* 📷 *(free Fri).* ♿ 🎦
🎵 *Concerts, lectures, films.*

THE SPERTUS MUSEUM, in the
Spertus Institute of Jewish
Studies, has one of the largest
permanent collections of
Judaic art in the US. Five
thousand years of religious

Interior of the Museum of Contemporary Photography

**Children excavating in a re-created
dig at the Spertus Museum**

and cultural history are
represented in the collection's
10,000 artifacts, arranged by
themes relating to holy days
and rituals. Ceremonial
objects, paintings, sculptures,
jewelry, and coins fill this
somewhat labyrinthine space,
covering two floors.

Highlights include ornate
torah arks and scrolls from
around the world. The 5-ft-
(1.5-m-) tall Aron Ha-Kodesh
torah ark (1913–23) from
Jerusalem is embellished with
etched and bas-relief brass
depicting biblical events
accompanied by Hebrew
quotations. Decorative
candelabras and Hanukkah
lamps include 18th-century
eastern European examples
and modern Israeli designs.

A computer in the deeply
moving Zell Holocaust
Memorial room lists the
names of people lost by
Chicago families in the
Holocaust; it takes a full day
to read the list. Shoes and a
spoon from Auschwitz and a
prisoner's outfit are likewise
haunting reminders of this
horrific period of history.
Temporary exhibitions are

held in the museum's second-
floor gallery.

Kids can excavate artifacts
in a 32-ft- (10-m-) long re-
created dig site in the
ARTiFACT Center – a hands-
on archeological adventure.

Asher Library, on the fifth
floor, is the largest public
Jewish library in the central
US, with over 100,000 books.

Museum of Contemporary Photography ❼

600 S Michigan Ave. **Map** 4 D3.
📞 663-5554. Ⓜ *Harrison.* ⭕
*10am–5pm Mon–Wed, Fri; 10am–
8pm Thu; noon–5pm Sat.* ⬤ *major
hols, Dec 25 –Jan 1.* 📷 ♿ *1st, 2nd
floors only.* 🎵 *Lectures, films.*

FOUNDED BY Columbia
College Chicago in 1984 to
collect, exhibit, and promote
contemporary photography,
the Museum of Contemporary
Photography is the only
museum in the Midwest
devoted exclusively to the
medium of photography.
Wide-ranging provocative

and innovative exhibitions,
housed in the college's
historic 1907 building,
change regularly as do
selections from the collection
of more than 5,000
American photographs pro-
duced since 1959.

Temporary exhibitions
explore photography's many
roles in contemporary culture: as artistic expression, as
documentary chronicler, as
commercial industry, and as
a powerful scientific and
technological tool. The Midwest Photographers Project,
work by regional photographers, rotates annually.

Grant Park ❽

From Randolph St to Roosevelt Rd,
between Michigan Ave & Lake
Michigan. **Map** 4 E2–E4.
Ⓜ *Randolph; Madison; Adams.*
📷 *See* **Through the Year** *pp30–33.*

GRANT PARK is the splendid
centerpiece of the 23-
mile- (37-km-) long band of
green stretching along the
Lake Michigan shoreline from
the city's south end to its

The main entrance to Grant Park, Ivan Mestrovic's *Bowman* to the right

View of Grant Park, looking north

northern suburbs. Although bisected by busy streets, the park offers a tranquil retreat from noisy downtown, serving as Chicago's "front yard" – playground, promenade, garden, and sculpture park all in one, and hosting summer concerts and festivals.

The park is built on landfill and debris dumped after the 1871 Fire. Originally called Lake Park, it was renamed in 1901 for the 18th US president, Ulysses S. Grant, who lived in Galena *(see p128)*. In

***Reading Cones* by Richard Serra in Grant Park**

1893, the World's Columbian Exposition was held in the south end of the park.

Although the park was intended as public ground, free of buildings, various structures were erected. Not until 1890, when businessman Aaron Montgomery Ward initiated a series of lawsuits which dragged on for more than 20 years, was the preservation of Grant Park for public recreation secured.

Daniel H. Burnham and Edward H. Bennett's 1909 Plan of Chicago *(see p28)* envisioned the park as the "intellectual center of

Chicago." The renowned landscape-architecture firm Olmsted Brothers designed the park in a French Renaissance style reminiscent of the gardens at Versailles. The symmetrical layout includes large rectangular "rooms," grand promenades, formal tree plantings, sculptures, and the central Buckingham Fountain.

A noteworthy footnote is that the park was the site of the 1968 Democratic Convention riots, when anti-Vietnam War protesters clashed with police.

Buckingham Fountain ❾

In Grant Park, east of Columbus Dr, at the foot of Congress Pkwy. **Map** 4 E3. **℄** *742-7529*. **Ⓜ** *Harrison*.

THROUGHOUT the summer, one of the showiest and most impressive sights in Chicago is the water shooting from the 133 jets of Grant

Park's Buckingham Fountain, culminating dramatically in a spray 135 ft (41 m) high. The fountain's one-and-a-half million gallons (5.7 million liters) of water recirculate through a computer-operated pumping system at a rate of 14,000 gallons (53,000 liters) per minute.

Hundreds of spotlights hidden within the fountain are used to create a dazzling show of colored lights. The 20-minute shows, set to music, are held from dusk to 11pm every hour on the hour, from April to October.

Financed by Kate Sturges Buckingham (1858–1937) in honor of her brother, Clarence (1854–1913), a trustee and benefactor of the Art Institute of Chicago, the fountain was designed by Marcel Francois Loyau (sculptor), Jacques Lambert (engineer), and Edward H. Bennett (architect).

The design, based on the Latona Basin in the gardens of Versailles but twice the size of that fountain, incorporates a ground-level pool 280 ft (85 m) wide, with three concentric basins rising above. In 1927, it was dedicated as the world's largest decorative fountain.

Constructed of pink marble, the Beaux-Arts fountain symbolizes Lake Michigan. The four pairs of 20-ft- (6-m-) tall seahorses diagonally across the fountain from each other represent the four US states bordering the lake: Illinois, Wisconsin, Indiana, and Michigan.

Buckingham Fountain, sculpted seahorses in the foreground

Field Museum ⑩

Xochipilli, Aztec
god of flowers

THE FIELD MUSEUM is one of the world's
great natural history museums, with a
collection of over 20 million specimens
(just under 5 percent are displayed).
Following the success of the 1893 World's
Columbian Exposition, a group of
prominent Chicagoans decided to create a
museum with objects from the fair. With
funding from Marshall Field *(see p77),*
they opened, in 1894, the Columbian
Museum of Chicago in Jackson Park's
Palace of the Fine Arts, one of the fair's
finest buildings. This lodging soon
proved too small for the museum. In
1921, its current home – a white-marble Neo-Classical
structure designed by Daniel H. Burnham – was built,
and the Field Museum, with its celebrated collection of
anthropological, botanical, zoological, and geological
artifacts, opened to the public.

★ **Underground
Adventure**
*Walk through worm
tunnels, meet giant bugs,
and feel reduced to insect
size in this "subterranean"
exhibit.*

**Egyptian Mummy
Mask**
*This decorative linen-
and-plaster burial
mask encased a
mummified child.*

KEY TO FLOORPLAN

- ☐ Animals, plants, and ecosystems
- ☐ Rocks and fossils
- ☐ Ancient Egypt
- ☐ Americas
- ☐ Pacific cultures
- ☐ Special exhibits
- ☐ Nonexhibition space

Ground Level

MUSEUM GUIDE

*The museum has three levels: ground, main,
and upper. Most of the exhibition galleries are
on the main and upper levels. Each level has
east and west wings; those of the main and
upper are bisected by a large central hall. The
upper level features exhibitions on nature
(plants and earth sciences), dinosaurs, and
Pacific cultures. Exhibits on the main level
focus on animals, birds, and American
Indians. The highlight of the ground level is
the Underground Adventure exhibition.*

Lions of Tsavo
*The two lions that, in 1898, terrorized a
Kenyan outpost, killing 140 workers before
being shot, are on display in the Mammals
of Africa gallery.*

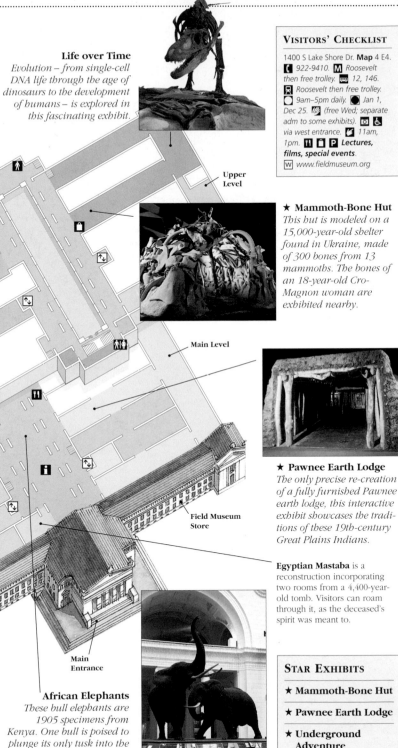

Life over Time

Evolution – from single-cell DNA life through the age of dinosaurs to the development of humans – is explored in this fascinating exhibit.

Upper Level

★ Mammoth-Bone Hut

This hut is modeled on a 15,000-year-old shelter found in Ukraine, made of 300 bones from 13 mammoths. The bones of an 18-year-old Cro-Magnon woman are exhibited nearby.

Main Level

★ Pawnee Earth Lodge

The only precise re-creation of a fully furnished Pawnee earth lodge, this interactive exhibit showcases the traditions of these 19th-century Great Plains Indians.

Field Museum Store

Egyptian Mastaba is a reconstruction incorporating two rooms from a 4,400-year-old tomb. Visitors can roam through it, as the deceased's spirit was meant to.

Main Entrance

African Elephants

These bull elephants are 1905 specimens from Kenya. One bull is poised to plunge its only tusk into the other as it rears.

STAR EXHIBITS

★ **Mammoth-Bone Hut**

★ **Pawnee Earth Lodge**

★ **Underground Adventure**

Exploring the Field Museum

WITH ITS ENCYCLOPEDIC COLLECTION of cultural objects and biological specimens from around the globe, the Field Museum warrants many trips. More than 40 permanent exhibitions are supplemented with fascinating temporary shows. Particular strengths of the museum are dinosaur fossils – highlighted by the recently opened exhibit on Sue, the most complete *Tyrannosaurus rex* skeleton ever found – American Indian artifacts, botanical specimens, and displays relating to mammals and birds. Major crowd pleasers, especially for children, are Underground Adventure, which explores the rich diversity of life in the soil, and Inside Ancient Egypt, focusing on that civilization's funerary practices.

Tlatilco female figurine

The monumental Neo-Classical entrance to the Field Museum

tropical aerial garden. Its reproductions made from wax, glass, and wire look remarkably lifelike.

ANIMALS, PLANTS, AND ECOSYSTEMS

ONE OF the museum's missions is to encourage prudent stewardship of our environment. This theme is highlighted in the animal, plant, and ecosystem exhibits, which emphasize the interconnectedness of all life on Earth. The Messages from the Wilderness gallery is a good place to start your exploration. Eighteen wilderness park settings, from the Arctic to Argentina, incorporate representative mammals and their habitats.

Also here is the Local Woodlands Four Seasons Diorama, completed in 1902 by taxidermist Carl Akeley, who transformed the way museums displayed animals.

For Akeley, habitat accuracy and the authenticity of background details were equally important. Thus, each of the 17,000 wax leaves in the diorama is cast separately from a real one.

The main-level galleries in the west wing provide an overview of animal biology, behavior, and habitats, with samples from the museum's 17 million zoological specimens. Outstanding exhibits are Mammals of Asia and Mammals of Africa. Suspended from the ceiling in the World of Mammals gallery is the massive skeleton of a right whale. The museum's collection of birds is also particularly strong, with its informative Bird Habitats, World of Birds, and North American Birds galleries.

A popular attraction is Bushman, a lowland gorilla brought from West Africa to Lincoln Park Zoo in the 1920s. So beloved by Chicagoans that the mayor gave him a voter's registration card, Bushman died in 1951. He was then moved to the museum where, preserved, he continues to delight visitors.

The museum's 2.6 million botanical specimens encompass all major plant groups and every continent. Particularly rich in flowering plants and ferns of the Americas, this is the world's largest museum exhibit dedicated exclusively to plants. Be sure to stop at the

A golden eagle clutching its prey, by taxidermist Carl Akeley

ROCKS AND FOSSILS

TWO OF THE TWELVE Martian meteorites on display in museums around the world are here at the Field Museum. You can touch non-Martian meteorite pieces on the upper floor, in the Earth Sciences galleries. Other fascinating

A collection of marine skeletons, exoskeletons, and fossils

and beautiful rocks in the 500-specimen display are a topaz the size of a pear, in the sparkling Grainger Hall of Gems, and a 312-lb (142-kg) block of lapis lazuli, one of the largest ever found and its origin still a puzzle.

The centerpiece of the museum's renowned collection of dinosaur fossils is 67-million-year-old Sue, the largest, most complete *Tyrannosaurus rex* skeleton ever found. It was discovered near the Black Hills of South Dakota in 1990 by fossil-hunter Sue Hendrickson. The

A gargantuan *Apatosaurus* skeleton in Genius Dinosaur Hall

restored skeleton, the skull alone weighing 750 lb (340 kg), was unveiled in 2000. Interactive exhibits tell the story of its discovery and preparation for exhibit. Scientists still do not know whether creatures preying on Sue's remains left the teeth marks on her skull or if these marks are the signs of a deadly battle with another *Tyrannosaurus rex,* the fiercest dinosaur known.

The Genius Dinosaur Hall showcases fossils of seven dinosaurs and the evocative Charles Knight murals. Commissioned by the Field Museum in 1927, these 28 striking paintings of dinosaurs, Ice Age mammals, and early humans were for years the standard depictions of prehistoric life.

ANCIENT EGYPT

THE MUSEUM'S Ancient Egyptian holdings consist of more than 1,400 rare artifacts, including statues, hieroglyphics, and mummies. The predynastic burial exhibit

Isty's Book of the Dead, an ancient papyrus scroll

reveals Egypt's intriguing burial practices before the development of intricate pharaonic tombs. Here, the remains of a 5,500-year-old woman are displayed, along with items such as pottery jars thought to be needed in the afterlife. A partial reconstruction of a *mastaba*, a multiroom "mansion of eternity," features a false door at which the earthbound and the wandering spirits meet.

Other extraordinary artifacts include the fully preserved inner coffin of Chenet-a-a, a woman who lived between 945 BC and 712 BC. It is not known what is inside the coffin since it has never been opened or X-rayed.

A Pacific Coast Indian carved figure, once a house entranceway

AMERICAS

THE MUSEUM'S HOLDINGS of artifacts from North American Indian tribes reflect one of the Field's main missions: to encourage improved understanding among cultures. Ceremonial objects and splendid totem poles – two Haida examples rise to the ceiling of Stanley Field Hall – are just some of the treasures in this exhibit.

The Pawnee Earth Lodge, a life-size reproduction, was built in conjunction with the Pawnee, a group of American Indians based in Oklahoma.

The 19th-century cedar Kwakiutl transformation masks are colorful and vivid. Such masks are often used

Ceremonial dance mask worn by Alaskan Eskimo shamans

during the ceremonies of this Pacific Northwest tribe. Panels on the mask are opened and closed by the dancer wearing it to show various faces.

PACIFIC CULTURES

THE HIGHLIGHT of the Pacific cultures exhibits, with a section on headhunting and a re-creation of a Tahitian market, is the sacred Maori meetinghouse, Ruatepupuke II. Built in 1881 in New Zealand, it was acquired by the museum in 1905. The 55-ft- (17-m-) long, beautifully carved house symbolizes the body of the Maori ancestor Ruatepupuke, credited with sharing the art of wood-carving with the world. The house's ridgepole represents his spine, the rafters his ribs, and the expansive roof-boards his arms, open in greeting. It is the only Maori meetinghouse in the western hemisphere and remains governed by Maori customs.

Spirit mask from Papua New Guinea

John G. Shedd Aquarium ⑪

See pp96–7.

Adler Planetarium and Astronomy Museum ⑫

See pp92–3.

Prairie Avenue Historic District ⑬

Prairie Ave, from 18th to Cullerton Sts. **Map** 6 D1. **M** *Cermak-Chinatown then bus 21.* **☑** *May–Oct weekends; call 326-1480.*

WHEN THE CITY of Chicago was incorporated in 1837, the area now known as the Prairie Avenue Historic District was not much more than a strip of sandy prairie bordering Lake Michigan. Its fortunes changed dramatically when the 1871 fire destroyed the city center. Chicago's wealthy, including George Pullman *(see p119)* and Marshall Field *(see p77),* moved to the Near South Side, building their grand mansions along Prairie Avenue. It remained a mecca for the city's socialites until the late 1800s and early 1900s, when the rapidly

The imposing Richardsonian Romanesque façade of Glessner House

growing Gold Coast area superseded Prairie Avenue as the address of choice. Many mansions fell to the wrecker's ball (plaques along Prairie Avenue mark the sites of demolished houses), but those that remain offer a glimpse into 19th-century splendor.

Along with Glessner House and Clarke House, highlights of the district include the Kimball House (No. 1801). This mansion, designed by Solon Spencer Beman in 1890, is one of the best remaining examples in the US of the Chateauesque style.

Elbridge G. Keith House (No. 1900) is the oldest extant mansion on Prairie Avenue. Built in 1870, it was designed by John W. Roberts in the Italianate style *(see p24).* Now home to the Woman Made Gallery, which exhibits contemporary art, it is one of the few mansions whose interior is open to the public.

At 1936 South Michigan Avenue is the magnificent neo-Gothic Second Presbyterian Church, designed by James Renwick in 1874. Inside are 22 stained-glass windows by Louis C. Tiffany and 2 windows painted by British Pre-Raphaelite artist Edward Burne-Jones.

The district is reputedly close to the site of a grim event: the 1812 massacre of settlers fleeing Fort Dearborn *(see p13).*

Elbridge G. Keith House on Prairie Avenue

Glessner House ⑭

1800 S Prairie Ave. **Map** 6 D1. **☎** *326-1480.* **M** *Cermak-Chinatown.* **☑** *mandatory: 1pm, 2pm, 3pm Wed–Sun (except public hols).* **☒** *(free Wed).* **☐** **Lectures.**

THE ONLY EXTANT residential design in Chicago by Boston architect Henry Hobson Richardson, whose signature style became known as Richardsonian Romanesque *(see p24),* Glessner House helped change the face of residential architecture.

Commissioned by farm-machinery manufacturer John J. Glessner and his wife, Frances, in 1885 and completed in 1887, the two-story house represented a radical departure from traditional design and created a furor in the exclusive Prairie Avenue neighborhood. George Pullman is said to have proclaimed: "I do not know what I have ever done to have that thing staring me in the face every time I go out of my door."

A fortress-like building of rough-hewn pinkish gray granite with three modified turrets, the house dominates its corner site. The main rooms and many of the large windows face a southern courtyard. The striking simplicity of the design is perhaps best reflected in the main entrance arch, which frames a heavy oak door ornamented with grillwork.

The beautifully restored interior boasts a world-class

collection of decorative accessories. Most were purchased or commissioned by the Glessners, who were keenly interested in the British Arts and Crafts movement of the late 19th and early 20th centuries. Adherents of the philosophy that everyday objects should be artistically crafted, they filled the house with tiles, draperies, and wallpaper designed by William Morris. Handcrafted pieces, from furniture to ceramics, by American designer Isaac E. Scott grace the rooms.

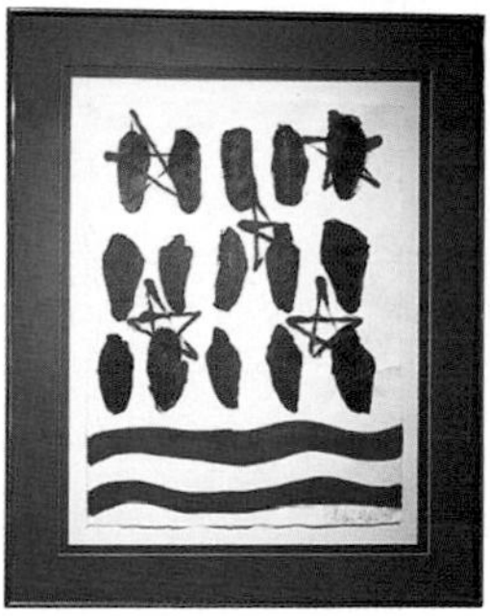

***Untitled* (1995) by Stephen Ham, at the Vietnam Veterans Art Museum**

National Vietnam Veterans Art Museum ⓯

1801 S Indiana Ave. **Map** 6 D1. *326-0270.* *Cermak-Chinatown then bus 21.* *11am–6pm Tue–Fri; 10am–5pm Sat; noon–5pm Sun.* *major hols.* *(for groups).*

The national Vietnam Veterans Art Museum is the only museum in the world with a permanent collection that focuses on the subject of war from a personal point of view. Bringing together more than 700 works of art in diverse media created by 115 artists who participated in one of America's most divisive wars, this collection presents a humanist statement on behalf of veterans of all wars.

This adamantly apolitical museum began when two Chicago veterans, Ned Broderick and Joe Fornelli, began collecting artworks created by fellow veterans. The City of Chicago donated an abandoned warehouse and the museum opened in its new home in 1996.

The artworks explore powerful themes with unflinching honesty. The belongings of prisoner-of-war Major General John L. Borling, who lived in captivity in North Vietnam for seven years, is documented in the display *My Cup Runneth Over*. There is also a comprehensive collection of North Vietnamese and Viet Cong medals, uniforms, and weapons.

Henry B. Clarke House ⓰

1827 S Indiana Ave. **Map** 6 D1. *326-1480.* *Cermak-Chinatown then bus 21.* *mandatory: noon, 1pm, 2pm Wed–Sun (departs from Glessner House).* *public hols.* *(free Wed).*

Built in 1836, Clarke House is Chicago's oldest surviving building, a Greek Revival-style house constructed for merchant Henry B. Clarke and his wife Caroline. The house originally stood on what is now South Michigan Avenue but was then an old Indian path. When the house sold in 1872, the new owners moved it 28 blocks south, to 4526 South Wabash Avenue. In 1977, the City purchased the house and then, in a feat of engineering, hoisted the 120-ton structure over the 44th Street "L" tracks, moving it to its present location one block southeast of the original Clarke property.

The dining room in the Henry B. Clarke House

Four Roman Doric columns mark the east entrance to the house. Solidly constructed of timber frame, with a white clapboard exterior, the two-story house was damaged in a 1977 fire. It now has been painstakingly restored, even adhering to the original color scheme, which researchers determined by delving under 27 layers of paint.

Now a museum showcasing an interior reflecting the period 1836–60, Clarke House offers a fascinating glimpse into early Chicago domestic life. It is so historically accurate that the first-floor lighting simulates gas lighting, and the upper floor has no artificial lights. A gallery in the basement documents the history of the house.

Behind the house is Clinton Women's Park, an outdoor cultural center named in honor of former first lady Hillary Rodham Clinton.

The classical façade of the Henry B. Clarke House

Adler Planetarium and Astronomy Museum ⑫

Diptych sundial, c.1665–1700

THE ADLER PLANETARIUM and Astronomy Museum has one of the finest astronomical collections in the world, with artifacts dating as far back as 12th-century Persia. It also has the world's first virtual-reality theater. Spectacular light shows complement displays on navigation, the solar system, and space exploration. State-of-the-art technology enables visitors to explore exhibits hands-on.

When the Adler opened in 1930, it was the first modern planetarium in the western hemisphere. Businessman Max Adler funded the 12-sided, granite-and-marble Art Deco structure, designed by Ernest Grunsfeld. This original building, with its copper dome and a bronze depiction of a sign of the zodiac on each of the 12 corners, is now a historical landmark.

★ StarRider Theater
The world's first digital theater offers an unrivaled virtual-reality environment in which visitors can participate in a journey beyond the solar system.

★ Atwood Sphere
Step into North America's only walk-in planetarium, built in 1913. Light enters through the 692 holes in the surface of this huge metal ball, representing the stars in Chicago's night sky. The "stars" move across the "sky" as the sphere, powered by a motor, slowly rotates.

Lower Level

KEY TO FLOOR PLAN

- Landmark exhibition space
- Sky Pavilion exhibition space
- Sky Pavilion special exhibits
- Zeiss Sky Theater
- StarRider Theater
- Nonexhibition space

History of Astronomy
Astronomical instruments, celestial charts, astrological calendars, and rare books – products of observation, speculation, and imagination – showcase a millennium of discovery.

Our Solar System
Investigate through interactive exhibits the worlds that orbit the Sun, and program a computer-activated Rover to move across simulated Martian terrain.

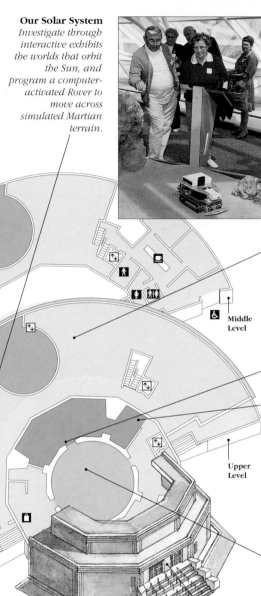

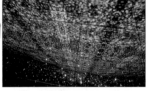

The Milky Way Galaxy

★ **Milky Way Galaxy**
Immerse yourself in a 3-D, computer-animated trip through the Milky Way.

Gateway to the Universe features interactive exhibits that explore the wonder of the universe through the scientific examination of light, gravity, motion, and energy.

♿ Middle Level

Upper Level

★ **Space Walk**
A mirrored, darkened room, dotted with light, simulates the exhilarating experience of stepping into infinite space.

Zeiss Sky Theater is the Adler's original planetarium theater. The night heavens are cast by a modern version of the historic Zeiss projector onto a screen suspended from its dome.

Main Entrance

Sky Pavilion
A stunning view of the city's skyline can be seen from Galileo's café, in the Sky Pavilion. This two-story 1999 addition to the east side of the landmark building also houses exhibition space and the StarRider Theater.

STAR FEATURES

★ **Atwood Sphere**

★ **Milky Way Galaxy**

★ **Space Walk**

★ **StarRider Theater**

A Chinatown grocery shop

Chinatown ⑰

S Wentworth Ave, south of Cermak Rd. **Map** 5 B1–C1. **C** *326-5320.* **M** *Cermak-Chinatown.* 🍴 *See* **Restaurants and Cafés** *p150.*

A RED AND GREEN gateway decorated with Chinese characters inscribed by Dr. Sun Yet-Sen, founder of the Republic of China, arches over Wentworth Avenue just south of Cermak Road. It marks the entrance to the largest Chinatown in the Midwest. A lively area full of Asian grocery and herbal shops, bakeries, and restaurants, this densely packed neighborhood of approximately 10,000 residents has been home to Chicago's highest concentration of Chinese people since just before World War I.

Traditional Chinese architecture is evident throughout the colorful streetscape. The temple-like **Pui Tak Center** (2216 South Wentworth Avenue) was originally the On Leong Chinese Merchants' Association Building; it is now a cultural center. Sculpted lions at the doorway guard its street-level shops; terra-cotta ornaments bedeck the walls. Modern **Chinatown Square Mall** (Archer, Cermak, 18th, and Wentworth) quarters shops and a plaza surrounded by zodiac sculptures and a mosaic mural.

Annual Chinatown celebrations include the Dragon Festival in June and the Moon Festival in September.

Detail of decorative tile on the Chinese Cultural Center

Illinois Institute of Technology ⑱

31st to 35th Sts, between Dan Ryan Expy & S Michigan Ave. **Map** 5 C4–D4. **C** *567-3075.* **M** *Sox-35th; 35-Bronzeville-IIT.*

T HE ILLINOIS INSTITUTE of Technology (IIT) is a world leader in engineering, technology, and architecture. The institute is the result of the 1940 merger of Armour Institute of Technology and the technical school Lewis Institute. During the late 1940s, IIT coplanned the urban renewal of 7 sq miles (18 sq km) of the Near South Side, which helped eradicate the area's slums. IIT has played a significant role in the community ever since.

The campus is an outstanding example of the work of influential architect Ludwig Mies van der Rohe *(see p28)*, who was hired by architect John A. Holabird to direct the Armour Institute's architecture school and design the new campus.

In the campus plan, along with the 22 IIT buildings he designed, Mies expressed his modernist view that form follow function. Geometric and unadorned glass-sheathed curtain-wall structures epitomize Mies' International style. One of Mies' masterpieces is the **S.R. Crown Hall** (1956). This glass-walled pavilion is an early example of a large clear-span structure, the four exterior columns supporting the girders from which the roof is hung. The building appears to float in space. Of it, Mies said: "This is the clearest structure we have done, the best to express our philosophy."

Alumni Memorial Hall, Mies' first classroom building on the campus, is another notable example of structure also functioning as ornament. The steel grid of the curtain wall suggests the steel structure within. In **Wishnick Hall**, the curtain wall stops short of the corner to reveal the load-bearing column.

St. Saviour's Chapel, waggishly known as the "God

S.R. Crown Hall on the Illinois Institute of Technology campus

box," is believed to be Mies' only church design.

The campus is also home to the magnificent redbrick Richardsonian Romanesque **Main Building**. Designed by Patten and Fisher (1891–3), it is IIT's most visible landmark.

The campus is explored easily on foot; maps are available at Hermann Union Hall (3241 S Federal Street).

Pilgrim Baptist Church ⓳

3301 S Indiana Ave. **Map** 6 D4. **Church** ☎ 842-5830; **Office** ☎ 842-4417. Ⓜ 35-Bronzeville–IIT. ◯ during services only. ♿

BUILT IN 1890–91 and designed by Adler and Sullivan for Chicago's oldest Jewish congregation, Kehilath Anshe Ma'ariv, this building has housed the Pilgrim Baptist Church since 1926.

The magnificent arched doorway – the only surviving example of an ecclesiastical arch by Adler and Sullivan – reflects the strong masonry forms of the exterior. Terracotta panels of foliage designs provide ornament. The opulent interior is notable for its tunnel-vaulted ceiling and richly ornamented balcony. The art glass windows were designed by Healy and Millet.

Calumet-Giles-Prairie District ⓴

Calumet to Prairie Aves, from 31st to 35th Sts. **Map** 6 D4. Ⓜ 35-Bronzeville–IIT.

THIS SMALL ENCLAVE of restored Victorian houses was granted national landmark status in 1980. Of particular interest is Joseph Deimel House (3141 South Calumet Avenue), designed in 1887 by Adler and Sullivan and the only remaining residential commission by the firm in this area.

The Joliet limestone row houses (3144–8 South Calumet Avenue), built in 1881, are a fine example of Victorian row-house architecture. However, only three of the original eight houses are still standing.

A block to the south are the only row houses Frank Lloyd Wright designed (1894) – the Robert W. Roloson Houses (3213–19 South Calumet Avenue). Like Robie House *(see pp102–103)*, Wright used Roman bricks for the walls, here decorated with terra-cotta panels between the upper-story windows.

A trio of Richardsonian Romanesque *(see p24)* townhouses in sandstone, greenstone, and limestone are found at 3356–60 South Calumet Avenue.

Ida B. Wells-Barnett House

Ida B. Wells-Barnett House ㉑

3624 S King Dr. **Map** 6 E5. Ⓜ 35-Bronzeville–IIT. ◯ to public.

CIVIL RIGHTS and women's suffrage advocate Ida B. Wells (1862–1931) lived in this house with her husband from 1919 to 1930. Born a slave in Mississippi, Wells became a teacher at age 14 but was dismissed for protesting segregation.

Wells' work as a columnist for *Memphis Free Speech* brought her to Chicago in 1893 to report on the lack of African-American representation at the World's Columbian Exposition. She moved to Chicago in 1895 and married Ferdinand Lee Barnett, the founder of Chicago's first Black newspaper, the *Conservator.*

Playing a key role in the 1909 founding of the National Association for the Advancement of Colored People, Wells is perhaps best known for her anti-lynching campaign, which brought national attention to the issue.

The house, designed in 1889 by Joseph A. Thain in the Romanesque style, was designated a national historic landmark in 1973 in Wells' honor. One of its most interesting features is the corner turret made of pressed metal.

Victory monument in the Calumet-Giles-Prairie District

Façade of the Pilgrim Baptist Church, with its distinctive doorway

John G. Shedd Aquarium ⓫

NEARLY 8,000 SALTWATER and freshwater animals, representing 650 species of fish, reptiles, amphibians, invertebrates, birds, and mammals, live at the John G. Shedd Aquarium. Named after its benefactor, an influential Chicago businessman, the aquarium opened in 1930 in a Neo-Classical building designed by the firm Graham, Anderson, Probst and White. The Oceanarium and its magnificent curved wall of glass face Lake Michigan, whose water flows into its tank. This marine-mammal pavilion showcases beluga whales and dolphins. The aquarium offers various viewpoints of its exhibits, including some beneath the water.

Neptune's trident atop the dome of the aquarium

Aerial view of the Shedd Aquarium, looking north toward Grant Park

Beluga Whales
Six whales live in the Oceanarium's Secluded Bay. Four are from Hudson Bay in central Canada; two were born at the aquarium.

The Nature Trail leads visitors along winding paths through a re-creation of a Pacific Northwest coastal forest, complete with streams and replicas of 70 species of plants.

KEY

- ☐ Aquarium
- ☐ Oceanarium
- ☐ Animal underwater viewing
- ☐ Special exhibits
- ☐ Nonexhibition space

STAR EXHIBITS

- ★ **Amazon Rising**
- ★ **Caribbean Reef**
- ★ **Oceanarium**

Sea Otter Cove features Habitat Chat about these smallest of marine mammals

★ Oceanarium

Pacific white-sided dolphins, Alaskan sea otters, tidal-pool creatures, and other marine animals live in this gigantic saltwater tank, which seems to extend into Lake Michigan, a dramatic effect created by the stunning 475-ft- (145-m-) long glass wall. Watch dolphins and whales during daily educational presentations, or come face to face with them in the Underwater Viewing gallery.

Harbor Seals
The seal bight is home to this vulnerable species now protected by US legislation.

VISITORS' CHECKLIST

1200 S Lake Shore Dr. **Map** 4 E4.
939-2438. Roosevelt then free trolley. 12, 127, 146. Roosevelt then free trolley. Memorial Day–Labor Day: 9am–6pm daily (Jun–Sep: 9am–9pm Thu). Labor Day–Memorial Day: 9am–5pm Mon–Fri; 9am–6pm Sat, Sun, public hols. Jan 1, Dec 25. (free Mon). *Lectures*.
www.shedd.org

Animals of Cold Coasts
Creatures of the northern saltwater tide pools and oceans, such as the red-belly piranha, are exhibited here.

Animals of the Great Lakes Region
showcases cold water fish, including the Lake Whitefish, that dwell in the Great Lakes.

★ Caribbean Reef
More than 250 tropical animals, including nurse sharks and barracudas, live in this reef habitat, one of the aquarium's most popular exhibits. Visitors can watch as a diver feeds the creatures.

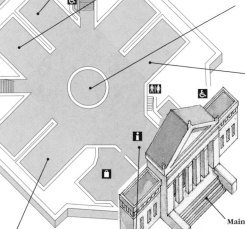

★ Amazon Rising
Experience all four seasons affecting the floodplain forest of the mighty Amazon River, and encounter stingrays, dart frogs, lizards, and many more creatures of the Amazon.

Main Entrance

Central Rotunda
Aquatic motifs on tiles, cornices, walls, and doorways grace the central rotunda of the building, designated a national historic landmark in 1987.

Asia, Africa, and Australia highlights fish such as the aggressive Nile knifefish that inhabit the warm freshwaters of the eastern hemisphere.

SOUTH SIDE

St. George and the dragon, detail from the University of Chicago

SETTLED IN the mid-1800s as suburban estates, the South Side was soon transformed when the 1893 World's Fair, held in Jackson Park, brought tourists, money, and real-estate and transit development. Hyde Park in particular experienced dramatic change, as the City's preparation for the fair led to an influx of Chicago's elite. By the 1920s, however, pollution from nearby industry and the encroachment of poorer neighborhoods caused the wealthy to depart. By the 1950s, Kenwood and Hyde Park were in decline. That same decade, the University of Chicago led a massive urban-renewal program. Today, the area contains many classic Prairie School homes, superb museums, and two of Chicago's largest greenspaces.

SIGHTS AT A GLANCE

Historic Buildings
Robie House ❷
Rockefeller Memorial
  Chapel ❶
University of Chicago
  Quadrangles ❺

Historic Districts
Hyde Park ❾
Kenwood ❿

Museums
DuSable Museum of African
  American History ❽
*Museum of Science and
  Industry pp106–109* ⓬
Oriental Institute Museum ❸
Smart Museum of Art ❹

Parks
Jackson Park ⓫
Midway Plaisance ❻
Washington Park ❼

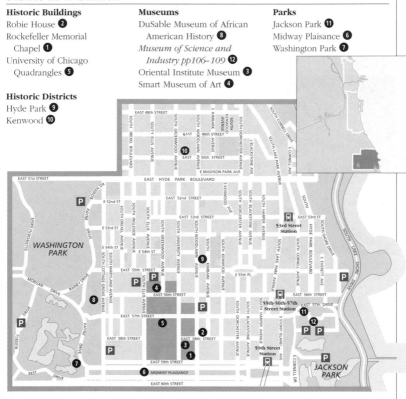

GETTING THERE

Eight miles (13 km) south of the Loop, the South Side is accessible by car via I-94/I-55 or South Lake Shore Drive. Metra trains depart from the Randolph Street, Van Buren Street, and Roosevelt Road stations to 55th-56th-57th and 59th Street stations. CTA buses 6 and 10 offer express service to the South Side. CTA green line trains also service the area.

KEY

■   Street-by-Street map
    See pp100–101

🚉   Metra train station

🅿   Parking

0 meters   500
0 yards   500

◁ **Lower cloister hall in the Chicago Theological Seminary, University of Chicago**

Street-by-Street: University of Chicago

Angel with harp, Bond Chapel

THE UNIVERSITY of Chicago, founded in 1891 on land donated by Marshall Field, opened its doors to students – male and female, White and Black – in 1892. Today, it has the greatest number of Nobel laureates among faculty, alumni, and researchers of any US university and is particularly lauded in the fields of economics and physics. Over the years, John D. Rockefeller gave $35 million to the university. Henry Ives Cobb designed 18 of the university's limestone buildings before the Boston firm Shepley, Rutan and Coolidge took over as the main architects in 1901. Today, the campus boasts the designs of more than 70 architects. While large, it is easily explored on foot (for walking tours, *see pp168–9*).

Nuclear Energy, by sculptor Henry Moore, marks the spot where, in 1942, a team of scientists led by Enrico Fermi ushered in the atomic age with the first controlled nuclear reaction.

Bond Chapel
(1926) contains beautiful stained-glass windows by Charles Connick and elaborate wood carvings.

Main Quadrangle
The university's tranquil central quadrangle is the largest of seven designed by Henry Ives Cobb ❺

Midway Plaisance
This is the site of the 1893 World's Columbian Exposition amusement park ❻

STAR SIGHTS
★ **Oriental Institute Museum**
★ **Robie House**
★ **Smart Museum of Art**

Cobb Gate
was donated to the university by Henry Ives Cobb, the campus' master planner. It is ornately decorated with gargoyles.

★ **Smart Museum of Art**
This light-filled, intimate museum offers a rich, balanced survey of Western art ❹

LOCATOR MAP
See Street Finder maps 7 & 8

KEY

- - - Suggested route

Regenstein Library,
the university's main library, holds treasured rare book and manuscript collections, along with millions of other volumes.

★ **Oriental Institute Museum**
Three millennia of ancient Near East civilization are showcased at this fascinating museum ❸

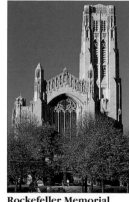

Rockefeller Memorial Chapel
Elaborate carvings and intricate stained-glass windows grace the interior of this limestone-and-brick chapel ❶

58TH STREET

WOODLAWN AVENUE

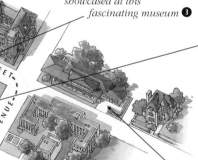

0 meters 100
0 yards 100

★ **Robie House**
This Frank Lloyd Wright-designed home (1906–1909) is a masterpiece of the Prairie School of architecture ❷

Rockefeller Memorial Chapel ❶

5850 S Woodlawn Ave. **Map** 7 C4.
[(773) 702-2100. **M** *Garfield
(green line) then bus 55.* **R** *59th.*
O *8am–4pm daily.* **†** *11am,
8:30pm Sun.* **&** **♪** *Concerts.*

ROCKEFELLER Memorial
Chapel is Bertram G.
Goodhue's 1928 interpretation
of Gothic *(see p24)*. The
chapel is topped with a 207-ft
(63-m) carillon tower. It is the
tallest building on campus:
John D. Rockefeller, as a
condition of his bequest,
required that this structure
representing religion be the
university's most dominant
feature.

Contributing to its tradition
of musical excellence is one
of Chicago's oldest choral
ensembles, and the stunning
E.M. Skinner organ. The 72-
bell tower, the bells weighing
from 10.5 lb (5 kg) to 18.5
tons, is the second-largest
carillon in the world. The
bells ring at 6pm weekdays,
after service, and during the

Bust of a Man (c.1840 BC), at the Oriental Institute Museum

Oriental Institute Museum ❸

1155 E 58th St. **Map** 7 C4. **[** (773)
702-9514. **M** *Garfield (green line)
then bus 55.* **R** *59th.* **O** *10am–
4pm Tue, Thu–Sat; 10am–8:30pm
Wed; noon–4pm Sun.* **●** *public
hols.* **&** **♪** **📷** *Special events.*

THE ORIENTAL Institute
Museum is the exhibition
arm of the Oriental Institute,
its scholars having excavated
in virtually every region of

the Near East since 1919. The
museum presents the institute's famed collection of
over 100,000 artifacts from
the earliest civilizations of
the world. It is also one of
only three places in the
world where you can see a
reconstruction of an Assyrian
palace (c.721–705 BC).

Other highlights of the
museum include a monu-
mental sculpture (c.1334–25
BC) of King Tutankhamen
from a Luxor temple. At 17 ft
(5 m), it is the tallest ancient

Robie House ❷

5757 S Woodlawn Ave. **Map** 8 D4.
[(708) 848-1976. **M** *Garfield
(green line) then bus 55.* **R** *59th.*
O *daily.* **●** *Jan 1, Thanksgiving, Dec
25.* **🎟** *(children free).* **♪** *mandatory: call for times.* **📷**

FRANK LLOYD WRIGHT's world-
famous Robie House is the
quintessential expression of
the Prairie School movement
(see p25). Designed in 1906
for Frederick Robie, a bicycle
and motorbike manufacturer,
and completed in 1909, the
home is one of Wright's last
Prairie School houses: Wright
left both his family and his
Oak Park practice during its
three-year construction.

Robie House has three
distinct parts combining to
create a balanced whole.
Two, two-story rectangular
concrete blocks sit parallel to
each other; a smaller square
third story is positioned at
their junction. There is no
basement and no attic.

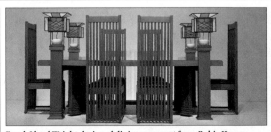

Frank Lloyd Wright-designed dining-room set from Robie House

The exterior design of the
house perfectly captures the
prairie landscape of flat, open
fields. The roof's sweeping
planes embody the house's
aesthetic of bold rectilinear
simplicity. Steel beams, some
60 ft (18 m) long, support the
overhanging roof. Their use
was unorthodox in
residential architecture at
the time.

Also bold but
simple, the interior is
furnished with Wright-
designed furniture.
The innovative dining-
room set is on view at

**Leaded stained-glass windows and
doors**, which run the length of the
living room, allow for both privacy
and natural light.

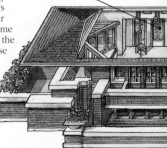

Egyptian statue in the western hemisphere.

The museum's Egyptian collection, which includes objects of ancient Egyptian daily life and religious and funerary practices, is one of the largest in the US.

Smart Museum of Art ❹

5550 S Greenwood Ave. **Map** 7 C4.
(773) 702-0200. **M** *Garfield (green line) then bus 55.* ◗ *10am–4pm Tue, Wed, Fri; 10am–9pm Thu; noon–6pm Sat, Sun.* ● *public hols.*
Special events.

IF YOU ARE FEELING overwhelmed by the crowds at Chicago's major museums, this is the place to come for an intimate encounter with art. Named after David and Alfred Smart, founders of *Esquire Magazine* and the museum's benefactors, the Smart Museum was established in 1974 as the art museum of the University of Chicago. It holds more than 7,500 artworks and artifacts,

**Henry Moore's *Nuclear Energy*,
outside the Smart Museum**

including antiquities and Old Master prints, Asian paintings, calligraphies, and ceramics. By displaying its works in rotating, thematic displays, the museum ensures its collection is made available to the public.

The museum also owns important post-war Chicago artwork, furniture and glass from Robie House, and early modern and contemporary painting and sculpture.

A 1999 renovation has allowed for more comprehensive displays of the museum's collection of

important 20th century and Asian artworks.

The museum's café, with tall windows overlooking the tranquil sculpture garden, is a great spot for a quiet lunch.

University of Chicago Quadrangles ❺

Bounded by 57th & 59th Sts, Ellis & University Aves. **Map** 7 C4.
M *Garfield (green line) then bus 55.*
R *59th.*

THE CLOISTERED quadrangle plan for the University of Chicago – in the 1890s, one of the first in the US – was developed by architect Henry Ives Cobb. He patterned the unified campus after British universities Cambridge and Oxford. Despite years of development and modification, the six broken quadrangles surrounding a seventh still reflect Cobb's vision.

Cobb Gate, at the north entrance, is a gargoyled ceremonial gateway donated by Cobb in 1900.

A huge chimney crowns the intersection of the house's three sections, uniting the parts.

A large hearth is the focal point of the living room.

the Smart Museum *(see p103)*. Created with the obsessive attention to detail typical of Wright, the house is a *Gesamtkunstwerk*, a total work of art. Every item in the house contributes to its beauty. The house is an organic whole, underscored

by the harmonious interplay between the exterior and interior and is admired by architects worldwide.

A massive restoration of Robie House was undertaken in early 2000 and is expected to take ten years. The house remains open for tours.

The long Roman bricks are a Wright signature.

Main Entrance

Robie House Shop

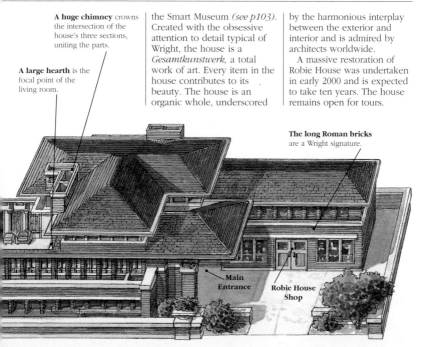

University students playing soccer on the Midway Plaisance

Midway Plaisance ⑥

Bounded by 59th & 60th Sts, Cottage Grove & Stony Island Aves. **Map** 7 B5–8 E5. 🚇 *59th.*

MIDWAY Plaisance, a mile- (1.6-km-) long greenway at the south end of the University of Chicago campus and the city's broadest boulevard, serves as the university's recreation grounds. The Midway is also an excellent vantage point from which to view the university's Gothic buildings.

Designed by Frederick Law Olmsted and Calvert Vaux as the link between Washington and Jackson parks, the Midway was the site of the 1893 exposition's Bazaar of Nations. It was here that the Ferris wheel – 250 ft (76m) high – made its debut.

Washington Park ⑦

Bounded by 51st & 60th Sts, Martin Luther King Jr. Dr & Cottage Grove Ave. **Map** 7 A2–A5. 🚇 *51st; Garfield (green line).*

NAMED AFTER the first US president, Washington Park was originally intended to be part of a grand South Park, comprising both Washington Park and Jackson Park, connected by a canal

running through Midway Plaisance. Landscape architects Frederick Law Olmsted and Calvert Vaux, designers of New York's Central Park, developed the South Park plan in 1871. The park commission balked at creating a canal and so the original plan was never realized in its entirety. In 1872, Horace W.S. Cleveland was hired to oversee the completion of Washington Park.

Combining expanses of meadows with borders of trees and shrubs, Washington Park's pastoral landscape also has a pond and lagoon. At the northeast end of the park is Drexel Fountain, one of the oldest fountains in Chicago. It was designed in 1881–2 by Henry Manger.

The park's most magnificent feature is the sculpture *Fountain of Time* at the south end, where Washington Park meets Midway Plaisance. Designed in 1922 by the Chicago artist Lorado Taft (1860–1936), this haunting monument depicts the cloaked figure of Time watching the endless march of humanity. It was erected to celebrate 100 years of US-British peace.

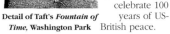

Detail of Taft's *Fountain of Time*, Washington Park

DuSable Museum of African American History ⑧

740 E 56th Pl. **Map** 7 B4. 📞 *(773) 947-0600.* Ⓜ *Garfield (green line) then bus 55.* 🕐 *10am–5pm Mon–Sat; noon–5pm Sun & major public hols.* 🎫 *(children under 6 free; free Sun).* ♿ 📷 *book in advance.* 🏠 🅿 **Lectures, films**.

AS PART OF ITS mission to celebrate the rich and diverse history and culture of African Americans and their contributions to the nation, the DuSable Museum highlights accomplishments of the ordinary and extraordinary

alike. Founded in 1961, the museum is the oldest such institution in the US.

The museum's permanent exhibit "Songs of My People" brings together diverse images by Black photojournalists to document the lives of African Americans.

Memorabilia from the life and political career of Chicago's first Black mayor, Harold Washington, make up the "Harold Washington in Office" exhibit.

Disturbing pop-culture materials are collected in "Distorted Images: Made in USA?," an exhibit focusing on contrived and demeaning images of African Americans. "Africa Speaks" presents art from Africa, much of which has a functional purpose. Handcrafted door panels, for example, are given to a Nigerian bride on her wedding day so she may close her boudoir while decorating it. The ritual masks from closed West African societies are particularly striking.

Hyde Park ⑨

Bounded by Hyde Park Blvd, 61st St, Washington Park, & Lake Michigan. **Map** 8 D3. 🚇 *53rd; 55th-56th-57th; 59th.* 📞 *call 922-3432.* 🍴 🏠

HYDE PARK is one of Chicago's most pleasant neighborhoods. The University of Chicago's presence contributes a collegiate atmosphere, while the many shops, restaurants, theaters, and galleries provide a broad array of attractions.

The area was open countryside in 1853 when Chicago lawyer Paul Cornell established the community on a swath of lakeside property.

Unruly gardens characteristic of the Rosalie Villas, in Hyde Park

Isidore Heller House, in Hyde Park, by Frank Lloyd Wright

The quiet suburb was transformed by three events: its 1889 annexation by the City of Chicago, the 1890 founding of the University of Chicago, and the 1893 World's Columbian Exposition. Many of the houses from this 1890s spurt of development survive. Isidore Heller House (5132 South Woodlawn Avenue) is a Frank Lloyd Wright design (1897) that precedes his celebrated Robie House *(see pp102–103)* by a decade yet reveals his characteristic Prairie style.

Rosalie Villas (Harper Avenue, from 57th to 59th), designed by Solon S. Beman between 1884 and 1890, was Hyde Park's first planned community. It consists of about 50 Queen Anne-style residences, each unique in architectural detail.

The retail heart of Hyde Park is 53rd Street, while ethnic restaurants cluster on 55th Street. Bookstores thrive in Hyde Park; it has been called the largest center for books in the Midwest.

Kenwood ⑩

Bounded by 47th St, Hyde Park & Drexel Blvds, & Blackstone Ave. **Map 7** C1. Ⓜ *47th (green line) then bus 28.* Ⓡ *47th.* 🚌 *call 922-3432.* 🍴 🛒

HISTORIC KENWOOD was established in 1856 when dentist Jonathan A. Kennicott bought and subdivided a large plot of land near 43rd Street. During the next three decades, it became one of the most fashionable South Side communities. In the 1920s, many middle-class African Americans moved to the area, but the late 1940s saw a period of decline. A massive urban renewal project, led by social planners from the University of Chicago, was begun in the early 1950s.

The neighborhood has some of the finest mansions constructed in Chicago, along with many Prairie School homes *(see p25)* homes. Two commissions Frank Lloyd Wright undertook while working for Adler and Sullivan include the George W. Blossom House (4858 Kenwood Avenue) and the Warren McArthur House (4852 Kenwood Avenue).

Noteworthy are the mansions on Greenwood Avenue between 49th and 50th, in particular the elegant Prairie style of the Ernest J. Magerstadt House (4930 South Greenwood Avenue), designed in 1908 by George W. Maher, as well as the ornate houses lining South Kimbark Avenue. One of Chicago's largest single-family homes is the Julius Rosenwald House (4901 South Ellis Avenue), built for the Sears, Roebuck magnate.

Jackson Park ⑪

Bounded by 57th & 67th Sts, Stony Island Ave & Lake Michigan. **Map 8** E5. Ⓡ *59th; 63rd.* 🚌 *call 922-3432; bird walk, call (773) 493-7058.*

JACKSON PARK was designed by Frederick Law Olmsted and Calvert Vaux in 1871 as part of the unrealized South Park plan *(see p104)*. Even though the park was redesigned after being chosen as the main site for the 1893 World's Fair, and again in 1895, its original aquatic theme is still evident.

Osaka Garden is a re-creation of the Japanese garden built for the fair. This serene spot on Wooded Island has a pavilion, waterfall, and gorgeous cherry trees. The island is considered the best place in Chicago for bird-watching: more than 120 species of birds have been sighted here.

In the center of the park, a smaller, gilded replica of the 65-ft- (20-m-) statue *The Republic* celebrates the fair's 25th anniversary.

There are also two beaches and several sports facilities.

Jackson Park's "Golden Lady," a replica of Daniel Chester French's *The Republic*

The contemplative Osaka Garden in Jackson Park

Museum of Science and Industry ⑫

T HE MUSEUM OF SCIENCE AND INDUSTRY celebrates the scientific and technological accomplishments of humankind, with an emphasis on achievements of the 20th century. Originally called the Rosenwald Industrial Museum, after the museum's benefactor, its name was soon changed at Julius Rosenwald's urging, who said that the museum belonged not to him but to the people. While the building, a monumental Neo-Classical structure dominating Jackson Park, is a nod to history *(see p109)*, the museum within has been the North American leader in modern, interactive displays, making the exploration of science and technology an accessible experience.

A carved stone figure over the north portal

Colleen Moore's Fairy Castle
This 9-sq-ft (0.8-sq-m) dollhouse is complete with miniature furniture and working electricity and plumbing.

Apollo 8 Command Module
This historic spacecraft played an important role in early US lunar missions, which culminated in the landing on the moon.

U-505 Submarine, a World War II U-Boat, sank eight allied ships before being captured on the high seas by the US Navy, in 1944.

Main Floor

Ground Floor

Circus
Roland Weber, a railroad worker, spent 33 years carving and casting the 22,000 figures that come to life in this tiny, animated circus.

Crown Entrance

Great Hall

STAR EXHIBITS

★ All Aboard the Silver Streak

★ The Heart

★ Take Flight

★ All Aboard the Silver Streak
Climb aboard the record-breaking 1930s train that revolutionized industrial design.

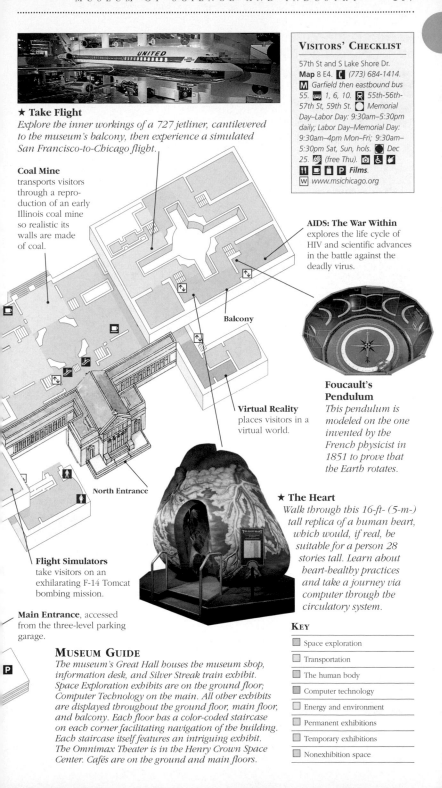

★ **Take Flight**
Explore the inner workings of a 727 jetliner, cantilevered to the museum's balcony, then experience a simulated San Francisco-to-Chicago flight.

Coal Mine
transports visitors through a reproduction of an early Illinois coal mine so realistic its walls are made of coal.

VISITORS' CHECKLIST

57th St and S Lake Shore Dr.
Map 8 E4. ☎ (773) 684-1414.
Ⓜ *Garfield then eastbound bus 55.* 🚌 *1, 6, 10.* 🚆 *55th-56th-57th St, 59th St.* 🕐 *Memorial Day–Labor Day: 9:30am–5:30pm daily; Labor Day–Memorial Day: 9:30am–4pm Mon–Fri; 9:30am–5:30pm Sat, Sun, hols.* ● *Dec 25.* 🎫 *(free Thu).* 🅿️ ♿ ⬛
🍴 🏪 🛍 🅿️ *Films.*
🆆 *www.msichicago.org*

AIDS: The War Within
explores the life cycle of HIV and scientific advances in the battle against the deadly virus.

Balcony

Foucault's Pendulum
This pendulum is modeled on the one invented by the French physicist in 1851 to prove that the Earth rotates.

Virtual Reality
places visitors in a virtual world.

North Entrance

★ **The Heart**
Walk through this 16-ft- (5-m-) tall replica of a human heart, which would, if real, be suitable for a person 28 stories tall. Learn about heart-healthy practices and take a journey via computer through the circulatory system.

Flight Simulators
take visitors on an exhilarating F-14 Tomcat bombing mission.

Main Entrance, accessed from the three-level parking garage.

MUSEUM GUIDE
The museum's Great Hall houses the museum shop, information desk, and Silver Streak train exhibit. Space Exploration exhibits are on the ground floor; Computer Technology on the main. All other exhibits are displayed throughout the ground floor, main floor, and balcony. Each floor has a color-coded staircase on each corner facilitating navigation of the building. Each staircase itself features an intriguing exhibit. The Omnimax Theater is in the Henry Crown Space Center. Cafés are on the ground and main floors.

KEY

☐ Space exploration
☐ Transportation
☐ The human body
☐ Computer technology
☐ Energy and environment
☐ Permanent exhibitions
☐ Temporary exhibitions
☐ Nonexhibition space

Exploring the Museum of Science and Industry

Caryatids grace the museum's exterior

THE MUSEUM OF SCIENCE and Industry, with its more than 800 exhibits and 2,000 interactive displays, encompasses everything from basic science to advanced technology. Space exploration and transportation are particularly strong areas. A few exhibits, such as the Circus, fall outside the museum's defined focus, but prove to be enduring crowd pleasers. With 300,000 sq ft (27,870 sq m) of exhibition space, there's more than enough to keep visitors of all ages engaged for a full day of investigation and discovery.

View of the Museum of Science and Industry from across Columbia Basin

SPACE EXPLORATION

THE HENRY CROWN Space Center is the epicenter of the museum's excellent display on space exploration. Here, you can view the Apollo 8 Command Module – the first manned spacecraft to circle the moon, orbiting ten times in December 1968. Less than 13 ft (4 m) in diameter and weighing 13,100 lb (6,000 kg), the cramped vessel still bears the scars of its epic journey on its pitted exterior.

The exhibit includes a replica of NASA's Apollo Lunar Module Trainer, which is used for astronaut training, and a 6.5-oz (185-g) piece of moon rock retrieved by the Apollo 17 mission.

The Space Center is also home to the Aurora 7 Mercury Space Capsule, one of the earliest manned

Henry Crown Space Center, showcasing US space exploration

spacecrafts to orbit the Earth – doing so four times consecutively in May 1962.

A 20-minute movie simulating the experience of blasting off in a space shuttle, complete with shaking seats, allows viewers to feel like astronauts, if only briefly.

TRANSPORTATION

PICK A MODE of transport – from train, plane, to automobile – and you can be sure the museum has an outstanding example, ready for visitors to climb aboard. Train-nostalgia buffs will enjoy the All Aboard the Silver Streak exhibit, which showcases the first diesel-electric, streamlined passenger train in America, the Pioneer Zephyr. Built in 1934, the Zephyr was the swiftest, sleekest train in the US, initiating the conversion from steam to diesel-electric locomotion and ushering in the era of luxury passenger rail travel. The Zephyr's interior was dramatically different from the opulent Pullman cars in use at the time (see p119) yet just as elegant in its simplicity. Visitors can get behind the

controls and pretend they are driving this historic train.

The museum also has one of the largest train models in the world. The 3,000-sq-ft (280-sq-m) model highlights the role of the railroad in the US economy.

The history of aviation is well represented in the museum's transportation zone. Look up to the balcony and you will see a rare Boeing 40B-2 airplane suspended from the ceiling.

Nearby is Take Flight, an exhibit explaining the scientific principles behind the wonder of flight, such as radar, aerodynamics, and engine and wing construction. This exhibit contains one of the museum's largest attractions, a cantilevered United Airlines Boeing 727. Visitors can board the aircraft to explore, and watch from the balcony its seven-minute simulated flight.

Adjacent to the Boeing 727 is Designed to Fly, an exhibit tracing the history of humans' efforts to fly, from the 15th century to the Wright Brothers' first successful powered flight, in 1903.

Another popular attraction is the U-505 Submarine, a World War II German submarine captured by US naval forces off the west coast of Africa in 1944. Tour this cramped, 252-ft- (77-m-) long vessel, now a memorial to

The Great Hall, the popular Silver Streak train in the background

Navy war veterans, in which sailors could not be taller than 5.5 ft (1.7 m) if they wished to stand upright.

Directly above, on the main floor, is the NAVY: Technology at Sea exhibit, where a high-tech flight simulator replicates a take-off and landing on the back of an aircraft carrier.

Fast machines in the museum's transportation zone

Closer to earth is the Auto Gallery's Spirit of America, the first car to break the 500 mph (800 kph) land speed barrier. On October 15, 1964, Craig Breedlove became the "fastest man on wheels" when he piloted this missile-like vehicle to spectacular speeds.

THE HUMAN BODY

UNDOUBTEDLY the weirdest and most compelling exhibit in the museum (for the strong of stomach only) is the Anatomical Slices, located on the blue staircase between the main floor and balcony. In the 1940s, the corpses of a man and woman who died of natural causes were frozen and then cut into 0.5-inch (1.25-cm) sections – the man, horizontally, and the woman, vertically – and preserved in fluid between glass. These unique displays allow you to look right inside the human body – in all its queasiness-inducing glory.

Equally dramatic – but less gory – is The Heart, a 16-ft- (5-m-) tall replica of a human heart. Walk through the model to see the heart from the perspective of a blood cell. Then check your blood pressure and calculate the number of times your heart has beaten since birth.

AIDS: The War Within is the world's first permanent museum exhibit on AIDS and HIV. It explores, in part through bold comic-book

FROM PLASTER TO STONE

Architect Charles B. Atwood *(see p28)* based his design of this majestic building – built as a temporary structure for the 1893 World's Fair and, today, the only surviving building from the fair – on classical Greek models. Over 270 columns and 24 caryatids, weighing 6 tons each, grace the exterior. Covered in plaster, with a roof of skylights, the building deteriorated badly after the fair. The Field Museum *(see pp86–9)* occupied it briefly, until 1920. The building then sat in a state of disrepair until the mid-1920s, when Julius Rosenwald, chairman of Sears, Roebuck and Co., campaigned to save it and founded the museum, donating millions of dollars to a massive reconstruction effort. Exterior plaster was replaced with 28,000 tons of limestone and marble in an 11-year renovation. The Museum of Science and Industry opened in 1933, in time for the Century of Progress World's Exposition.

The original building during the 1893 World's Columbian Exposition

artwork, the nine stages of the AIDS virus and the efforts of scientists to control it. Interactive displays encourage visitors to learn about viruses, the ecology of disease, and the human immune system.

COMPUTER TECHNOLOGY

ALTHOUGH the museum makes effective use of computers in its many interactive displays, relatively little space is devoted specifically to the subject of computer technology. A fascinating exception is Imaging: The Tools of Science. This installation explores computer-imaging procedures such as MRIs (which produce the image of a cross-section of an object) and CT scans (soft-tissue X-rays). Visitors can delve into radiosurgery and forensic science through hands-on exhibits.

Don goggles in the main floor's Virtual Reality exhibit and become part of an environment created by computer technology. A video camera, real-time digitizer,

and recorded images will place you in a virtual world, where you can "play" a drum or "bounce" a ball.

ENERGY AND ENVIRONMENT

ONE OF THE MUSEUM'S most popular exhibits is Coal Mine. It is worth waiting for in the inevitable lineup. This re-creation of a 1933 Illinois coal mine is remarkably life-like. The 20-minute tour begins at the top of a mineshaft, where an elevator takes visitors down in semi-darkness to a bituminous coal seam and a fascinating demonstration of coal-mining machinery. A short ride on a mine train ends this unique, if somewhat claustrophobic, experience. Environmental issues are front and center at the Reusable City. Interactive displays encourage visitors to learn more about the Earth's ozone layer, climate change, and pollution. A periscope allows visitors to see inside a "landfill," down to its decades-old contents.

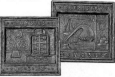

Bronze plaques on the main doors honor the sciences

FARTHER AFIELD

CHICAGO'S OUTLYING areas offer a wealth of sight-seeing opportunities. For lovers of architecture, Oak Park is a must-see for its Frank Lloyd Wright designs. Other Chicago neighborhoods, such as Wicker Park and Lakeview, each with its own distinct character, are ideal day-trip destinations. Pullman is one of the US's best-preserved

Mexican sugar skull, Pilsen

19th-century neighborhoods. A little farther is Brookfield Zoo, renowned for its realistic animal habitats. Walking paths lead through varied landscapes at Morton Arboretum. Visitors with more time can traverse the canal corridor, which runs alongside the 1848 historic canal and encompasses extensive recreational trails and several fine museums.

SIGHTS AT A GLANCE

Historic Buildings, Districts, and Canals
Hull-House **6**
Illinois and Michigan Canal National Heritage Corridor **10**
Oak Park **4**
Pullman Historic District **11**

Neighborhoods
Lakeview and Wrigleyville **2**

Lower West Side **7**
Near West Side **5**
Wicker Park **3**

Zoos and Botanic Gardens
Brookfield Zoo **8**
Lincoln Park Zoo *pp112–13* **1**
Morton Arboretum **9**

KEY

☐	Urban area
▬	Interstate highway
▬	State highway
═	Major road

5 miles = 8 km

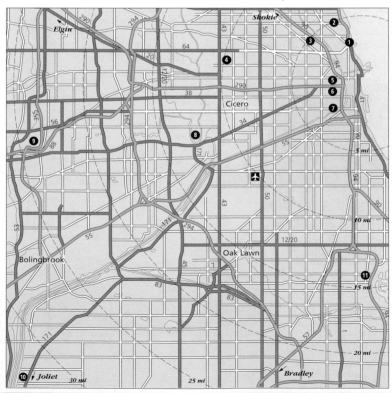

◁ **Pink flamingos at Lincoln Park Zoo**

Lincoln Park Zoo ❶

Statue of Abraham Lincoln in Lincoln Park

Established in 1868 with the gift of two swans from New York's Central Park, Lincoln Park Zoo is the US's oldest free public zoo. Today, more than 1,000 mammals, reptiles, and birds from around the world live here, in realistic habitats. The zoo's status as a world leader in wildlife conservation is evident in its educational exhibits, as well as in its many international efforts to save endangered species. Although it is not Chicago's largest zoo (see Brookfield Zoo *p117*), Lincoln Park Zoo, in the heart of Lincoln Park, is easily accessible from the Downtown Core. The park, Chicago's largest, offers walking and biking paths that wind along groves of native trees, paddle-boating ponds, lagoons, and sandy beaches.

West Entrance

Lincoln Park Conservatory
This stunning conservatory (1890–95), designed by architect Joseph L. Silsbee, houses many exotic plants, including orchids. Thousands of flowers for use in the park are grown here.

★ Regenstein Small Mammal-Reptile House
This exhibit showcases 40 species, including African Dwarf crocodiles.

Waterfowl Lagoon
Flamingos and other waterfowl find refuge in this peaceful lagoon, one of the zoo's earliest features.

Café Brauer was designed in 1908 by Dwight Perkins, a leading architect of the Prairie School. The building was restored in 1989. Its Great Hall has spectacular chandeliers and a skylight.

STOCKTON DRIVE

Star Features

- ★ **Farm in the Zoo**

- ★ **Lester E. Fisher Great Ape House**

- ★ **Regenstein Small Mammal-Reptile House**

★ Farm in the Zoo
The five barns of this working farm shelter cows, horses, chickens, and pigs. Children especially enjoy the daily milking in the Dairy Barn and horse-grooming demonstrations.

**McCormick Bear and
Wolf Habitat**
*The zoo's polar bear pool is one
of the largest in the world.*

**East
Entrance**

Gateway Building, at the
zoo's main east entrance,
houses the information
and security desk.

Kovler Lion House
*Rare cats, including Siberian tigers,
inhabit this 1912 historic building.*

★ **Lester E. Fisher Great Ape House**
*The zoo's collection of lowland gorillas
is one of the largest in the US –
testimony to the zoo's extraordinarily
successful breeding program.*

**Antelope and
Zebra Area**
*Various hoofed
animals live in 11
outdoor habitats by the
zoo's south pond,
including the
threatened Grevy's
zebra from Africa and
the endangered
Bactrian camel from
Mongolia, as well as
rare gazelles, antelopes,
deer, and alpacas.*

**South
Entrance**

0 meters 100

0 yards 100

Wrigley Field baseball stadium, home of the famous Chicago Cubs

Lakeview and Wrigleyville ❷

West of Lake Michigan to Ashland Ave, from Diversey Ave to W Irving Park Rd. **M** *Belmont (red, brown, purple lines).* 🚌 *8, 22, 36.* 🎭 *See* **Entertainment** *p163.*

LAKEVIEW AND Wrigleyville make up one of Chicago's most colorful neighborhoods. Now a cultural melting pot, the area was settled by German immigrants in the 1830s. Farms dotted the landscape until the mid-1800s, when the area began to develop as a residential neighborhood of working-class Swedish immigrants. After annexation by the City in 1889, a spurt of development established the area as one of the liveliest in Chicago – a distinction it continues to hold today.

Wrigleyville, the northern half of Lakeview, is named after Wrigley Field, home of the famous Chicago Cubs baseball team. This charming stadium, designed by Zachary Taylor Davis in 1914, is the oldest National League ballpark. The community resisted electric lighting of the stadium into the late 1980s.

Lakeview hosts a thriving theater scene and excellent restaurants, coffeehouses, bars, specialty shops, and bookshops. Trendy boutiques line Belmont Avenue between Halsted and Sheffield Streets. Lakeview is also the heart of Chicago's gay community.

To sample Lakeview's architectural heritage, visit

Alta Vista Terrace, between Grace and Byron Streets. This block of turn-of-the-century row houses was designed by Joseph C. Brompton in 1904 and was the first area in Chicago to be designated a historic district. Hawthorne Place, north of Belmont Avenue, east of Broadway, is a rare surviving Victorian-era residential design typical of the area's early development.

Beautiful tombstones mark the resting places of Chicago's notables in **Graceland Cemetery** (4001 North Clark Street), just north of Lakeview. Buried here are Louis Sullivan *(see p28)* and George Pullman *(see p119),* among others. A site map is available at the cemetery's office; call 922-8687 for tour information.

Rapp House, one of Wicker Park's architectural gems

Wicker Park ❸

Bounded by Schiller & Leavitt Sts, Damen & Milwaukee Aves. **M** *Damen (blue line).* 🚌 *56.* 🎭 *Around the Coyote (Sep).*

IF YOU ARE LOOKING for the trendy area of Chicago, Wicker Park is it. Along with nearby Bucktown to the northeast, Wicker Park has enjoyed a cultural renaissance for the last few decades. It is brimming with alternative galleries, boutiques, coffeehouses, restaurants, and nightclubs. Real-estate values here are escalating faster than anywhere else in the city.

Originally working-class, the area experienced its first upscale surge in the late

1800s, when German and Scandinavian immigrants built Victorian mansions here. Many mansions remain, making Wicker Park a great place for an architectural tour, either on foot or by car.

Particularly interesting streets are Caton Street (west of Milwaukee Avenue, south of Wabansia Avenue, to Leavitt Street), Leavitt Street, and Pierce Avenue, all of which feature late-19th-century mansions. John Rapp House (1407 North Hoyne Avenue) is a fine example of Second Empire architecture, an ornate French style characterized by mansard roofs and dormer windows.

The funky retail center of Wicker Park is at the intersection of North, Damen, and Milwaukee Avenues.

Oak Park ❹

Bounded by N Chicago Ave, S Randolph St, E Harlem & W East Aves. **ℹ** *(708) 848-1500.* **M** *Oak Park (green line); Harlem/Lake (green line).* 🚃 *Oak Park (Union Pacific/West line).* **Visitors' center***: 158 N Forest Ave.* ◐ *10am–5pm daily (Thanksgiving–Mar: 10am–4pm).* ● *Jan 1, Thanksgiving, Dec 25.* 🅿 🎟 **Frank Lloyd Wright Home and Studio Foundation** **ℂ** *(708) 848-1978.* 🎟

IN 1889, FRANK LLOYD Wright moved to Oak Park, at the age of 22. During the next 20 years here, he created many groundbreaking buildings as his legendary Prairie School style evolved. This tranquil community is now home to 25 Wright-designed buildings – the largest grouping of his work anywhere. Oak Park is

Frank Lloyd Wright's Home and Studio, his residence for 20 years

Unity Temple, Frank Lloyd Wright's "little jewel"

also known for its literary association: famed American writer Ernest Hemingway *(see p29)* was born here in 1899.

The best place to feast on Wright's achievement is the **Frank Lloyd Wright Home and Studio**. Designed by Wright in 1889, the magnificently restored residence and workspace is where the architect developed his influential Prairie style.

Nearby are two private homes that reveal Wright's versatility. Thc **Arthur Heurtley House** (1902) is typically Prairie style, with its row of windows spanning the low roofline and its simple but elegant entrance arch. The **Moore-Dugal House** (1895) is a hybrid of styles, rich with Tudor Revival and Gothic elements.

At the southern end of Oak Park is the masterful **Pleasant Home**, a 30-room Prairie-style mansion designed in 1897 by George W. Maher. The house contains extraordinary art glass (designed panels of leaded glass), intricate woodwork, and decorative motifs, as well as a display on the area's history.

Wright was particularly proud of **Unity Temple**, his design for the Unitarian Universalist Congregation. He called this church, one of his most important designs, his first expression of an "entirely new architecture." It was built between 1906 and 1908 using a then-unusual technique of poured reinforced concrete, in part because of a budget of only $45,000. Unity Temple is a masterpiece of powerful simplicity wedded with functional ornamentation. The use of interior space, with its multiple receding planes, is truly remarkable.

Ernest Hemingway lived in Oak Park until the age of 18. The **Ernest Hemingway Birthplace**, a grand Victorian home with turn-of-the-century furnishings, has displays on this Nobel Prize winner's life. The **Ernest Hemingway Museum** features artifacts from Hemingway's early life, including a childhood diary.

The Victorian house in which Ernest Hemingway was born

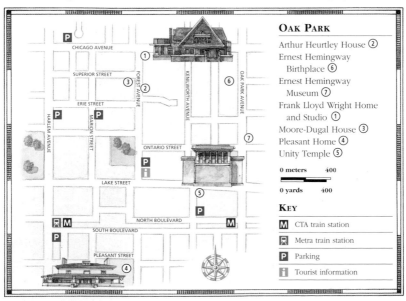

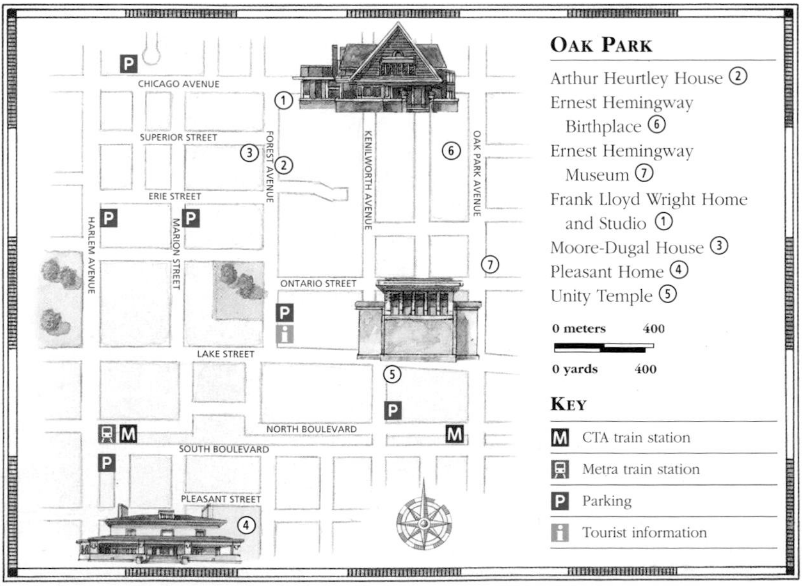
CHICAGO AVENUE
SUPERIOR STREET
ERIE STREET
ONTARIO STREET
LAKE STREET
NORTH BOULEVARD
SOUTH BOULEVARD
PLEASANT STREET
HARLEM AVENUE
MARION STREET
FOREST AVENUE
KENILWORTH AVENUE
OAK PARK AVENUE
OAK PARK
Arthur Heurtley House ②
Ernest Hemingway Birthplace ⑥
Ernest Hemingway Museum ⑦
Frank Lloyd Wright Home and Studio ①
Moore-Dugal House ③
Pleasant Home ④
Unity Temple ⑤
0 meters 400
0 yards 400
KEY
[M] CTA train station
Metra train station
[P] Parking
[i] Tourist information

Jane Addams' Hull-House Museum, seen from the courtyard

Near West Side ❺

Bounded by Chicago River, 16th & Kinzie Sts, & Ogden Ave. **Map** 3 A1–A5. **M** *UIC-Halsted*. 🚌 *8, 60.*

Over the years, Chicago's Near West Side has experienced waves of successive immigrant settlement. Today, it is one of the best places to experience the city's many ethnic communities.

It was settled in the 1840s and 1850s by working-class Irish immigrants. The Great Chicago Fire of 1871 began here, on DeKoven Street (No. 558), in the O'Leary barn. Appropriately (or ironically, depending on how you look at it), the **Chicago Fire Academy** is now located on the site. An arresting bronze sculpture of flames marks the spot where the devastating fire reportedly began.

Following the fire, Russian and Polish Jews settled the area in the 1890s, while to the north, a lively Greek Town developed, centered along Halsted Street, between Madison and Van Buren Streets. To the west, Little Italy, centered around Taylor Street at Halsted Street, flourished.

The **University of Illinois at Chicago** holds a prominent position in the area. Walter A. Netsch Jr. designed the university in the 1960s, in the modern style known as Brutalism. The campus is characterized by unadorned concrete buildings with rows of narrow vertical windows.

Hull-House ❻

800 S Halsted St. 📞 *413-5353*. **Map** 3 A3. **M** *UIC-Halsted*. 🚌 *7, 8, 60.* 📷 🎥 *mandatory: 10am–4pm weekdays; noon–5pm Sun.* 🅿

Jane Addams' Hull-House Museum, now part of the University of Illinois campus, celebrates the pioneering work of Addams *(see p29)*, who won the 1931 Nobel Peace Prize for her social-justice work and advocacy and became perhaps the most famous woman in the US. In her pioneering work with the poor, Addams fought for child-labor laws, a minimum wage, and better public sanitation, among other social causes.

It was in this 1856 mansion in the then industrial center of Chicago that Addams and Ellen Gates Starr established, in 1889, a settlement house to provide social services to immigrants, the poor, and the dispossessed. The house's interior has been restored to look as it did in its early days, with original furnishings. Exhibits document the history of the settlement and the work of its residents.

Egon Weiner's sculpture at the Chicago Fire Academy

Lower West Side ❼

Bounded by Chicago River, 16th St, & Pulaski Rd. **M** *18th.* 🚌 *9, 18, 60.*

The Lower West Side, like the Near West Side, developed as an industrial, working-class neighborhood after the 1871 fire. Immigrants from Bohemia were the first to arrive, in the 1870s, followed in the early 20th century by Germans, Poles, and Yugoslavians. In the 1950s, an influx of Mexican and Puerto Rican immigrants brought a Hispanic flavor to the community.

Today, the neighborhood of Pilsen, centered along 18th Street between South Damen Avenue and South Halsted Street, is home to many fine Mexican restaurants, bakeries, and specialty shops. The sounds of salsa are everywhere, the inviting scent of corn tortillas emanates from tortillerias, and colorful murals brighten the streetscape. Artists, lured here by low rents in the 1980s, contribute a touch of eclecticism to the area.

The best way to experience this vibrant district is to stroll along 18th Street, admire the late-19th-century buildings – one of the most interesting is the Romanesque-style Thalia Hall at the corner of Allport Street – and perhaps stop at a street vendor for a tasty cob of roasted corn.

For more substantial fare, one of the best restaurants in Pilsen is Nuevo León (No. 1515), where the food is tasty and the portions huge. Café Jumping Bean (No. 1439) exhibits work by local artists

Café Jumping Bean on Chicago's Lower West Side

and serves up delicious snacks. Panaderia El Paraiso (No. 1156) is an excellent local bakery.

The cultural heart of Pilsen is the **Mexican Fine Arts Center Museum** (1852 West 19th Street; call 738-1503 for hours), the largest Mexican arts institution in the US. The museum rotates a broad range of exhibitions, covering subjects as diverse as ancient Mexico and young avant-garde artists. The more than 1,500 works in the permanent collection include Mexican masters such as Diego Rivera.

A Capuchin monkey at Tropic World watching visitors

Signs for Mexican bakeries and eateries lining the streets of Pilsen

Brookfield Zoo ❽

First Ave & 31st St, Brookfield.
📞 (708) 485-0263. 🚉 Hollywood (Burlington Northern Santa Fe line).
🕐 Memorial Day–Labor Day: 9:30am–6pm daily. Labor Day–Memorial Day: 10am–5pm daily.
🎟 (free Oct–Mar: Tue, Thu; separate adm to some exhibits). 📷 ♿
🔲 🚻 🍴 🎁 🅿 Lectures, daily special events.

B ROOKFIELD ZOO, opened in 1934, is one of the largest zoos in the US. More than 2,800 animals representing approximately 450 species, gathered from around the world, roam realistic habitats.

Many of the animal exhibits are outdoors, along the zoo's 15 miles (24 km) of trails, but there are also a number of fascinating indoor displays, such as the Living Coast and Tropic World.

The Fragile Kingdom comprises two indoor exhibits – an African desert and an Asian rainforest, with indigenous bats, squirrels, and foxes – and an outdoor display featuring large cats, including a Siberian tiger.

Nearby is the 2,000-seat Dolphinarium. Shows featuring Atlantic bottlenose dolphins are offered here daily. To the north of the Dolphinarium is the Seven Seas Seascape: outdoor pools containing sea lions, harbor seals, and walruses.

At the southeast corner of the grounds is the Children's Zoo, where kids can pet barnyard animals and watch cow and goat milking.

Another children's favorite is Tropic World, one of the largest indoor mixed-species exhibits in the world. Here, rainforest creatures and primates from South America, Asia, and Africa swing through trees and wander the forest floor while visitors watch from the observation deck. The Brazilian tapir, with a flexible snout; the giant anteater, with a 2-ft- (0.6-m-) long tongue; and Ramar, the 365-lb (165-kg) silverback gorilla and Tropic World's largest resident, are particularly impressive.

Close by is the Swamp, an indoor re-created cypress swamp with egrets, storks, and a 10-ft- (3-m-) long American alligator, which sleeps with its eyes open.

The Living Coast features three habitats of South America's western coast: open ocean, near-shore waters, and rocky shores. Jellyfish, turtles, and penguins are just a few of the creatures to be found here.

At the interactive Be a Bird exhibit, visitors can learn about bird anatomy and behavior, and test their own ability to fly.

One of the most spectacular exhibits is Habitat Africa! This re-created savanna is complete with giraffes and wild dogs. A "danger game" trail allows visitors to pretend they're thirsty animals walking to a waterhole, their steps activating taped sounds of predators.

Along the zoo's northern boundary are enclosures for large animals, including the unusual Grevy's zebras. To the south, near Roosevelt Fountain, is Pachyderm House, home to elephants, rhinos, and hippos.

A hippopotamus grazing in the Pachyderm House

Morton Arboretum ⑨

4100 Illinois Route 53, Lisle.
📞 (630) 719-2400. 🚉 Lisle
(Burlington Northern Santa Fe line).
🕐 Apr–Oct: 7am–7pm daily;
Nov–Mar: 7am–5pm daily. 🎫
(discount Wed). 🖥 ♿ 🚻 🍴 🎁
🅿 **Workshops, library**.

MORTON ARBORETUM is home to more than 3,600 species of trees, shrubs, and flowers from around the world. Eight lakes and ponds dot this 2.5-sq-mile (6.5-sq-km) outdoor museum, providing wonderful picnic settings.

Founded in 1922 by Joy Morton of the Morton Salt Company, the arboretum's mission is educational. It conducts scientific research as well as providing informative public displays. Collections are grouped according to plant families and habitats, allowing visitors to learn about each species' unique features and to compare related plants.

The arboretum's Daffodil Glade is particularly stunning in spring. Its Schulenberg Prairie, radiant in summer, is a pioneering landscape restoration begun in the early 1960s by Ray Schulenberg. The prairie is admired throughout the Midwest as a fine re-creation of this now-endangered prairie that covered the region before settlement. The maples are dramatic in the fall; the evergreen trees striking in winter.

If you do not have time to hike along any of the 12 miles (19 km) of trails, you can drive through the arboretum in about 50 minutes via 11 miles (18 km) of one-way roads. Open-air tram tours are offered daily.

Begin your visit at the visitors' center, located near the entrance. The center lists daily events and seasonal bloom information. It also has an excellent bookstore.

The arboretum's Thornhill Education Center (open weekdays) houses displays about Joy Morton and the Morton family. The Sterling Morton Library has a wide range of publications on plants, gardening and landscaping, and natural history. The library's holdings also include rare botanical books and prints.

Illinois and Michigan Canal National Heritage Corridor ⑩

From Chicago's south branch of Chicago River to LaSalle-Peru.
📞 (815) 942-0796. See **The History of Chicago** p15.

THE FIRST EUROPEANS to explore the Chicago region – Louis Jolliet and Father Jacques Marquette – urged, in their 1673 expedition report, the building of a canal to connect Lake Michigan to the Des Plaines and Illinois Rivers.

St. James of the Sag, burial place of many canal laborers

They believed that such a transportation link would be of great economic benefit to the region. It took a century and a half for their prediction to come true, and the loss of many – mostly Irish – canal laborers to diseases such as dysentery and cholera, but when the Illinois and Michigan (I&M) Canal opened in 1848, it did indeed transform the area's economy. It also established Chicago as the transportation center of the Midwest.

As the use of rail to transport freight became increasingly popular, however, canal traffic declined. Carrying waste away from Chicago became the canal's primary purpose, until the Sanitary and Ship Canal took over this function, in 1914. The I&M Canal, with its 15 locks, was abandoned entirely in 1933 when the Illinois Waterway replaced it as a connection between the Great Lakes and Mississippi River.

Fifty years later, in 1984, the canal was designated a national heritage corridor. Today, with almost 100 miles (160 km) of multiuse trails running alongside the canal, the canal route offers abundant recreational opportunities, from bird-watching to biking, hiking, and canoeing. The route passes through more than 40 towns and cities, sites of historic buildings and fascinating museums.

A good place to begin your exploration is the town of Lockport, 30 miles (48 km) southwest of Chicago. During

Lush trees reflected in one of Morton Arboretum's several lakes

the canal's heyday, this town thrived as the center of the boat-building and -repair trades. The visitors' center (200 West 8th Street) in Lockport's historic Gaylord Building, the oldest industrial structure along the waterway, offers maps and information. Adjacent to the center is a restored pioneer settlement, its buildings characteristic of those built during the development of the canal.

Will County Historical Society Museum is located in Lockport's scenic 1837 canal headquarters building. Tour guides tell stories of the canal and explain historic artifacts.

Pullman Historic District ⓫

Bounded by 111th & 115th Sts, Ellis & Cottage Grove Aves. Ⓜ 95/Dan Ryan then bus 111. Ⓡ 111th St (Electric District line). ⓘ 11141 S Cottage Grove Ave. Ⓒ (773) 785-3828. ⏰ noon–2pm Mon ·Fri; 11am–2pm Sat; noon–3pm Sun. 🎫 May–Oct 12:30pm, 1:30pm 1st Sun of month; call (773) 785-3828.

PULLMAN HISTORIC District, one of Chicago's best-preserved 19th-century communities, is the site of a fascinating – if ultimately unsuccessful – experiment. The town, the first of its kind in the US, was built by George M. Pullman, founder of the luxury rail-carriage manufacturer Pullman Palace Car Company, to house his employees. In 1879, Pullman purchased 6.25 sq miles

Interior of Hotel Florence, typical of the town's Queen Anne-style elegance

(16 sq km) of marshland in Chicago's far south side, 14 miles (22.5 km) south of downtown Chicago. He hired architect Solon S. Beman and landscape architect Nathan F. Barrett to plan the company town. Most of the more than 1,700 row houses and apartment units were constructed between 1880 and 1885.

Workers rented the living quarters from Pullman, who expected to realize a 6 percent profit by collecting rent on all the buildings, including the church and library. The homes were modern by contemporary standards. This was the first development to offer the working class indoor plumbing, gas, and recreational facilities.

The experiment ended in acrimony when Pullman laid off workers and cut wages without lowering rents during

Ornate west window of Greenstone Church

the 1893 depression. A huge strike, which eventually spread across the entire nation, ensued. The US government intervened, sending in federal troops. The workers lost the seven-week strike, but Pullman's experiment was tainted with failure. He died three years later, in 1897, still resentful. By 1907, all the houses in Pullman had been sold to private buyers.

Plans in 1960 to demolish the area's buildings and create an industrial park were defeated by residents. The district of Pullman was designated a national landmark in 1971. Today, many of the row houses have been restored. The town is easily explored in an afternoon; maps are available at the visitors' center.

Hotel Florence, named for Pullman's favorite daughter, is a superb 1881 example of Queen Anne style. Now a museum housing artifacts from the town's labor struggles, it is undergoing a $3-million renovation.

The mansions lining 111th and 112th Streets were built for Pullman executives; the Pullman colors of maroon and green frame the windows and doors. The Greenstone Church and the curved Beman-designed Colonnade Apartments and Town Houses by Market Hall are also worth a look. The apartments (1892) provided extremely narrow bachelor units for workers.

Building once housing several Pullman Palace Car Company workers

BEYOND CHICAGO

Exploring Beyond Chicago

VISITORS EAGER TO DISCOVER more of Illinois won't be disappointed by the rich mix of historical sights, recreational activities, and picturesque countryside Chicago's environs have to offer. Excursions to the attractive North Shore towns of Evanston, Wilmette, Glencoe, and Lake Forest will take you along the shoreline of Lake Michigan, affording stunning views.

For those wishing to venture farther, the resort area of Lake Geneva awaits just across the Wisconsin state line. The delightful, historic town of Galena lies near the Iowa border, a three-and-half hour drive west of Chicago. The drive to both leads through rural farmland dotted with small towns and state parks. The typically flat Midwestern terrain gives way to rolling hills just outside Galena.

A picturesque circular barn near Highway 20, West Galena

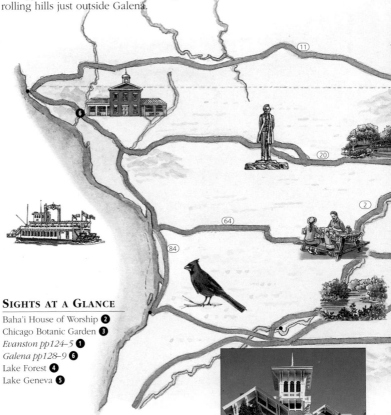

SIGHTS AT A GLANCE

Baha'i House of Worship **2**

Chicago Botanic Garden **3**

Evanston pp124–5 **1**

Galena pp128–9 **6**

Lake Forest **4**

Lake Geneva **5**

GETTING AROUND

Chicago has excellent Metra commuter rail links to the northern suburbs. The Union Pacific/North line, departing from the Ogilvie Transportation Center, services Evanston, Wilmette, Glencoe, and Lake Forest, with frequent trains during rush hour and every one to three hours at other times. The CTA purple line also services Evanston. You will need a car to reach Lake Geneva and Galena. Highway I-94 leads north from Chicago; I-90 is the western route.

Galena's Belvedere Mansion *(see p128)*

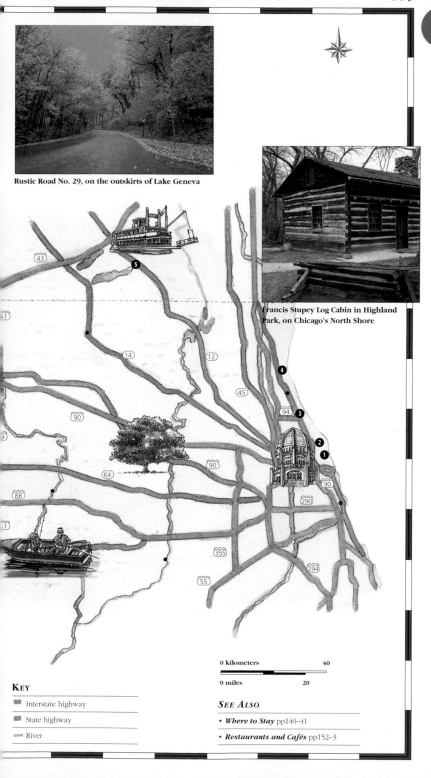

Rustic Road No. 29, on the outskirts of Lake Geneva

Francis Stupey Log Cabin in Highland Park, on Chicago's North Shore

KEY

■ Interstate highway

■ State highway

～ River

SEE ALSO

• *Where to Stay* pp140–41

• *Restaurants and Cafés* pp152–3

Evanston ➊

EVANSTON, ON THE SHORES of Lake Michigan, 14 miles (22 km) north of Chicago, offers stunning beaches, charming boutiques and restaurants, and exciting museums, art galleries, and theater. Originally known as Ridgeville, it began as a community of farmers from New England, and Irish and German immigrants. In 1850, a group of Chicago Methodists bought a large tract of lakefront land, opening Northwestern University five years later. Ridgeville changed its name to Evanston in 1857 to honor John Evans, one of the university's founders. By the 1870s, wealthy Chicagoans, is search of cleaner neighborhoods, were moving to Evanston. Many of their mansions still stand.

Charles Gates Dawes House, overlooking Lake Michigan

Exploring Evanston

Many of Evanston's attractions, including shops, restaurants, and art galleries, are concentrated in the historic downtown around Grove Street and Sherman Avenue, an area easily explored on foot. Other interesting districts include that at Central Street, and at Chicago Avenue and Dempster Street. The large lakefront university campus, the buildings of which reflect widely varied architectural styles, provides greenspace ideal for strolling. Or you can saunter along Forest Avenue to see the historic mansions built for Chicago's wealthy.

🏛 Charles Gates Dawes House

225 Greenwood St. 🄲 (847) 475-3410. ◯ 1–5pm Thu–Sun. ◉ major public hols. 🈺 (children under 6 free). 🎫 mandatory. ♿

This massive Chateauesque mansion was designed in 1894 by Henry Edwards-Ficken for Robert Sheppard,

treasurer of Northwestern University. Sheppard sold it in 1909 to Charles Gates Dawes, who went on to become US vice-president under Calvin Coolidge. The restored 28-room house, home to the Evanston Historical Society, showcases the period 1925–9.

🏛 Rest Cottage

1730 Chicago Ave. 🄲 (847) 864-1396. ◯ Mar–Dec: 1–4pm 1st Sun of month or by appt. ◉ major public hols. 🈺 🎫 mandatory. 🚻

Pioneering suffragist and Women's Christian Temperance Union (WCTU) activist Frances Willard lived at Rest Cottage from 1865 until her death in 1898.

This quaint, Gothic-style *(see p24)* cottage, built by Willard's father in 1865, is now a museum devoted to Willard's life and the history of the WCTU. The world's oldest voluntary, nonsectarian women's organization, the WCTU is best known for its campaign against alcohol.

🏛 Block Sculpture Garden

1967 S Campus Dr. 🄲 (847) 491-4000. ◯ year round.

The Block Museum's sculpture garden showcases 20th-century sculpture. Among the garden's treasures are two large, bronze abstract sculptures by British artist Barbara Hepworth (1903–1975) and an intriguing movable bronze sculpture by Spanish artist Joan Miró (1893–1983).

🏛 Mary and Leigh Block Museum of Art

1967 S Campus Dr. 🄲 (847) 491-4000. ◯ noon–5pm Tue, Wed; noon–8pm Thu–Sun. ◉ major hols. ♿ 🎫 call for details. **Lectures, films, concerts**.

Artwork from the 14th century onward and thematic historical displays are featured at this art museum of Northwestern University, one of the US's top university museums. Major national exhibits also often stop here.

🚩 Grosse Point Light Station

2601 Sheridan Rd. 🄲 (847) 328-6961. ◉ hol weekends. 🈺 🎫 mandatory: Jun–Sep: 2–5pm Sat, Sun.

This lighthouse was built in 1873 in response to one of the worst maritime disasters on the Great Lakes – the 1860 sinking of the paddle wheeler *Lady Elgin,* in which nearly 300 people died.

During the summer, visitors can climb to the top of the lighthouse for wonderful views of the town and lake.

A maritime museum is on the lower floor. Plants native to Illinois are grown in the Wildflower Trail Garden, on the grounds of the station.

Grosse Point Light Station, guiding ships since 1873

Interior of the Mitchell Museum of the American Indian

🏛 Evanston Art Center

2603 Sheridan Rd. ☎ *(847) 475-5300.* 🕐 *10am–4pm, 7–10pm, Mon–Thu; 10am–4pm Fri, Sat; 2–5pm Sun.* ● *major public hols & 4th Thu evening of month.* $ *by donation.* 📷 ♿ *1st-floor gallery.* 👉 ***Lectures, workshops****.*

Housed in a 1926 mansion, the gallery of this community art center exhibits regional contemporary artwork by both established and emerging artists. Gallery talks by exhibiting artists are offered regularly. The center's annual spring art auction is a great opportunity to acquire work by Midwest artists.

The lovely grounds of the center were designed by the Prairie School-influenced landscape architect Jens Jensen, designer of several parks in Chicago, including Columbus Park and the conservatory in Garfield Park, on Chicago's west side.

Visitors' Checklist

[M] *Davis.* 🚆 *Davis (Union Pacific/North line).* ℹ *1560 Sherman Ave.* ☎ *(847) 328-1500.* [W] *www.evanston-illinois.org.* 🎭 *Ethnic Arts (Jul); Lakeshore Arts (Aug); Jump & Verve Jazz Festival (Sep).*

🏛 Mitchell Museum of the American Indian

2600 Central Park Ave. ☎ *(847) 475-1030.* 🕐 *10am–5pm Tue, Wed, Fri, Sat; 10am–8pm Thu; noon–4pm Sun.* ● *major public hols.* $ *by donation.* 📷 ♿ 👉 🛍 ***Lectures, concerts, films****.*

The Mitchell Museum showcases North American Indian cultures from prehistoric to contemporary times. More than 6,000 domestic objects, including pottery, baskets, clothing, and textiles, are on display. The Mitchell is particularly rich in artifacts of Indians of the Midwest. Temporary exhibitions at the museum highlight ancient and present-day Native crafts.

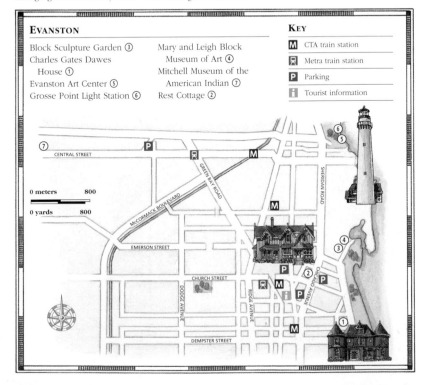

Evanston

Block Sculpture Garden ③
Charles Gates Dawes House ①
Evanston Art Center ⑤
Grosse Point Light Station ⑥
Mary and Leigh Block Museum of Art ④
Mitchell Museum of the American Indian ⑦
Rest Cottage ②

Key

[M] CTA train station
🚆 Metra train station
[P] Parking
ℹ Tourist information

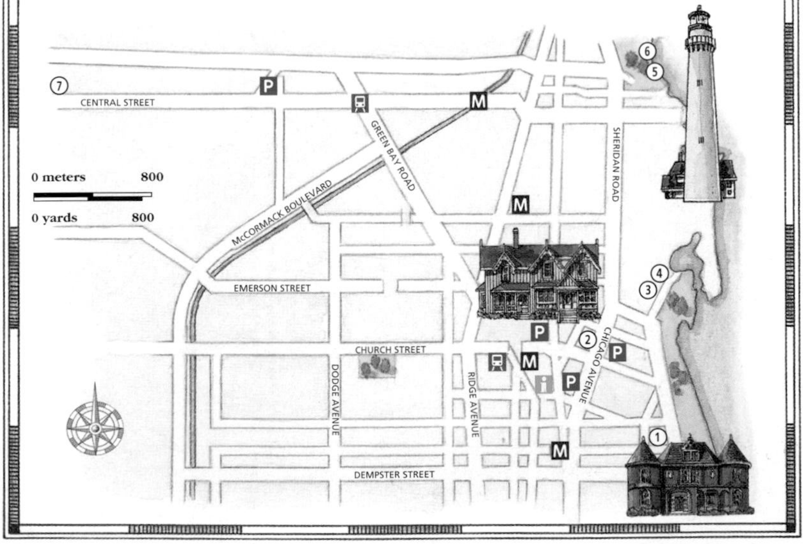
CENTRAL STREET
GREEN BAY ROAD
SHERIDAN ROAD
McCORMACK BOULEVARD
0 meters 800
0 yards 800
EMERSON STREET
CHURCH STREET
DODGE AVENUE
RIDGE AVENUE
CHICAGO AVENUE
DEMPSTER STREET

Baha'i House of Worship ②

100 Linden Ave, Wilmette. **[** (847) 733-3469. **M** Linden. **R** Wilmette (Union Pacific/North line) then bus 421, 422. **◯** May 1–Sep 30: 10am–10pm daily. Oct 1–Apr 30: 10am–5pm daily. **Devotions**: 12:15pm Mon–Sat; 1:15pm Sun. **& P** **w** www.us.bahai.org

THE BAHA'I HOUSE of Worship, gleaming like a white beacon, is the North Shore's most striking building. There are seven major Baha'i houses of worship in the world; this is the only major one in North America. The Baha'i faith, based on the teachings of the 19th-century Persian prophet Baha'u'llah, promotes unity among all people and religions.

Construction of the house, which began in 1920, wasn't completed until 1953. Adhering to Baha'i requirements, there are nine sides to this building designed by French-Canadian architect Louis Bourgeois. An entrance door is on each side. Quotations from Baha'u'llah are carved into the stone, one above each entrance and each of the nine alcoves. Elaborate filigree-like carvings adorn the exterior. A dramatic dome of quartz and white cement rises 135 ft (41 m) above the central auditorium, which seats almost 2,000 people. The colorful, symmetrical gardens are lovely to stroll in.

A short video at the visitors' center introduces the Baha'i faith and the house's history.

The Baha'i House of Worship, with its beautifully filigreed dome

Fountains and pools dot the serene grounds of the Chicago Botanic Gardens

Chicago Botanic Garden ③

1000 Lake Cook Rd, Glencoe. **[** (847) 835-5440. **R** Braeside; Glencoe (Union Pacific/North line) then bus 213. **◯** 8am–sunset daily. **●** Dec 25. **⊙ & ✎ ▣ ⛔ P** **Lectures, exhibits**. **w** www.chicago-botanic.org

THE CHICAGO Botanic Garden, 25 miles (40 km) north of downtown Chicago, is dazzling with its 20 themed gardens and 3 native habitats of flowers, vines, shrubs, and trees. Opened in 1972, the Garden contains 1.5 million specimens representing 8,000 plant families from around the world. Eight lagoons and nine islands dot the Garden's attractive grounds.

The audiovisual presentation at Gateway Center is a useful introduction to the Garden. The center, which is near the entrance, also leads to the main island, the site of the majority of themed gardens.

The English Walled Garden consists of a secluded enclosure with six garden "rooms," each reflecting a

Chicago Botanic Garden banners

different English gardening style. The Heritage Garden is modeled after Europe's first botanical garden. Intoxicating scents of the Rose Garden's 5,000 rose bushes accompany the colorful blooms.

Unsurprisingly, the jewel of the Waterfall Garden is a 45-ft (14 m) waterfall. Sansho-En, or "garden of three islands," reflects the tranquil minimalism of Japanese garden design. One of the islands is tantalizingly out of reach.

The Botanic Garden's mission of conservation is well represented in the Endangered Species Garden; native plants threatened with extinction thrive here.

The Garden's three natural habitat areas (an oak woodland, a prairie, and a riverscape) offer wonderful walking trails through secluded sections of the grounds.

Lake Forest ④

R Lake Forest (Union Pacific/North line). **R** 472. **Deer Path Golf Course** **[** (847) 615-4290. **Forest Park Beach** **[** (847) 615-4284.

LAKE FOREST is one of Chicago's most affluent suburbs, about 30 miles (48 km) north of Chicago's Downtown Core. The town was established in the 1850s by a group of Presbyterians who planned to build a college. The St. Louis landscape architect hired to plan the town took full advantage of the area's beautiful prairie lands, ravines, and hills, designing streets to follow the natural curves of the landscape.

Presbyterian Lake Forest College, established in 1857,

has many grand, late-1800 buildings. The Romanesque-style Hotchkiss Hall was designed by Henry Ives Cobb (*see p24*) in 1890 and named after the town's planner.

The First Presbyterian Church was designed by Charles Frost in 1887. The church's unusual design is an adaptation of the New England cottage style, known as Shingle style.

Market Square, in downtown Lake Forest, is one of the first planned suburban shopping centers in the US. Designed in 1916 by Howard Van Doren Shaw, this pleasant town square has a quaint English character.

The charming Market Square in Lake Forest

The best way to experience Lake Forest is to drive on meandering Sheridan Road. Along the route are many beautiful homes on spacious, landscaped grounds.

Golfers can take advantage of Deer Path Golf Course, while at Forest Park Beach, beachgoers can enjoy the cooling waters of Lake Michigan during the summer heat.

***Belle of the Lake,* a reproduction of a Mississippi paddle wheeler**

Lake Geneva ❺

ℹ 201 Wrigley Dr, WI. **☏** *(414) 248-4416.* **◷** *9am–5pm Mon–Fri; 10am–4pm Sat, Sun.* **✅ 🍴 ♿**
ⓦ *www.lakegenevawi.com*

L AKE GENEVA, 70 miles (113 km) north of Chicago, nestles on the shores of a spring-fed lake of the same name. There is much to keep you occupied for a weekend in this picturesque resort town and its surrounding rural communities. Boating on the wide lake, hiking, and ballooning are just a few of the possibilities.

Lake Geneva is also a shopper's and diner's paradise. Many of the charming boutiques and antique stores are in turn-of-the-century buildings. Several of the town's restaurants, particularly those along Wrigley Drive, provide spectacular views of the lake.

In autumn, the countryside is ablaze with fall foliage. It is an ideal backdrop to the 21-mile (34-km) trail encircling the lake, a trail that once connected Indian camps. On the western edge of town is a state-designated "Rustic Road," an ideal route for a leisurely drive through the country. In winter, skiing and snowmobiling are popular activities. However, accommodations fill up quickly in summer and traffic is heavy.

Lake Geneva has a rich history. The Oneota tribes of the now-extinct Hopewell Culture Indians, an agricultural people, lived in the area as long ago as 1000 BC. In 1836, the local Potawatomi tribe was evicted from the area, and pioneer Christopher Payne built the first log cabin in town. The site is marked with a plaque on Center Street, north of White River.

The town, laid out in 1837, was originally a sawmill town. Following the Civil War, it became a resort for wealthy Chicagoans, who built their homes on the lakefront.

One of the best ways to see these mansions is by boat. Geneva Lake Cruise Line's fleet of ships includes replicas of a Southern paddle wheeler and a turn-of-the-century lake steamer. The *Walworth II* operates as a US mail boat, one of the last in service. A mail carrier jumps off and onto the moving boat, delivering mail during the tour.

Geneva Lake Area Museum of History (818 Geneva Street) displays interesting historical photographs and artifacts.

Riviera Docks, departure point for Lake Geneva boat cruises

Galena ❻

The old town hall, built in 1872, in historic East Galena

A VISIT TO GALENA, "the town that time forgot," is like stepping into a bygone era. More than 85 percent of this town, in Jo Daviess County, is on the National Register of Historic Places. Its architectural gems, museums, and unique landscape make Galena a great weekend destination.

As early as the 1600s, Indians were mining the area's rich deposits of lead and ore. In the 1820s, as prospectors flocked to Galena, the town became one of the US's most important mining centers. By the mid-1800s, it was a major Mississippi River port. But as rail displaced shipping as the mode of freight transportation, the town went into decline. The expense of tearing down the old buildings ensured that its historic core remained intact.

Statue of Ulysses S. Grant

Exploring Galena

The best way to explore Galena is on foot or by trolley tour. Downtown parking is limited; it is best to park at the lot by the visitors' center at the old railroad depot.

Galena has a number of noteworthy historic churches. The **Union Baptist Church** (1854) features a Romanesque Revival doorway, whereas the

A trolley tour is one of the best ways to explore Galena

enchanting **First Presbyterian Church** (1838) has a Georgian spire. The 1838 Erban organ is still played at the Gothic Revival-style *(see p24)* **Grace Episcopal Church**.

The **Galena post office** (1857–9) is the second-oldest continuously operating post office in the US.

🚩 Old Illinois Central Railroad Depot

101 Bouthillier St. 📞 (815) 777–4390. ☐ 9am–5pm Mon–Thu; 9am–7pm Fri, Sat; 10am–5pm Sun. ♿
Originally Galena's station for passenger rail service, it was from here that former US president Ulysses S. Grant departed for war while a Civil War colonel. The 1857 Italianate *(see p24)* building now houses the Visitor Information Center; watch its informative video on the town's history.

🏛 Belvedere Mansion

1008 Park Ave. 📞 (815) 777-0747. ☐ 11am–4pm Sun–Fri; 11am–5pm Sat. ⬤ Oct–Memorial Day. 🎟 📷 mandatory.
Built in 1857 for J. Russell Jones, a steamship owner and US ambassador to Belgium, the Italianate-style Belvedere Mansion is the largest house in Galena.

Completely restored to its original condition, the 22 rooms contain Victorian furnishings. Pieces include furniture once belonging to former US president Theodore Roosevelt, and a gold-painted cabinet once owned by entertainer Liberace.

🏛 Washburne House

908 Third St. 📞 (815) 777-3310. ☐ 10am–4pm (closed noon–1pm) Fri–Sun. ⬤ Jan 1, Thanksgiving, Dec 25. 🎟 📷 mandatory: on the hour and half-hour. ♿
A stunning example of Greek Revival architecture, this house was built in 1843 for prominent Galena attorney

and later US congressman Elihu Washburne (1816–87). Washburne was a comrade of Abraham Lincoln and a strong supporter of the career of Ulysses S. Grant. It was in the library of Washburne's home that Grant first heard the news that he had won the 1868 US presidential election.

The restored interior of the house reflects Victorian middle-class elegance.

🏛 Ulysses S. Grant Home

500 Bouthillier St. 📞 (815) 777-3310. ☐ 9am–5pm daily. ⬤ major public hols. 🎟 📷 mandatory. ♿
This two-story, brick Italianate *(see p24)* house designed by William Dennison was constructed in 1860. It was given to returning Civil War hero General Ulysses S. Grant by a group of prominent Galena citizens in 1865.

Even though Grant spent little time in the house after being elected US president in 1868, it has been restored to its 1870s appearance and contains furnishings used by the Grant family. Costumed guides lead visitors through the house while telling Grant's story.

The Old Illinois Central Railroad Depot now housing Galena's visitors' center

View of Galena looking northeast from the pedestrian bridge

Dowling House

220 Diagonal St. ☎ *(815) 777-1250.* 🕐 *May–Oct: 10am–4pm Sun–Fri; 10am–5pm Sat. Apr, Nov, Dec: 10am–4pm Fri–Sun.* $ 🚶 *mandatory.*

This 1826 example of vernacular architecture is Galena's oldest house. Built of limestone, it originally served as a miner's trading post and rather crude residence. It has been restored to reflect the era of Galena's early pioneers.

DeSoto House Hotel

230 S Main St. ☎ *(815) 777-0090.* ♿ 🍴 🍸 [P]

This hotel was considered the largest, most luxurious hotel west of New York City when it opened its doors in 1855. It was built by Galena merchants in preparation for the boom that accompanied the 1854 arrival of Illinois Central Railroad service in Galena. Many famous Americans, including writer Mark Twain, have stayed here. Abraham Lincoln made a speech from its balcony in 1856, and it was from the DeSoto House Hotel that Ulysses S. Grant ran his 1868 presidential campaign.

Old Market House

123 N Commerce St. ☎ *(815) 777-3310.* 🕐 *9am–5pm Thu–Mon.* ● *Jan 1, Thanksgiving, Dec 25.* $ 🚶 *mandatory.* ♿

The recently restored Greek Revival-style Market House was built by the City of Galena in 1846. One of the Midwest's oldest extant market houses, it was buzzing with activity until the early 1900s. Farmers sold produce inside and out, city offices were on the second floor, and the city jail was in the basement. Today, a first-floor exhibition space is dedicated to displays of historical interest.

VISITORS' CHECKLIST

Hwy 20. 🚌 *Greyhound bus.* [i] *101 Bouthillier St.* ☎ *(815) 777-4390.* 🚶 *by trolley.* 🎉 *Irish Heritage (Mar), Galena Arts Festival (Jul), Fall Harvest (Sep–Oct), County Fair (Oct).* [w] *www.galena.org*

Galena/Jo Daviess County Historical Society and Museum

211 S Bench St. ☎ *(815) 777-9129.* 🕐 *9am–4:30pm daily.* ● *Jan 1, Thanksgiving, Dec 25.* $ *(children under 10 free).* 🛍

This 1858 Italianate mansion, designed by William Dennison, was built for merchant Daniel Barrows. It is now occupied by a museum specializing in the area's history.

The creation of the stunning geology of Jo Daviess County – rugged hills, rocky bluffs, and riveting vistas – is depicted in a large landform model, which shows how Ice Age glaciers detoured around the land, sparing this hilly part of Illinois while flattening the surrounding area.

A display on the Galena River tells the story of the Army Corps of Engineers' building of the town's flood dike and massive gate.

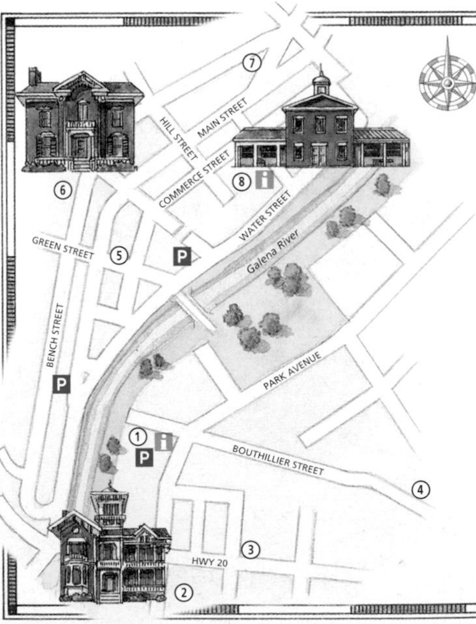

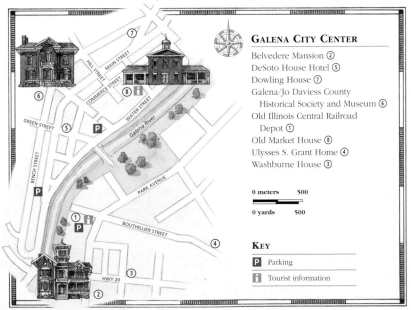

GALENA CITY CENTER

Belvedere Mansion ②
DeSoto House Hotel ⑤
Dowling House ⑦
Galena/Jo Daviess County Historical Society and Museum ⑥
Old Illinois Central Railroad Depot ①
Old Market House ⑧
Ulysses S. Grant Home ④
Washburne House ③

0 meters 500
0 yards 500

KEY

[P] Parking
[i] Tourist information

TRAVELERS' NEEDS

WHERE TO STAY

CHICAGO HAS A ROOM for every taste and budget. The top hotels are good value by international standards. For those travelers on a budget, there are many inexpensive and comfortable hotels and youth hostels in the city. Two-room suites are suitable for families, and some have kitchenettes, for those visitors who want to do their

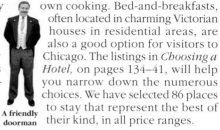

A friendly doorman

own cooking. Bed-and-breakfasts, often located in charming Victorian houses in residential areas, are also a good option for visitors to Chicago. The listings in *Choosing a Hotel,* on pages 134–41, will help you narrow down the numerous choices. We have selected 86 places to stay that represent the best of their kind, in all price ranges.

Hotel Burnham's lobby, modeled on the 1891 original (see p134)

WHERE TO LOOK

MOST OF CHICAGO's hotels are clustered in two areas: the Downtown Core and the North Side. Many are both good and moderately priced. Downtown hotels are particularly convenient for visitors interested in Chicago's cultural sights such as the Chicago Art Institute, the Museum Campus, and the theater district, as well as those attending conventions at McCormick Place. This area can become quiet at night, though. By contrast, hotels on the North Side, just north of the Loop, are in one of the liveliest areas of the city. Many of the city's finer hotels are on the Magnificent Mile and the Gold Coast.

Business travelers often favor the chain hotels near O'Hare and Midway airports. Bed-and-breakfasts are scattered throughout the city. The **Illinois Bureau of Tourism** will mail you information about hotels in Chicago and Illinois.

FACILITIES

AIR-CONDITIONING and cable TV are both standard in Chicago hotels. Fax and photocopy service, computer modem hook-up, in-room speaker-phones, exercise facilities, and a swimming pool are amenities to inquire about. Be sure you understand the charges; some hotels offer these facilities for free, other hotels will charge handsomely for them.

The many conventions and trade shows held in the city provide Chicago's hotels with a major part of their business, so most hotels offer an array of business meeting rooms.

HOTEL RATES AND DISCOUNTS

HOTEL PRICES in Chicago are competitive, but keep in mind when booking that hotels charge a steep 14.9 percent room tax.

Some hotels offer discounts to visitors attending a convention or major exhibition. Hotels may also offer corporate rates and discounts to persons in

the military, senior citizens, teachers, automobile-club members, and frequent flyers. Business travelers often leave the city on weekends, and hotels will offer special weekend rates to encourage more business. Be sure to ask.

Hotels in Chicago do not usually include meals in the room rate, though meal plans are sometimes available.

Two notable discount reservation agencies in Chicago are **Hot Rooms** and **Hotel Reservations Network**. Both charge a fee if you cancel for any reason.

HIDDEN COSTS

ROOM RATES are usually quoted assuming double occupancy. But always ask; some hotels quote single-occupancy rates and charge as much as $20 per night for a second person.

Keep in mind, too, that a room with a view will likely come at a premium.

Convenience costs money. Parking at your hotel can add as much as $20 a day to your bill. You will also pay a steep

Guests relaxing in their suite at Palmer House Hilton (see p134)

Lobby of Hotel Allegro, inspired by the building's 1920 design *(see p134)*

premium for any drinks and snacks you take from the room's mini-bar.

A telephone call made from your room will cost substantially more than a telephone call made from the pay phone in the hotel lobby.

How to Reserve

IF THERE IS one secret to finding a good room, it is planning. Reserve as far in advance as possible. Hotels can fill up quickly when a convention is in town.

Reservations usually require a deposit by credit card. You will be given a confirmation or reservation number when you book. Always confirm your reservation before arriving at the hotel.

If you have special requirements, such as a quiet room away from busy streets, elevators, and ice machines, make these known when booking a room.

Notify the hotel if you expect to arrive later than 5 pm, or you may lose your reservation. If you need to cancel your reservation, it is advisable to record the cancelation number you are given, in case you are later charged for the room. Most hotels do not charge a cancelation fee if you give 24 or 48 hours' notice. Without sufficient notice, you may be charged for the room.

Travelers with Disabilities

HOTELS IN THE US are by law required to provide facilities for wheelchair-bound persons (some older properties are exempt). Most establishments are eager to provide rooms and assistance to travelers with disabilities. Persons with visual impairments may bring guide dogs into hotels.

Traveling with Children

CHILDREN ARE WELCOME in all Chicago hotels, and few charge extra when one or two children under 12 stay in their parent's room. Ask about family rates when making reservations, and make sure the room is suitable. The hotel may offer a room with two beds or a sofa that easily converts to a bed. Many hotels will provide a cot for an additional $10 to $15 a night. Suite hotel rooms are also a good option.

French Deco living room, Hotel Monaco *(see p134)*

Bed-and-Breakfasts

A BED-AND-BREAKFAST is a charming alternative to a hotel. Primarily in residential neighborhoods, such accommodations range from rooms in Victorian homes to rooms in high-rise buildings. Some have private bathrooms. In general, bed-and-breakfasts are very reasonably priced. For information call **Bed and Breakfast Chicago**.

Tourist Offices

Illinois Bureau of Tourism
C *(800) 226-66328.*
W *www.enjoyillinois.com*

Reservation Agencies

Hot Rooms
C *(773) 468-7666 or (800) 468-3500.*

Hotel Reservations Network
C *(800) 964-6835.*
W *www.hoteldiscounts.com*

Bed-and-Breakfasts

Bed and Breakfast Chicago
C *(773) 248-0005 or (800) 375-7084.*
W *www.chicago-bed-breakfast.com*

Youth Hostels

American Youth Hostels
2232 W Roscoe St, Chicago, IL 60618.
C *(773) 327-8114.*
FAX *(773) 327-4287.*

Hosteling International Chicago
24 E Congress Pkwy, Chicago, IL 60690.
Mailing address for reservations:
PO Box 0452, Chicago, IL 60690.
C *360-0300.*
FAX *360-0313.*

Airport Hotels

See page 177 for details of hotels at O'Hare and Midway airports.

Choosing a Hotel

THESE HOTELS HAVE BEEN SELECTED across a wide price range for their good value, facilities, and location. Rooms have private bath, TV, and air-conditioning, and are wheelchair accessible unless otherwise noted. Fitness facilities and pool may be off-site. Some hotels are pet-friendly; ask when making a reservation. Hotels are listed by area, starting with downtown. For map references, see pages 190–97.

DOWNTOWN CORE

Hotel	Number of Rooms	Business Facilities	Restaurant	Concierge
TRAVELODGE DOWNTOWN CHICAGO. Map 4 D3. [$] 65 E Harrison St, Chicago, IL 60605. ☎ *427-8000 or (800) 525-9055.* [FAX] *427-8261.* [W] *www.travelodge.com* This budget hotel offers all the conveniences of downtown: within walking distance of shopping in the Loop, theaters, and museums. The hotel is not fully wheelchair accessible. 🚭 [P] 👪 🍸 💳	200		■	
HOTEL ALLEGRO. Map 3 C1. [$][$][$] 171 W Randolph St, Chicago, IL 60601. ☎ *236-0123 or (800) 643-1500.* [FAX] *236-0917.* [W] *www.allegrochicago.com* This Art Deco hotel, part of the Kimpton chain, is located in Chicago's theater district. Rooms are bright and colorful. Live music in the lobby accompanies the nightly wine reception. Ask about weekend specials that include tickets to local shows. 🚭 [P] 👪 🍸 🏋 💳	483	●	■	●
HOTEL BURNHAM. Map 3 C1. [$][$][$] 1 W Washington St, Chicago, IL 60601. ☎ *782-1111 or (877) 294-9712.* [FAX] *782-0899.* [W] *www.burnhamhotel.com* Originally designed by Daniel Burnham in 1895 *(see p50)*, the remodeled steel-and-glass Reliance Building offers elegant rooms just minutes from the theater district. A Kimpton hotel. 🚭 [P] 👪 🍸 🏋 💳	122		■	●
HOTEL MONACO. Map 4 D1. [$][$][$] 225 N Wabash Ave, Chicago, IL 60601. ☎ *960-8500 or (800) 397-7661.* [FAX] *960-1883.* [W] *www.monaco-chicago.com* The front desk, modeled after a steamer trunk, epitomizes the travel theme of this Kimpton-chain hotel. Goldfish are available to keep you company in your room; wine is served in the evening. The hotel's limited business facilities include a meeting room. 🚭 [P] 👪 🍸 🏋 💳	192		■	●
PALMER HOUSE HILTON. Map 3 C2. [$][$][$] 17 E Monroe St, Chicago, IL 60603. ☎ *726-7500 or (800) 445-8667.* [FAX] *431-6900.* [W] *www.hilton.com* Exquisite paintings on the ceiling complete the rich decor in this upscale hotel's lobby. Rooms are pleasant but not quite as splendid. Minutes from the Art Institute of Chicago and Grant Park. 🚭 [P] 👪 🍸 🏋 🏊 💳	1640	●	■	●
RENAISSANCE CHICAGO HOTEL. Map 3 C2. [$][$][$] 1 W Wacker Dr, Chicago, IL 60601. ☎ *372-7200 or (800) 228-9290.* [FAX] *372-0093.* [W] *www.renaissancehotels.com* Friendly service and richly appointed rooms overlooking the river. The fee for Club Level, which includes complimentary breakfast and evening hors d'oeuvres, is worth it. 🚭 [P] 👪 🍸 🏋 🏊 💳	553	●	■	●
SWISSOTEL CHICAGO. Map 4 E1. [$][$][$] 323 E Wacker Dr, Chicago, IL 60601. ☎ *565-0565 or (800) 637-9477.* [FAX] *565-0450.* [W] *www.swissotel.com* This hotel has a handsome wood-trimmed lobby and oversized luxury rooms with breathtaking views of Lake Michigan or Grant Park. The marble bathrooms come with all the extras. 🚭 [P] 👪 🍸 🏋 🏊 💳	630	●	■	●
EXECUTIVE PLAZA. Map 4 D1. [$][$][$][$] 71 E Wacker Dr, Chicago, IL 60601. ☎ *346-7100 or (800) 621-4005.* [FAX] *346-4549.* [W] *www.executive-plaza.com* This hotel overlooking the Chicago River offers comfort, location, and convenience, close to Michigan Avenue. Guests staying in the hotel's tower are treated to many extras. 🚭 [P] 👪 🍸 🏋 💳	420	●	■	●
FAIRMONT HOTEL. Map 4 D1. [$][$][$][$] 200 N Columbus Dr, Chicago, IL 60601. ☎ *565-8000 or (800) 866-5577.* [FAX] *856-1032.* [W] *www.fairmont.com* Contemporary rooms with large bathrooms and all the extras. Guests may use the Illinois Center Athletic Club for a fee. Room rates may be much lower on the weekend than on weekdays. 🚭 [P] 🍸 🏋 🏊 💳	692	●	■	●
HYATT REGENCY CHICAGO. Map 4 D5. [$][$][$][$] 151 E Wacker Dr, Chicago, IL 60601. ☎ *565-1234 or (800) 233-1234.* [FAX] *565-2966.* [W] *www.hyatt.com/usa* This hotel offers immaculate, contemporary rooms in a spectacular downtown setting. Its beautiful atrium contains a sparkling fountain surrounded by palm and ficus trees. 🚭 [P] 🍸 🏋 💳	2019	●	■	●

Price categories for a standard double room per night, including tax and service (prices will fluctuate depending on arrival date and availability):

$ under $100
$$ $100–$180
$$$ $180–$260
$$$$ over $260

BUSINESS FACILITIES
Message service; desk and telephone in each room; meeting room, Internet access, and fax and copy machine within the hotel.

RESTAURANT
Hotel restaurant or dining room, usually also open to nonresidents.

CONCIERGE
Available to advise, make reservations, secure tickets.

	NUMBER OF ROOMS	BUSINESS FACILITIES	RESTAURANT	CONCIERGE

THE SILVERSMITH. Map 4 D2. $$$$
10 S Wabash St, Chicago, IL 60605. 372-7696 or (800) 227-6963. FAX 372-7320.
www.basshotels.com/crowneplaza This Arts-and-Crafts-style Crowne Plaza hotel, in a historic building, offers comfort and excellent service. Rooms have high windows and ceilings, and oversized bathrooms.

	143	●	■	●

W CHICAGO CITY CENTER. Map 3 C2. $$$$
172 W Adams St, Chicago, IL 60603. 332-1200 or (800) 621-2360. FAX 332-5909.
www.w-hotels.com Formerly the Midland Hotel, this hotel's recent refurbishing offers guests spacious, comfortable rooms, some with velvet chaise longues. The day spa provides pampering, for a fee.

	340	●	■	●

NORTH SIDE

CASS HOTEL. Map 2 D4. $
640 N Wabash Ave, Chicago, IL 60611. 787-4030 or (800) 781-4030. FAX 787-8544.
www.casshotel.com This hotel, dating from 1927, offers reasonably priced rooms. Rooms with a sink and refrigerator are handy for families. Data ports in rooms; free guest parking. Not fully wheelchair accessible.

	155		■	

OHIO HOUSE MOTEL. Map 1 C5. $
600 N LaSalle St, Chicago, IL 60610. 943-6000. FAX 943-6063.
This 1950s-style hotel, located in one of the most popular areas of the city, near Magnificent Mile shopping, is a true gem for the price. Rooms are clean, if plain; the staff helpful. Not wheelchair accessible. Free guest parking.

	50	●		●

BEST WESTERN INN OF CHICAGO. Map 2 D5. $$
162 E Ohio St, Chicago, IL 60611. 787-3100 or (800) 528-1234. FAX 557-2378.
www.bestwestern.com This hotel, a member of the famous Best Western chain, offers comfortable rooms just one block from the Magnificent Mile and shopping splendor. Also close to nightlife and Navy Pier.

	357	●	■	●

BEST WESTERN RIVER NORTH HOTEL. Map 2 D5. $$
125 W Ohio St, Chicago, IL 60610. 467-0800 or (800) 727-0800. FAX 467-1665.
www.bestwestern.com Clean, comfortable accommodation in the heart of the city. Rooms have tiled bathrooms and floor-to-ceiling windows that open; beds have cozy duvets and four pillows each. The rooftop sundeck offers a fantastic view of the city. Free parking for guests.

	150		■	●

GOLD COAST GUEST HOUSE. Map 1 C3. $$
113 W Elm St, Chicago, IL 60610. 337-0361. FAX 337-0362. www.bbchicago.com
Located in an 1873 townhouse, this hotel is quaint and comfortable. A secluded garden, living room, and dining room provide quiet elegance. Complimentary continental breakfast. Not wheelchair accessible.

	4	●		●

HOJO MOTOR INN. Map 1 C4. $$
720 N LaSalle St, Chicago, IL 60610. 664-8100 or (800) 446-4656. FAX 664-2365.
www.hojo.com This classic Howard Johnson two-story is perfect for those adverse to high prices and tall buildings. The hotel is not wheelchair accessible. Some business facilities; limited free guest parking.

	71		■	

HOLIDAY INN CHICAGO CITY CENTER. Map 2 E5. $$
300 E Ohio St, Chicago, IL 60611. 787-6100 or (800) 465-4329. FAX 944-7539.
www.basshotels.com/holiday-inn This hotel offers clean rooms and one of the finest hotel-connected spa and sports clubs in the city. It tends to cater to business travelers during the week, to tourists on the weekends. Families will find their stay here comfortable. Minutes to Navy Pier.

	500	●	■	●

MOTEL 6 CHICAGO DOWNTOWN. Map 2 D4. $$
162 E Ontario St, Chicago, IL 60611. 787-3580 or (800) 466-8356. FAX 787-1299.
www.motel6.com Excellent value and comfort for the price; kids stay free with adult. The rooms are not fancy, but the motel is in a good location, close to Michigan Avenue and Navy Pier.

	191		■	

For key to symbols see back flap

<table>
<tr><td>
Price categories for a standard double room per night, including tax and service (prices will fluctuate depending on arrival date and availability):

Ⓢ under $100
ⓈⓈ $100–$180
ⓈⓈⓈ $180–$260
ⓈⓈⓈⓈ over $260
</td><td>
BUSINESS FACILITIES
Message service; desk and telephone in each room; meeting room, Internet access, and fax and copy machine within the hotel.

RESTAURANT
Hotel restaurant or dining room, usually also open to nonresidents.

CONCIERGE
Available to advise, make reservations, secure tickets.
</td></tr>
</table>

	NUMBER OF ROOMS	BUSINESS FACILITIES	RESTAURANT	CONCIERGE
OLD TOWN BED AND BREAKFAST. Map 1 C1. ⓈⓈ 1442 N North Park Ave, Chicago, IL 60610. ☏ 440-9268. 🖷 440-2378. ⊞ www.oldtownbandbchicago.com This B & B, in an Art Deco mansion on a tree-lined residential street, is close to prime shopping and the beach. It prides itself on having hypoallergenic facilities. Continental breakfast (complimentary); free guest parking. Not wheelchair accessible. 🕭 P 📶 ✉	4	●		
SENECA HOTEL. Map 2 D4. ⓈⓈ 200 E Chestnut St, Chicago, IL 60611. ☏ 787-8900 or (800) 800-6261. 🖷 988-4438. ⊞ www.senecahotel.com Originally an apartment complex, the building housing this hotel boasts spacious deluxe rooms and suites, each with crown molding and high ceilings. Excellent personal service, and conveniently located between Water Tower Place and the John Hancock Center. 🕭 P 🏃 ⅄ 📶 ✉	130	●	■	●
AMBASSADOR WEST. Map 1 C2. ⓈⓈⓈ 1300 N State Pkwy, Chicago, IL 60610. ☏ 787-3700 or (800) 996-3426. 🖷 640-2967. ⊞ www.wyndham.com Although not quite as upscale as the Omni Ambassador East (see p137), to which it is connected by a walkway, the Ambassador West offers a charming old-world atmosphere and elegance. 🕭 P 🏃 ⅄ 📶 ✉	260	●	■	●
CLARIDGE HOTEL. Map 1 C1. ⓈⓈⓈ 1244 N Dearborn Pkwy, Chicago, IL 60610. ☏ 787-4980 or (800) 245-1258. 🖷 266-0978. ⊞ www.claridgehotel.com This hotel, on a tree-lined street, is a short walk from the best shopping, dining, and nightlife Chicago has to offer. Comfortable, elegant rooms. Complimentary continental breakfast. 🕭 🏃 ⅄ 📶 ≋ ✉	163	●		●
COURTYARD BY MARRIOTT CHICAGO DOWNTOWN. Map 2 D5. ⓈⓈⓈ 30 E Hubbard St, Chicago, IL 60611. ☏ 329-2500 or (800) 321-2211. 🖷 329-0293. ⊞ www.courtyard.com Large, comfortable rooms, each with desk, work chair, and data ports, provide space to work or plan the next day's sightseeing. Located on a quiet street in the busy River North neighborhood, the hotel is close to Navy Pier and the Magnificent Mile. 🕭 P ⅄ 📶 ≋ ✉	334	●	■	
DAYS INN LAKE SHORE DRIVE. Map 2 E4. ⓈⓈⓈ 644 N Lake Shore Dr, Chicago, IL 60611. ☏ 943-9200 or (800) 329-7466. 🖷 255-4411. ⊞ www.daysinn.com Breathtaking views of Chicago's skyline or lakefront can be enjoyed from all the rooms in this hotel, within walking distance of Water Tower Place and the lake. Data ports in rooms. 🕭 P 🏃 ⅄ 📶 ≋ ✉	578	●		
HILTON GARDEN INN DOWNTOWN NORTH. Map 2 D5. ⓈⓈⓈ 10 E Grand Ave, Chicago, IL 60611. ☏ 595-0000 or (800) 445-8667. 🖷 597-1989. ⊞ www.hilton.com Opened in 1999, this hotel features a 24-hour business center. Rooms have oversized desks and two telephones, as well as a refrigerator and microwave. Near the Magnificent Mile. 🕭 P 🏃 ⅄ 📶 ≋ ✉	357	●	■	●
HOUSE OF BLUES HOTEL. Map 1 C5. ⓈⓈⓈ 333 N Dearborn St, Chicago, IL 60610. ☏ 245-0333 or (877) 569-3742. 🖷 923-2444. ⊞ www.loewshotels.com/houseofblueshome.html The eclectically designed Moroccan-style rooms come with many extras, including stereo systems and VCRs. The hotel is connected to a bowling alley with 36 lanes and to the House of Blues music hall (see p165). 🕭 P 🏃 ⅄ 📶 ✉	367	●	■	●
LENOX SUITES. Map 2 D4. ⓈⓈⓈ 616 N Rush St, Chicago, IL 60611. ☏ 337-1000 or (800) 445-3664. 🖷 337-7217. ⊞ www.lenoxsuites.com Each suite has a kitchen. Fine accommodations for the price, in an excellent location. Complimentary morning muffin and juice. The hotel is not fully wheelchair accessible. 🕭 P 🏃 ⅄ 📶 ✉	324	●	■	●
MARRIOTT RESIDENCE INN. Map 2 D3. ⓈⓈⓈ 201 E Walton St, Chicago, IL 60611. ☏ 943-9800 or (800) 331-3131. 🖷 943-8579. ⊞ www.marriott.com Close to Chicago's top tourist destinations, here you'll find comfortable, clean rooms, each with a kitchen. Meals on demand from local restaurants; complimentary continental breakfast. 🕭 P 🏃 📶 ≋ ✉	221	●		

OMNI AMBASSADOR EAST. Map 1 C2. $$$ 1301 N State Pkwy, Chicago, IL 60610. ☎ *787-7200 or (800) 843-6664.* FAX *787-4760.* [W] *www.omnihotels.com* This hotel, in a historic building, recently underwent a $20-million restoration and now offers some of the most lavish guest rooms in Chicago. A favorite of celebrities and authors. 🚭 [P] 🚸 🍸 🍴 💳	285	●	■	●
PARK HYATT CHICAGO. Map 2 D4. $$$ 800 N Michigan Ave, Chicago, IL 60611. ☎ *335-1234 or (800) 233-1234.* FAX *239-4000.* [W] *www.hyatt.com/usa* The rooms in this new European-style hotel, the Park Hyatt's flagship, boasts custom-designed furniture, including the BRNO chair by Ludwig Mies van der Rohe. Other details reflect the styles of 20th-century architects Frank Lloyd Wright and Le Corbusier. 🚭 [P] 🚸 🍸 🍴 🏊 💳	203	●	■	●
RAPHAEL HOTEL. Map 2 D3. $$$ 201 E Delaware Pl, Chicago, IL 60622. ☎ *943-5000.* FAX *943-9483.* This elegant hotel offers old-world charm and superb service. The medieval-style lobby complements the building's brick façade. Guests may use the fitness center at the nearby Tremont Hotel *(see p137).* 🚭 [P] 🚸 🍸 🍴 💳	172		■	
REGAL KNICKERBOCKER HOTEL. Map 2 D3. $$$ 163 E Walton Pl, Chicago, IL 60611. ☎ *751-8100 or (800) 222-8888.* FAX *751-9205.* [W] *www.millennium-hotels.com* Luxurious rooms and personalized pampering are just two of the features of this hotel, which also claims to serve the best martini in town. Located near fashionable Oak Street. 🚭 [P] 🚸 🍸 🍴 💳	305	●	■	●
SUMMERFIELD SUITES. Map 2 D4. $$$ 166 E Superior St, Chicago, IL 60611. ☎ *787-6000 or (800) 833-4353.* FAX *787-4331.* [W] *www.wyndham.com* This hotel, in a concrete high-rise, offers many extras, such as in-room hair drier, iron and ironing board, VCR, and complimentary breakfast buffet. Excellent views from the rooftop deck. 🚭 [P] 🚸 🍸 🍴 🏊 💳	120			●
TALBOTT HOTEL. Map 2 D3. $$$ 20 E Delaware Pl, Chicago, IL 60611. ☎ *944-4970 or (800) 825-2688.* FAX *944-7241.* [W] *www.talbotthotel.com* Converted in 1989 from a 1920s apartment building to an upscale hotel, the Talbott is a soothing oasis in the city. All extras, such as nightly turn-down and morning paper accompanying a complimentary continental breakfast, are included. 🚭 🚸 🍸 🍴 🏊 💳	149	●	■	●
TREMONT HOTEL. Map 2 D4. $$$ 100 E Chestnut St, Chicago, IL 60611. ☎ *751-1900 or (800) 621-8133.* FAX *751-9253.* Located just off Michigan Avenue, this European-style hotel offers cozy, comfortable lodgings. The lobby, with its carved-wood ceiling, has an English-country atmosphere. Many rooms come with VCR, stereo system, and fax machine. Not fully wheelchair accessible. 🚭 [P] 🚸 🍸 🍴 💳	135		■	
ALLERTON CROWNE PLAZA. Map 2 D4. $$$$ 701 N Michigan Ave, Chicago, IL 60611. ☎ *440-1500 or (800) 227-6963.* FAX *440-1819.* [W] *www.allertoncrowneplaza.com* Following a $39-million restoration, this hotel, in a historic building, features European decor and luxurious amenities. Some rooms have fireplaces. Complimentary continental breakfast. 🚭 [P] 🚸 🍸 🍴 💳	465	●	■	●
CHICAGO MARRIOTT DOWNTOWN. Map 2 D5. $$$$ 540 N Michigan Ave, Chicago, IL 60611. ☎ *836-0100 or (800) 228-0265.* FAX *836-6139.* [W] *www.marriott.com/marriott/CHIDT* This hotel on the Magnificent Mile has a shopping galleria and gourmet coffee shop in its lobby. Great views of Lake Michigan from the upper floors. 🚭 [P] 🚸 🍸 🍴 🏊 💳	1176	●	■	●
DOUBLETREE GUEST SUITES. Map 2 D3. $$$$ 198 E Delaware Pl, Chicago, IL 60611. ☎ *664-1100 or (800) 222-8733.* FAX *664-9881.* [W] *www.doubletree.com* Your stay at this hotel begins with warm chocolate-chip cookies upon check-in. Each room is wired and furnished for business. Located across the street from John Hancock Center. 🚭 [P] 🚸 🍸 🍴 🏊 💳	345	●	■	●
DRAKE HOTEL. Map 2 D3. $$$$ 140 E Walton Pl, Chicago, IL 60611. ☎ *787-2200 or (800) 553-7253.* FAX *787-1431.* [W] *www.thedrakehotel.com* From your first step into the lobby, it is apparent that the Drake lives up to its reputation for service and luxury. Each spacious room is individually designed and offers an excellent view. 🚭 [P] 🚸 🍸 🍴 💳	537	●	■	●
EMBASSY SUITES CHICAGO. Map 2 D4. $$$$ 600 N State St, Chicago, IL 60610. ☎ *943-3800 or (800) 362-2779.* FAX *943-5979.* [W] *www.embassy-suites.com* Handsome Biedermeier furnishings in each of the two-room suites. Enjoy a complimentary cooked-to-order breakfast in the atrium beside a waterfall. Not fully wheelchair accessible. 🚭 [P] 🚸 🍸 🍴 🏊 💳	358	●	■	●

For key to symbols see back flap

Price categories for a standard double room per night, including tax and service (prices will fluctuate depending on arrival date and availability):

$ under $100
$$ $100–$180
$$$ $180–$260
$$$$ over $260

Business Facilities
Message service; desk and telephone in each room; meeting room, Internet access, and fax and copy machine within the hotel.

Restaurant
Hotel restaurant or dining room, usually also open to nonresidents.

Concierge
Available to advise, make reservations, secure tickets.

	Number of Rooms	Business Facilities	Restaurant	Concierge
Four Seasons Hotel. Map 2 D3. $$$$ 120 E Delaware Pl, Chicago, IL 60611. ☎ *280-8800 or (800) 332-3442.* FAX *280-1748.* [W] *www.fourseasons.com* The Four Seasons Hotel provides unparalleled service and accommodations. This location has the only hotel outdoor rooftop jogging track in the city. 🚭 [P] ♿ 🍸 🏋 ≋ 💳	343	●	■	●
Hotel Inter-Continental Chicago. Map 2 D5. $$$$ 505 N Michigan Ave, Chicago, IL 60611. ☎ *944-4100 or (800) 628-2112.* FAX *944-1320.* [W] *www.chicago.interconti.com* The magnificent decor at this hotel includes art from around the world. The South Tower, the epitome of historic elegance, features a bar with a 1920s atmosphere *(see p62)*. The rooms in the rather nondescript North Tower have excellent views. 🚭 [P] ♿ 🍸 🏋 ≋ 💳	845	●	■	●
Omni Chicago Hotel. Map 2 D4. $$$$ 676 N Michigan Ave, Chicago, IL 60611. ☎ *944-6664 or (800) 843-6664.* FAX *266-3015.* [W] *www.omnihotels.com* Mahogany and imported marble accentuates the vaulted ceilings and Art Deco furnishings in this hotel's common areas. Each room includes a parlor separated from the bedroom by French doors. Complimentary cocktails and weekday bar buffet. 🚭 [P] ♿ 🍸 🏋 ≋ 💳	347	●	■	●
Ritz-Carlton Chicago. Map 2 D4. $$$$ 160 E Pearson St, Chicago, IL 60611. ☎ *266-1000 or (800) 241-3333.* FAX *266-1194.* [W] *www.fourseasons.com* Located above Water Tower Place, Ritz-Carlton (owned by the Four Seasons chain) provides the service and satisfaction one expects from a world-renowned hotel company. 🚭 [P] ♿ 🍸 🏋 ≋ 💳	435	●	■	●
Sheraton Chicago Hotel and Towers. Map 2 E5. $$$$ 301 E North Water St, Chicago, IL 60611. ☎ *464-1000 or (800) 325-3535.* FAX *464-9140.* [W] *www.sheratonchicago.com* Ideally situated, this hotel has beautifully appointed guest rooms overlooking the Chicago River and Lake Michigan. Tower guests receive deluxe treatment. 🚭 [P] ♿ 🍸 🏋 ≋ 💳	1204	●	■	●
Sutton Place Hotel. Map 2 D3. $$$$ 21 E Bellevue Pl, Chicago, IL 60611. ☎ *266-2100 or (800) 606-8188.* FAX *266-2103.* [W] *www.suttonplace.com* This hotel's stunning Art Deco interior features original prints by American photographer Robert Mapplethorpe. Mahogany furnishings, stereo, and jazz recordings in rooms. 🚭 [P] ♿ 🍸 🏋 💳	246	●	■	●
Westin Michigan Avenue. Map 2 D3. $$$$ 909 N Michigan Ave, Chicago, IL 60611. ☎ *943-7200 or (800) 228-3000.* FAX *397-5580.* [W] *www.westinmichiganave.com* Providing all the comforts of home, this hotel recently upgraded its beds to feature 1-foot- (30-cm-) thick mattresses. Complimentary continental breakfast. 🚭 [P] ♿ 🍸 🏋 💳	767	●	■	●
Westin River North. Map 1 C5. $$$$ 320 N Dearborn St, Chicago, IL 60610. ☎ *744-1900 or (800) 937-8461.* FAX *527-2637.* [W] *www.westinrivernorth.com* All rooms have an elegant, residential atmosphere. The large marble bathrooms include hair driers, magnifying mirrors, robes, and exclusive toiletries. Gourmet coffee in all rooms. 🚭 [P] ♿ 🍸 🏋 💳	424	●	■	●
Whitehall Hotel. Map 2 D3. $$$$ 105 E Delaware Pl, Chicago, IL 60611. ☎ *944-6300 or (800) 948-4255.* FAX *573-6250.* [W] *www.whitehallhotel.com* Following an extensive renovation, this hotel offers technological conveniences along with old-world charm and excellent service. Not fully wheelchair accessible. 🚭 [P] ♿ 🍸 🏋 💳	221	●	■	●

South Loop and Near South Side

	Number of Rooms	Business Facilities	Restaurant	Concierge
Best Western Grant Park Hotel. Map 4 D4. $$ 1100 S Michigan Ave, Chicago, IL 60605. ☎ *922-2900 or (800) 472-6875.* FAX *922-8812.* [W] *www.bestwestern.com.* The prime location of this older high-rise hotel allows for easy access to Grant Park, as well as to the Museum Campus and McCormick Place. Data ports in each room. 🚭 [P] ♿ 🏋 ≋ 💳	172		■	

Congress Plaza Hotel. **Map** 4 D3. ⓢⓢ 843
520 S Michigan Ave, Chicago, IL 60605. 〖 *427-3800 or (800) 635-1666.* ℻ *427-3307.*
ⓦ *www.congresshotel.com* This hotel has much of the same charm it had when
it was built in 1893 for the World's Fair. Rooms are large, some with views of
Grant Park and the lake. Not fully wheelchair accessible. ⚡ P 🏃 Y 🍴 🐾

Essex Inn. **Map** 4 D3. ⓢⓢ 255
800 S Michigan Ave, Chicago, IL 60605. 〖 *939-2800 or (800) 621-6909.* ℻ *922-6153.*
ⓦ *www.sagehospitality.com* An intimate, informal hotel near Grant Park. Many
rooms have an excellent view of the city and lake. Courtesy shuttle bus to
the Loop, Magnificent Mile, and State Street shops. ⚡ P 🏃 Y 〰 🐾

Hyatt on Printer's Row. **Map** 3 C3. ⓢⓢⓢ 161
500 S Dearborn St, Chicago, IL 60605. 〖 *986-1234 or (800) 233-1234.* ℻ *939-2468.*
ⓦ *www.hyatt.com* Large, comfortable rooms in a historic landmark building
that was once a print shop. Business travelers receive excellent extras for a
small fee. Its Prairie restaurant *(see p150)* is award winning. ⚡ P 🏃 Y 🐾

Hyatt Regency McCormick Place. **Map** 5 E2. ⓢⓢⓢ 800
2233 S Martin Luther King Jr. Dr, Chicago, IL 60616. 〖 *567-1234 or (800) 233-1234.*
℻ *528-4000.* ⓦ *www.hyatt.com/usa* This hotel is connected to McCormick
Place via a walkway that leads to all the exposition buildings. Fifty rooms
have telescopes for great views of the lake and skyline. ⚡ P 🏃 Y 🍴 〰 🐾

Hilton Chicago. **Map** 4 D3. ⓢⓢⓢⓢ 1544
720 S Michigan Ave, Chicago, IL 60605. 〖 *922-4400 or (800) 445-8667.* ℻ *663-6528.*
ⓦ *www.chicagohilton.com* The Hilton provides spacious rooms and excellent
service. The rooms in the tower come with many extras worth the higher
price. Located close to museums and nightlife. ⚡ P Y 🍴 〰 🐾

South Side

Ramada Inn Lake Shore. **Map** 7 E1. ⓢⓢ 184
4900 S Lake Shore Dr, Chicago, IL 60615. 〖 *(773) 288-5800 or (800) 228-2828.*
℻ *(773) 288-5745.* ⓦ *www.ramada.com* Newly renovated rooms designed with
casual elegance provide comfort and convenience at an affordable price.
Courtesy shuttle bus to popular sights; free guest parking. ⚡ P 🏃 Y 〰 🐾

Wooded Isle Suites. **Map** 7 F5. ⓢⓢ 13
5750 Stony Island Ave, Chicago, IL 60637. 〖 *(773) 288-6305 or (800) 290-6844.* ℻ *(773)
288-8972.* ⓦ *www.woodedisle.com* Vintage-style suites in the Hyde Park neighborhood. Kitchenettes; free guest parking. Not wheelchair accessible. ⚡ P 🏃 🐾

Farther Afield

Lakeview: *Best Western Hawthorne Terrace*. ⓢⓢ 59
3434 N Broadway St, Chicago, IL 60657. 〖 *(773) 244-3434 or (888) 675-2378.*
℻ *(773) 244-3435.* ⓦ *www.bestwestern.com* The fireplace in the Colonial-style
lobby warms up guests after a day of touring. Standard rooms, many with
microwave and refrigerator. Complimentary continental breakfast. ⚡ P 🍴 🐾

Lakeview: *City Suites*. ⓢⓢ 45
933 W Belmont Ave, Chicago, IL 60657. 〖 *(773) 404-3400 or (800) 248-9108.* ℻ *(773)
404-3405.* ⓦ *www.cityinns.com* This Neighborhood Inn of Chicago (one of
three) has been restored to Art Deco style. Data ports in rooms;
complimentary continental breakfast. Not wheelchair accessible. ⚡ P 🏃 🐾

Lakeview: *House of Two Urns*. ⓢⓢ 5
1239 N Greenview Ave, Chicago, IL 60622. 〖 *(773) 235-1408.* ℻ *(773) 235-1410.*
ⓦ *www.twourns.com* This B & B offers cozy rooms decorated with antiques,
original artworks, and family heirlooms. Shared bathroom; complimentary
continental breakfast; free parking. Not wheelchair accessible. ⚡ P 🏃 🐾

Lakeview: *Majestic Hotel*. ⓢⓢ 52
528 W Brompton Ave, Chicago, IL 60657. 〖 *(773) 404-3499 or (800) 787-3108.* ℻ *(773)
404-3495.* ⓦ *www.cityinns.com* This English-style Neighborhood Inn (one of
three) provides comfort at a reasonable price. Data ports in rooms;
complimentary continental breakfast. Not wheelchair accessible. ⚡ P 🍴 🐾

Lincoln Park: *Arlington House International Hostel and Hotel*. ⓢ 101
616 W Arlington Pl, Chicago, IL 60614. 〖 *(773) 929-5380 or (800) 467-8355.* ℻ *(773)
665-5485.* ⓦ *www.arlingtonhouse.com* Both dormitory and private rooms are
available at this hostel, which offers 24-hour check-in, linen rental, and
luggage storage. Hostel membership or student ID may be required. ⚡ 🏃 🐾

Price categories for a standard double room per night, including tax and service (prices will fluctuate depending on arrival date and availability): ⑤ under $100 ⑤⑤ $100–$180 ⑤⑤⑤ $180–$260 ⑤⑤⑤⑤ over $260	**BUSINESS FACILITIES** Message service; desk and telephone in each room; meeting room, Internet access, and fax and copy machine within the hotel. **RESTAURANT** Hotel restaurant or dining room, usually also open to nonresidents. **CONCIERGE** Available to advise, make reservations, secure tickets.	**NUMBER OF ROOMS**	**BUSINESS FACILITIES**	**RESTAURANT**	**CONCIERGE**
LINCOLN PARK: *Comfort Inn of Lincoln Park.* 601 W Diversey Pkwy, Chicago, IL 60614. **(** (773) 348-2810 or (800) 228-5150. **FAX** (773) 348-1912. **W** www.choicehotels.com An affordable, clean inn. Breezes from the lake provide the only air-conditioning. Complimentary continental breakfast is a pleasant start to a day of touring. Not wheelchair accessible. **⚡ P ♿ ☕**	⑤⑤	74			
LINCOLN PARK: *Days Inn Lincoln Park North.* 644 W Diversey Pkwy, Chicago, IL 60614. **(** (773) 525-7010 or (800) 576-3297. **FAX** (773) 525-6998. **W** www.daysinn.com This winner of the Days Inn Chairman's Award for consistent quality has been recently remodeled and finely appointed. Complimentary continental breakfast. **⚡ P ♿ Y 🍴 ≋ ☕**	⑤⑤	130	●	■	
LINCOLN PARK: *The Willows.* 555 W Surf St, Chicago, IL 60657. **(** (773) 528-8400 or (800) 787-3108. **FAX** (773) 528-8483. **W** www.cityinns.com The floral decor of this Neighborhood Inn (one of three) exudes 19th-century French-country charm. Data ports in rooms; complimentary continental breakfast. Not wheelchair accessible. **⚡ P ♿ ☕**	⑤⑤	55			●
LINCOLN PARK: *Windy City Bed and Breakfast Inn.* 607 W Deming Pl, Chicago, IL 60614. **(** (773) 248-7091 or (877) 897-7091. **FAX** (773) 248-7090. **W** www.chicago-inn.com Windy City combines Victorian details, such as fireplaces in the rooms (and no TVs), with modern luxury, such as whirlpool baths. The inn is not wheelchair accessible. **⚡ P ☕**	⑤⑤	8	●		●
LINCOLN PARK: *Belden-Stratford Hotel.* 2300 N Lincoln Park W, Chicago, IL 60614. **(** (773) 281-2900 or (800) 800-8301. **FAX** (312) 787-0573. **W** www.beldenstratford.com If the vintage façade of this hotel does not pique your interest, its dramatic three-story lobby will. Located across from Lincoln Park Zoo and close to the theater district. Rooms come with data ports. Not wheelchair accessible. **⚡ P ♿ Y 🍴 ☕**	⑤⑤⑤	30		■	
LINCOLN PARK: *City Scene Bed and Breakfast.* 2101 N Clifton Ave, Chicago, IL 60614. **(** (773) 549-1743. **FAX** (773) 529-4711. **W** www.cityscenebb.com This B & B, in a Victorian building, offers one eclectically furnished suite, rented as either a one or two bedroom (shared bath). Guests prepare breakfast in the well-stocked kitchen. Not wheelchair accessible. **⚡ P**	⑤⑤⑤	2			
OAK PARK: *Carleton of Oak Park Hotel.* 1110 Pleasant St, Oak Park, IL 60302. **(** (708) 848-5000 or (888) 227-5386. **FAX** (708) 848-0537. **W** www.carletonhotel.com Pleasant accommodations minutes from specialty shops and boutiques. New conference facilities and complimentary use of a nearby health club. Free guest parking. **⚡ P ♿ Y 🍴 ≋ ☕**	⑤⑤	154		■	

BEYOND CHICAGO

EVANSTON: *Homestead Hotel.* 1625 Hinman Ave, Evanston, IL 60201. **(** (847) 475-3300. **FAX** (847) 570-8100. **W** www.homesteadev.com Built in 1927 in the Williamsburg Colonial style, this hotel, near Northwestern University, offers genuine hospitality. Complimentary continental breakfast and guest parking. Not wheelchair accessible. **⚡ 🍴 ≋ ☕**	⑤⑤	90		■	
EVANSTON: *Margarita European Inn.* 1566 Oak Ave, Evanston, IL 60201. **(** (847) 869-2273. **FAX** (847) 869-2353. **W** www.margaritainn.com Friendly, cozy accommodations in a Georgian mansion. Relax in the library or on the rooftop deck, with its great view of downtown, and enjoy the award-winning restaurant, Va Pensiero *(see p153).* Complimentary continental breakfast. Some rooms with shared bathroom. **⚡ P ♿ ☕**	⑤⑤	44	●	■	
EVANSTON: *Omni Orrington Hotel.* 1710 Orrington Ave, Evanston, IL 60201. **(** (847) 866-8700 or (800) 529-9100. **FAX** (847) 866-8724. **W** www.omnihotels.com An upscale hotel near public transit. Rates include services at a health club and spa located at Northwestern University. Some rooms have a private terrace. **⚡ P ♿ Y 🍴 ≋ ☕**	⑤⑤⑤	277	●	■	●

GALENA: *Best Western Quiet House and Suites.* ⓈⓈ 42
9923 US Highway 20 W, Galena, IL 61036. 【 *(815) 777-2577 or (800) 528-1234.*
FAX *(815) 777-0584.* Ⓦ *www.bestwestern.com* This Best Western offers oversized rooms and suites with theme decors ranging from northwest frontier to high tech. Free parking for guests. ⚡ P 🏃 📺 ≋ 🖉

GALENA: *Chestnut Mountain Resort.* ⓈⓈ 120 ● ■
8700 W Chestnut Rd, Galena, IL 61036. 【 *(815) 777-1320 or (800) 397-1320.*
FAX *(815) 777-1068.* Ⓦ *www.chestnutmtn.com* A resort 8 miles (13 km) southeast of Galena, overlooking the Mississippi River. Prime skiing with 17 runs, and ski apparel and equipment rental. Free guest parking. ⚡ P 🏃 Y ≋ 🖉

GALENA: *Early American Settlement Log Cabin Lodging.* ⓈⓈ 12
9401 Hart John Rd, Galena, IL 61036. 【 *(815) 777-4200 or (800) 366-5647.* Ⓦ *www. easll.com* Replica one-room log cabins with period decor are situated on lovely grounds. Each cabin has a gas fireplace, VCR, refrigerator, and adjacent modern bathroom. Two cabins are wheelchair accessible. Free guest parking. P 🏃

GALENA: *Stoney Creek Inn.* ⓈⓈ 76 ●
940 Galena Square Dr, Galena, IL 61036. 【 *(815) 777-2223 or (800) 659-2220.*
FAX *(815) 777-6762.* Ⓦ *www.stoneycreekinn.com* This inn offers charming, rustic lodgings. Children under 18 stay free with adult. Complimentary continental breakfast, free parking, and shuttle service for guests. ⚡ P 🏃 Y 📺 ≋ 🖉

GALENA: *Eagle Ridge Inn and Resort.* ⓈⓈⓈ 470 ● ■ ●
444 Eagle Ridge Dr, Galena, IL 61036. 【 *(815) 777-2444 or (800) 892-2269.* FAX *(815) 777-4502.* Ⓦ *www.eagleridge.com* A favorite destination in northern Illinois, 6 miles (10 km) east of Galena, this resort offers cross-country skiing, and golf on its award-winning courses. Free guest parking. ⚡ P 🏃 Y 📺 ≋ 🖉

LAKE GENEVA: *Budget Host Diplomat Motel.* Ⓢ 23
1060 Wells St, Lake Geneva, WI 53147. 【 *(262) 248-1809 or (800) 264-5678.* FAX *(262) 248-2455.* Ⓦ *www.budgethost-lakegeneva.com* This motel offers comfortable rooms. Recreation grounds include volleyball, badminton, and picnicking areas. First floor is wheelchair accessible. Free guest parking. ⚡ P 🏃 ≋ 🖉

LAKE GENEVA: *Best Western Harbor Shores.* ⓈⓈ 108 ■
300 Wrigley Dr, Lake Geneva, WI 53147. 【 *(262) 248-9181 or (888) 746-7371.*
FAX *(262) 248-1885.* Ⓦ *www.bestwestern.com* Enjoy a fabulous view from one of the lakefront rooms or relax by the lobby's fireplace after a day of activities. Complimentary continental breakfast; free guest parking. ⚡ P 🏃 Y 📺 ≋ 🖉

LAKE GENEVA: *Pederson Victorian Bed and Breakfast.* ⓈⓈ 4 ●
1782 Highway 120 N, Lake Geneva, WI 53147. 【 *(262) 248-9110.* FAX *(262) 249-9830.*
Ⓦ *www.singingwolf.com/pederson.shtml* This Victorian home whisks visitors back to the 1880s with its vintage furnishings (and no TVs or telephones). Breakfasts made with wholesome, organic foods. Some rooms with shared bathroom; free guest parking. Not wheelchair accessible. ⚡ P 🖉

LAKE GENEVA: *Geneva Inn.* ⓈⓈⓈ 37 ■ ●
N2009 State Rd 120, Lake Geneva, WI 53147. 【 *(262) 248-5680 or (800) 441-5881.*
FAX *(262) 248-5685.* Ⓦ *www.genevainn.com* An intimate inn with English charm. Cognac and chocolates with nightly turn-down are part of the personal service. Complimentary continental breakfast; free guest parking. ⚡ P 🏃 Y 📺 🖉

LAKE GENEVA: *Grand Geneva Resort and Spa.* ⓈⓈⓈ 355 ● ■ ●
7036 Grand Geneva Way, Lake Geneva, WI 53147. 【 *(262) 248-8811 or (800) 558-3417.*
FAX *(262) 249-4763.* Ⓦ *www.grandgeneva.com* "Grand" is the operative word at this upscale resort. After skiing at the resort's Mountain Top ski slopes or shopping in town, relax in the spacious lobby, complete with fireside bar. Weekend packages are available. Free parking for guests. ⚡ P 🏃 Y 📺 ≋ 🖉

LAKE GENEVA: *Lake Lawn Resort.* ⓈⓈⓈ 284 ● ■ ●
2400 E Geneva St, Delavan, WI 53115. 【 *(262) 728-7950 or (800) 338-5253.* FAX *(262) 728-7976.* Ⓦ *www.lakelawnresort.com* You will find rustic luxury at this resort, a 15-minute drive northwest of Galena. Its spa offers packages designed to indulge the body and spirit, and its wooded grounds alongside Lake Delavan are ideal for a scenic hike. Free guest parking. ⚡ P 🏃 Y 📺 ≋ 🖉

LAKE GENEVA: *T.C. Smith Inn Bed and Breakfast.* ⓈⓈⓈ 8
865 Main St, Lake Geneva, WI 53147. 【 *(262) 248-1097 or (800) 423-0233.* FAX *(262) 248-1672.* Ⓦ *www.tcsmithinn.com* This inn, in a historic downtown building, offers elegant theme rooms, many with fireplace and whirlpool bath. Breakfast buffet; free parking. Not fully wheelchair accessible. ⚡ P 🏃 📺 ≋ 🖉

For key to symbols see back flap

RESTAURANTS AND CAFÉS

CHICAGO IS A BIG CITY and many establishments, from coffee shops to four-star restaurants, ask big-city prices. However, with thousands of places to eat and drink in Chicago, competition between restaurants is fierce, and visitors *can* find great food at reasonable prices. The city's immigrant roots mean you can sample dishes

A waiter serving champagne

from around the world, from Greek and Italian dishes to Vietnamese and Korean specialties. If you're in Chicago during the annual Taste of Chicago festival *(see p31)*, you will be able to sample cuisine from dozens of Chicago's restaurants. Those in our listings, *Choosing a Restaurant* (pages 146–53), have been selected as the best Chicago offers.

CHICAGO'S RESTAURANTS

CHICAGO restaurants represent the many cultures that make up the city. Some ethnic restaurants are clustered together, such as those in Chinatown *(see p94)* or on Greek Town's Halsted Street. Italian eateries abound on Taylor Street between Halsted and Western Avenues.

However, restaurants on the city's major streets offer a broad range of cuisine. Those in the Loop tend to cater to office workers, though many are staying open later as the area's theater district blossoms. River North is home to many of the city's premier restaurants. Numerous restaurants are situated farther north along Wells Street in Old Town and along nearby Lincoln and Halsted Avenues.

Although there are few strictly vegetarian restaurants in Chicago, most establishments offer vegetarian dishes. The menus at Amitabul *(see p151)* and Chicago Diner *(see p151)*, however, exclusively focus on vegetarian dishes.

Many restaurants are wheelchair accessible *(see p169)*.

RESTAURANT MENUS

MOST MENUS offer three courses: appetizer (starter), entrée (main course), and dessert. Almost all restaurants, except fast-food, serve bread and butter at no charge. Water glasses are filled with (free) tap water; bottled water is usually available.

Most Italian menus list pasta as a first course before a main course of meat or fish, but many restaurants also treat pasta as an entrée.

Coffee and dessert conclude the meal. If you have coffee, your cup may be refilled until you refuse any more.

OTHER PLACES TO EAT

DELICATESSENS offering soups, salads, and sandwiches are mostly found downtown. Hotdog stands

The handsome bar at the Omni Ambassador East Hotel *(see p137)*

and no-frills lunch counters are a quick, inexpensive alternative to restaurants.

Most malls have food courts, selling a variety of dishes. Some don't rise above fast-food fare, but a few are excellent, notably Foodlife at Water Tower Place, and 7 on Seven at Marshall Field's.

Brew pubs are popular in Chicago. They serve beer brewed on site, as well as "pub grub" such as hamburgers or fish and chips. Many taverns that appear to be only bars serve steaks, pasta, fish, and sandwiches.

ALCOHOL

THE LEGAL DRINKING age in Chicago is 21 and is strictly enforced. Alcohol is served until 2am most days. Some bars have late-night licenses and pour until 4am. On Sunday, alcohol is not served before 11am.

The grand mahogany and crystal Pump Room *(see p150)*

The Berghoff restaurant, family operated since 1898 *(see p146)*

HOURS AND PRICES

THE CITY OPENS early: coffee shops and diners at 6am. Coffee and a roll costs about $3.50. A breakfast of bacon and eggs is about $5 in diners and twice that in hotel restaurants. Sunday brunch, served between 11am and 2pm, costs about $20 per person.

Lunch is offered between 11am and 2pm. Restaurants catering to office workers may offer weekday lunch specials in the $5 to $8 range.

Most restaurants open for dinner at 5:30pm. Kitchens close once business tapers, around 10pm on weekdays, later on weekends. The most difficult time to secure a table is from 7:30pm to 9:30pm.

Salads and appetizers generally cost between $5 and $8 each, entrées between $9 and $25. Many restaurants offer superb wines by the glass for between $5 and $9.

Ethnic restaurants offer good value for the money. Mexican and Thai restaurants are always a good bet, as are pizzerias. Indian and Greek food is often a good bargain.

Some restaurants, especially Thai ones, let you "bring your own bottle" of wine, which can cut costs dramatically. A corkage fee is unlikely unless the restaurant has a bar.

Valet parking, offered by many restaurants, costs between $6 and $8.

PAYING AND TIPPING

THE CHECK will be brought to the table after you have finished eating. This is not meant to hurry you. Nearly all restaurants accept major

credit cards. Traveler's checks are accepted with appropriate identification. Personal checks are not welcome. *(See p172.)*

A sales tax of 9.75 percent will be added to meal checks in downtown Chicago; 8.75 percent in surrounding areas.

Sign for a Mexican restaurant specializing in seafood

You are expected to tip servers 15 percent for average service, 20 percent for excellent service. The gratuity is usually added to the check for parties of six or more. Be careful not to tip twice.

An especially helpful wine steward may be tipped $2 or $3. There is no need to tip the host or hostess. Nor will slipping him or her money get you a better table or position on the waiting list.

DRESS CODES

FEW RESTAURANTS have dress codes. Some hotel and country-club establishments expect men to wear a jacket and tie, and women to be dressed-up. At trendier spots, diners are expected to be fashionably attired. Inquire when making reservations.

RESERVATIONS

TRY TO MAKE a reservation at any restaurant you plan to eat at unless it's fast-food. If booking more than a day in advance, confirm the booking on the day of your reservation. Some restaurants will not accept reservations for parties of less than six.

Even with a reservation, expect to wait up to an hour at the bar for your table at the most popular restaurants. You may be seated sooner by accepting a table in the smoking section *(see p168)*.

CHILDREN

ALL RESTAURANTS in the city are happy to serve well-behaved children. Many are particularly kid-friendly, supplying high chairs and offering children's portions or menus. However, you may feel uncomfortable bringing children to some of the more fashionable spots. In general, Italian, Greek, Mexican, and chain restaurants are more family-oriented. Children may accompany adults to taverns and pubs if food is ordered.

Goose Island Clybourn Brewpub, brewing beer on the premises *(see p165)*

What to Eat and Drink in Chicago

GOOD FOOD is something that Chicago takes pride in. Whether it's pizza or martinis, the mention of food or drink will always spark lively debate about who makes it the best. The city's immigrant roots mean you can sample delicacies from around the world, ranging from authentic Chinese *dim sum* to back-country barbecue. The highest-quality regional ingredients are brought to Chicago restaurant kitchens every day, as is fresh produce and seafood from both US coasts. And while Chicagoans are concerned with health, it's a democratic city: you are likely to find fried chicken on the same menu as delicate, low-calorie creations.

Classic martini

Pancakes, *made of batter that has been fried until thick and fluffy, are served with whipped butter and maple syrup for breakfast. Fruit such as blueberries may be mixed into the batter before cooking.*

Bacon and eggs *is a classic Chicago breakfast dish. Eggs are prepared in a variety of styles, shown here "over easy," and served with sausage or bacon, home fries, and toast.*

Waffles, *made of batter baked in a waffle iron, are topped with fresh berries and whipped cream, with syrup on the side. They are offered on breakfast and brunch menus.*

Deli sandwiches *are custom-made from a large choice of breads and fillings, such as meat and cheese. They are available at most delicatessens.*

Meat and vegetable toppings   Cheese

Spiced tomato sauce

Thick, deep crust

Deep-dish pizza
Created in Chicago, deep-dish pizza satisfies the hungriest. The high crust creates a perfect container for layers of mozzarella and Parmesan cheese, spiced tomato sauce, vegetables such as mushrooms and olives, and sausage. Topped with olive oil, it is then baked in a hot oven.

Mixed green salad *is made of fresh lettuce and a variety of garnishes, such as feta cheese and tomatoes. The choice of dressings includes oil-and-vinegar and Italian.*

Fried calamari *are tender deep-fried rings of squid. They are served with fresh lemon wedges and tangy tartar, yogurt, or seafood-cocktail sauce.*

Thai green curry, *chicken and rich coconut milk mixed with spices and basil, is a Chicago favorite.*

Hot dog, *the arche-typical American dish, as well as other types of sausages, such as Polish, are sold by street vendors all over the city. Garnishes include sauerkraut, pickles, and onions.*

Charbroiled steak, *flame-grilled Midwest beef, some of the most tender meat in the world, is served with French fries or a baked potato.*

Quesadillas *are a Mexican dish of grilled corn or wheat tortillas, stuffed with cheese or other filling such as chicken, beef, or seafood.*

Sushi *is a Japanese specialty consisting of fresh raw fish on cakes of vinegar-flavored cold rice. Pickled ginger and fiery wasabi complement the dish.*

Burger with fries *is popular pub food. The ground-beef burger, with various garnishes, may also be served with salad.*

Spaghetti all'Amatriciana *is a tasty pasta dish made with bacon, tomatoes, and onion, and topped with cheese.*

Dim sum, *served for brunch, consists of a variety of steamed Chinese dumplings stuffed with seafood, meat, or vegetables.*

Nachos, *a Mexican snack of fried corn chips covered with melted cheese, is typically accompanied by salsa, a spicy chunky tomato sauce.*

Cheesecake, *a rich baked dessert, may be served plain or topped with strawberries or other fruit. Flavored varieties are also widely available.*

Tiramisù, *consisting of layers of ladyfingers, coffee, and mascarpone sprinkled with chocolate, is a delightful traditional Italian dessert.*

COCKTAILS AND DRINKS

The dry martini remains a favorite, though designer martinis are very fashionable. Mimosas, orange juice with champagne, are popular at brunch, while the lime-and-tequila margarita is a happy-hour favorite. Manhattans, made of whiskey and red vermouth, are a classic. Local breweries provide superb beers, and excellent wines from the western states are on good wine lists. Italian coffee drinks and artificially flavored regular coffees are popular.

Espresso

Cappuccino

Caffe latte

Iced cola

Beer

Mimosa

Manhattan

Margarita

Choosing a Restaurant

These restaurants have been selected across a wide price range for their good value, facilities, and location. They are listed area by area, starting with Chicago's Downtown Core and moving on to restaurants farther outside the center. Most restaurants are wheelchair accessible and provide nonsmoking seating areas. For map references, see pages 190–97.

Downtown Core

Heaven on Seven. Map 4 D1. [$]
Garland Building, 111 N Wabash Ave (7th Fl), Chicago, IL 60602. ☎ *263-6443.*
A spicy tingle in your mouth on your first bite is a good indication that you're in for real Cajun cooking here. That, and the 1,165 bottles of hot sauces on the wall. The gumbo is truly heavenly. Lunch only. ● *Sun.* 🚸

Miller's Pub. Map 3 C2. [$]
134 S Wabash Ave, Chicago, IL 60603. ☎ *263-4988.*
The high ceilings and paintings on the wall lend this pub a comfortable saloon-like atmosphere. Canadian baby back ribs and the Diamond Jim Brady cut of prime rib are on the menu. 🚸 🌙 💳

Taza's. Map 4 D2. [$]
39 S Wabash Ave, Chicago, IL 60603. ☎ *425-9988.*
Serving perhaps the best cafeteria food you'll ever taste, Taza's is a good alternative to the usual fast-food outlets. Closes at 7pm. ● *Sun.* 🚸

The Berghoff. Map 3 C2. [$][$]
17 W Adams St, Chicago, IL 60603. ☎ *427-3170.*
This restaurant, owned by the same family for more than 100 years, serves delectable schnitzel, grilled fish, and pasta, and its own beer and draft root beer. Wait staff are attired in waistcoats and bow ties. ● *Sun.* 🚸 💳

La Cantina. Map 3 C2. [$][$]
71 W Monroe St, Chicago, IL 60603. ☎ *332-7005.*
This cozy spot is the first in a trilogy of Italian restaurants at this location known as Italian Village. The kitchen specializes in fresh seafood and hearty traditional Italian dishes. Not wheelchair accessible. ● *Sun.* 🚸 🌙 💳

The Village. Map 3 C2. [$][$]
71 W Monroe St, Chicago, IL 60603. ☎ *332-7005.*
One of three restaurants at Italian Village. Twinkling lights and cozy alcoves complement a traditional Italian menu. Not wheelchair accessible. 🚸 🌙 💳

Rhapsody. Map 4 D2. [$][$][$]
65 E Adams St, Chicago, IL 60603. ☎ *786-9911.*
This spacious room with its understated elegance is a great place to dine before the symphony. The cooking is American with French flourishes, the presentation imaginative, the service efficient. ● *dinner Sun & Mon, Jun–Sep.* 🚸 💳

Trattoria No. 10. Map 3 C1. [$][$][$]
10 N Dearborn St, Chicago, IL 60602. ☎ *984-1718.*
A stylish, subterranean spot with an unusual and interesting variety of ravioli and northern Italian dishes. Convenient before a show downtown. ● *Sun.* 🚸 💳

Vivere. Map 3 C2. [$][$][$]
71 W Monroe St, Chicago, IL 60603. ☎ *332-4040.*
Another in the trilogy of restaurants at Italian Village, Vivere features upscale regional Italian cooking. Stylized Vs for "Vivere" are embedded in the sensuous, flamboyant decor. ● *Sun.* 🚸 💳

Russian Tea Time. Map 4 D2. [$][$][$][$]
77 E Adams St, Chicago, IL 60604. ☎ *360-0000.*
The red decor exudes luxury while the menu reflects the best of Russian cuisine. A popular destination before or after the symphony. 🚸 🌙 💳

Everest. Map 3 C2. [$][$][$][$][$]
One Financial Plaza, 440 S LaSalle St, Chicago, IL 60605. ☎ *663-8920.*
On the 40th floor, the chef's talents at preparing continental cuisine provide what many rank as one of the best, and most expensive, meals they have ever eaten. Notable is a pre-theater tasting menu. Dinner only. ● *Sun, Mon.* 🚸 💳

Restaurant	Vegetarian Specialties	Good Wine List	Outdoor Seating	Live Music
Heaven on Seven	●			■
Miller's Pub	●			
Taza's	●			
The Berghoff	●			
La Cantina	●			
The Village	●			
Rhapsody	●	■	●	
Trattoria No. 10	●			
Vivere	●	■		
Russian Tea Time	●			
Everest		■		

Price categories for a three-course evening meal and a half bottle of house wine, including taxes and service:
[$] under $30
[$][$] $30–$45
[$][$][$] $45–$65
[$][$][$][$] $65–$90
[$][$][$][$][$] over $90

VEGETARIAN SPECIALTIES
Denotes a vegetarian restaurant, or restaurant with vegetarian selections.

GOOD WINE LIST
Denotes a wide range or specialized selection of wines.

OUTDOOR SEATING
Facilities for eating on a terrace, or in a garden or courtyard.

LIVE MUSIC
Indicates live music, usually piano or small jazz ensembles, during dinner on weekends, sometimes on weeknights.

NORTH SIDE

		VEGETARIAN SPECIALTIES	GOOD WINE LIST	OUTDOOR SEATING	LIVE MUSIC
CORNER BAKERY. Map 1 C5. 516 N Clark St, Chicago, IL 60610. ☎ *644-8100.* When Corner Bakery first opened, it sold European breads off racks. As the menu expanded to include breakfast and lunch items, so did the number of locations. Alert staff keep the cafeteria-style line moving. No bar. 💳	[$]	●		●	
ED DEBEVIC'S. Map 1 C4. 640 N Wells St, Chicago, IL 60610. ☎ *664-1707.* The menu, from meatloaf to milkshakes, is painted on the wall outside. Inside, there is plenty of fun. A disc jockey spins 1950s tunes while costumed wait staff sing, dance, and dish out sassy attitude with the fries. 🧒 [D] 💳	[$]	●			
EDWARDO'S. Map 1 C3. 1212 N Dearborn St, Chicago, IL 60614. ☎ *337-4490.* This upscale chain is known for its stuffed pizza, baked with lots of cheese, the crust top covered with tomato sauce once out of the oven. As is often the case with chains, service ranges from good to poor. 🧒 💳	[$]	●			
FLAT TOP GRILL. Map 1 C1. 319 W North Ave, Chicago, IL 60610. ☎ *787-7676.* Asian ingredients and sauces that customers have chosen from a self-serve bar are stir-fried on a Mongolian grill. All you can eat. Reservations aren't accepted, so arrive early to avoid waiting in line. One of five locations. 🧒 [D] 💳	[$]	●			
GIORDANO'S. Map 2 D4. 730 N Rush St, Chicago, IL 60611. ☎ *951-0747.* A pizzeria with a wholesome, collegiate atmosphere. Some claim Giordano's has the best pizza in town. One of many locations. 🧒 [D] 💳	[$]	●			
JOHNNY ROCKETS. Map 2 D3. 901 N Rush St, Chicago, IL 60611. ☎ *337-3900.* A 1950s-style diner, with wait staff sporting snappy soda-jerk caps. Somehow, this re-creation of yesteryear works. The menu is limited to a few well-prepared items, such as burgers, milkshakes, and apple pie. No bar. 🧒 [D] 💳	[$]	●		●	
MITY NICE GRILL. Map 2 D4. Water Tower Place, 835 N Michigan Ave, Chicago, IL 60611. ☎ *335-4745.* This cozy 1940s-style diner serves burgers, turkey burgers, grilled flatbread, and a low-fat Enlightened Caesar salad, among other items. 🧒 💳	[$]	●			
NOOKIES. Map 1 C1. 1746 N Wells St, Chicago, IL 60614. ☎ *337-2454.* The original Nookies, like Nookies Too and Nookies Tree, is a clean, upbeat neighborhood restaurant where you can order breakfast all day, a good sandwich, or simply a cup of coffee. No bar. 🧒	[$]	●		●	
OLD JERUSALEM. Map 1 C2. 1411 N Wells St, Chicago, IL 60610. ☎ *944-0459.* This Old Town establishment draws a varied crowd, but everyone agrees that this is how falafel is supposed to taste. Bring your own wine. 🧒 💳	[$]	●		●	
ROCK 'N' ROLL McDONALD'S. Map 1 C4. 600 N Clark St, Chicago, IL 60610. ☎ *644-7940.* This McDonald's is chockablock full of rock-and-roll memorabilia and 1950s kitsch. It is slightly more expensive than other locations, but if you're going to eat fast food, this is the place to do so. 🧒	[$]				
CARSON'S FOR RIBS. Map 1 C4. 612 N Wells St, Chicago, IL 60610. ☎ *280-9200.* Famous nationwide for its ribs, Carson's also offers outstanding Greek chicken and pork chops. Seating is ample and comfortable. 🧒 💳	[$][$]			●	■

Price categories for a three-course evening meal and a half bottle of house wine, including taxes and service:
[$] under $30
[$][$] $30–$45
[$][$][$] $45–$65
[$][$][$][$] $65–$90
[$][$][$][$][$] over $90

Vegetarian Specialties
Denotes a vegetarian restaurant, or restaurant with vegetarian selections.

Good Wine List
Denotes a wide range or specialized selection of wines.

Outdoor Seating
Facilities for eating on a terrace, or in a garden or courtyard.

Live Music
Indicates live music, usually piano or small jazz ensembles, during dinner on weekends, sometimes on weeknights.

Restaurant	Price	Vegetarian Specialties	Good Wine List	Outdoor Seating	Live Music
Cheesecake Factory. Map 2 D3. 875 N Michigan Ave, Chicago, IL 60611. ☎ *337-1101.* Nothing will prepare you for this restaurant's comic-book decor or extensive menu featuring omelets, pizzas, and salads. And then there is the cheesecake, all 40 varieties. Located in the John Hancock Center. 🧒 🌙 💳	[$][$]	●		●	
Fireplace Inn. Map 1 C2. 1448 N Wells St, Chicago, IL 60610. ☎ *943-7427.* For 25 years, people have been returning to this Old Town institution for ribs and a lodge-like atmosphere. The stained-glass chandelier draws almost as many remarks as the great mashed potatoes and gravy. 🧒 🌙 💳	[$][$]			●	
Heaven on Seven on Rush. Map 2 D4. 600 Michigan St, Chicago, IL 60611. ☎ *280-7774.* This restaurant serves up the same fiery Cajun food as its sister restaurant in the Downtown Core *(see p146)*. ● *Sat, Sun.* 🧒 💳	[$][$]	●			
Papagus Greek Taverna. Map 1 C4. 620 N State St, Chicago, IL 60610. ☎ *642-8450.* The restaurant team of Lettuce Entertain You has created an interesting and fun environment at this rustic taverna. A wide selection of delicious *mezes* (appetizers), as well as lamb, seafood, and pasta entrées. 🧒 🌙 💳	[$][$]	●		●	
Pizzeria Uno. Map 2 D4. 29 E Ohio St, Chicago, IL 60611. ☎ *321-1000.* This is the home of Chicago-style pizza, also known as deep-dish pizza. A plaque at the door tells the whole story, which you'll have plenty of time to read, since there is almost always a waiting line. Not wheelchair accessible. 🧒 🌙 💳	[$][$]	●		●	
Rainforest Café. Map 1 C4. 605 N Clark St, Chicago, IL 60610. ☎ *787-1501.* Here you'll find talking trees, giant mushrooms, rainstorms, and live parrots. The fare – burgers, pizza, ribs – is standard, but kids love it. 🧒 💳	[$][$]	●			
Trattoria Dinotto. Map 1 C1. 163 W North Ave, Chicago, IL 60610. ☎ *787-3345.* Grapevines intertwined with tiny lights circle the ceiling, creating an intimate atmosphere that some may find too crowded. The usual Italian fare, from *polenta con funghi* to *vitello saltimbocca,* receives good grades. 🧒 💳	[$][$]				
Twin Anchors. Map 1 B1. 1655 N Sedgwick St, Chicago, IL 60614. ☎ *266-1616.* Arrive at this neighborhood bar and restaurant early or be prepared for a long wait. Fans recommend the ribs and coleslaw. Seafood is also on the menu, not surprisingly, given the nautical decor. Not wheelchair accessible. 🧒 🌙 💳	[$][$]			●	
Bistro 110. Map 2 D4. 110 E Pearson St, Chicago, IL 60611. ☎ *266-3110.* Brass, mirrors, murals, and the bustle of a Parisian bistro. Standard bistro fare (onion soup, mussels, and steak *frites*) and daily specials that go a little out of bistro bounds, but deliciously so. A good Sunday brunch with live jazz. 💳	[$][$][$]	●		●	
Brasserie Jo. Map 1 C5. 59 W Hubbard St, Chicago, IL 60610. ☎ *595-0800.* Reminiscent of elegant train-station dining rooms in days of old. The menu offers delicious, hearty Alsatian food, such as *choucroute garnie* or onion tart, as well as custom-brewed beer. Surprising touches in the service. 🧒 💳	[$][$][$]	●	■	●	
Café Luciano. Map 2 D3. 871 N Rush St, Chicago, IL 60611. ☎ *266-1414.* Beautiful antiques create a comfortable setting in which to enjoy authentic Italian dishes such as *giambotta* (a hearty stew of vegetables, chicken, and sweet sausage). Cigar lounge upstairs. Not wheelchair accessible. 🧒 💳	[$][$][$]			●	■

CAFÉ SPIAGGIA. Map 2 D3. $$$
980 N Michigan Ave, Chicago, IL 60611. 280-2764.
The Italian food here is simpler and less expensive than at Spiaggia next
door (see p150), but the decor, preparation, and service remain exceptional.
The pastas are made fresh each day. Sunday brunch. 🚹 🖼

CAPITAL GRILLE. Map 2 D4. $$$
633 N St. Clair St, Chicago, IL 60611. 337-9400.
With its tasteful decor of antiques, hand-crafted woodwork, and leather
furnishings, this steakhouse provides the perfect setting in which to entertain
clients or celebrate special occasions. 🚹 🖼

CARMINE'S. Map 2 D3. $$$
1043 N Rush St, Chicago, IL 60611. 988-7676.
This classy Italian restaurant serves huge portions of steaks, chops, seafood,
and pasta. There is a piano bar downstairs, a dining room more conducive to
conversation upstairs. Carmine's is very popular on weekends. 🚹 🌙 🖼

CENTRO RISTORANTE. Map 1 C4. $$$
710 N Wells St, Chicago, IL 60610. 988-7775.
The plush, comfortable dining room isn't stuffy, though it can be very busy,
and the traditional Italian menu has something for everyone. Specialties
include lamb chops and chicken Vesuvio. Large portions. 🚹 🖼

LE COLONIAL. Map 2 D3. $$$
937 N Rush St, Chicago, IL 60611. 255-0088.
With its ceiling fans whirling above the rattan furniture and palm trees,
Le Colonial has the elegant, sultry atmosphere of 1920s French Colonial
Vietnam. Dishes have the flavors of Asia crafted with French finesse. Food is
also served in the intimate upstairs lounge. Formal attire. 🌙 🖼

FRONTERA GRILL. Map 1 C5. $$$
445 N Clark St, Chicago, IL 60610. 661-1434.
Less expensive than Topolobampo at the same address (see p150), Frontera
Grill has earned a national reputation for its commitment to fine Mexican
cuisine. Even the tortillas are made from scratch daily. The dining room is
decorated with museum-quality folk art. ● Sun, Mon. 🚹 🖼

ROSEBUD ON RUSH. Map 2 D4. $$$
720 N Rush St, Chicago, IL 60611. 266-6444.
Visit this classy Italian restaurant when in need of some Frank Sinatra music and
a great *marinara*. The upstairs dining room is romantic and cozy; the bar and
dining area downstairs has live entertainment. Not wheelchair accessible. 🌙 🖼

SALPICÓN. Map 1 C2. $$$
1252 N Wells St, Chicago, IL 60610. 988-7811.
Colorful paintings by local artists set an upbeat atmosphere for contemporary
cooking that reflects the various regions of Mexico. Dishes include beef
tenderloin in spicy *tomatilla* sauce, and shrimp with fresh mango. 🖼

SHAW'S CRAB HOUSE. Map 1 C5. $$$
21 E Hubbard St, Chicago, IL 60611. 527-2722.
In the main dining room of this restaurant, you'll find fresh seafood, served
in a pleasant, formal atmosphere. The adjoining Blue Crab Lounge, offering a
lighter menu, provides a casual atmosphere with booth seating. 🚹 🖼

ZINFANDEL. Map 1 C5. $$$
59 W Grand Ave, Chicago, IL 60610. 527-1818.
Everything at this restaurant is American, even the vodka. The menu offers a
survey of regional American cuisine, featuring monthly regional menus,
cooked with care and presented with flair. The decor is fun, ranging from
petroglyphs to model airplanes. ● Sun. 🚹 🖼

COCO PAZZO. Map 1 C5. $$$$
300 W Hubbard St, Chicago, IL 60610. 836-0900.
A loft space with dark blue curtains and track lighting makes for a stylish
dining room equally suited for talking business or romance. The staff is not
overly friendly, but the Tuscan cooking is pure and simple. 🚹 🖼

GIBSON'S STEAKHOUSE. Map 1 C3. $$$$
1028 N Rush St, Chicago, IL 60611. 266-8999.
A popular restaurant with the city's business elite, as well as with local
celebrities, Gibson's is a handsome restaurant that serves strong drinks and
good steaks in a stylish atmosphere. Dinner only. 🚹 🌙 🖼

Price categories for a three-course evening meal and a half bottle of house wine, including taxes and service:
$ under $30
$$ $30–$45
$$$ $45–$65
$$$$ $65–$90
$$$$$ over $90

VEGETARIAN SPECIALTIES
Denotes a vegetarian restaurant, or restaurant with vegetarian selections.

GOOD WINE LIST
Denotes a wide range or specialized selection of wines.

OUTDOOR SEATING
Facilities for eating on a terrace, or in a garden or courtyard.

LIVE MUSIC
Indicates live music, usually piano or small jazz ensembles, during dinner on weekends, sometimes on weeknights.

	VEGETARIAN SPECIALTIES	GOOD WINE LIST	OUTDOOR SEATING	LIVE MUSIC
PUMP ROOM. Map 1 C2. $$$$ Omni Ambassador East Hotel, 1301 N State Pkwy, Chicago, IL 60610. 266-0360. One of the great classic dining rooms in Chicago, with a fine continental menu. Its mahogany-toned decor is accented with lush greenery and crystal chandeliers. Live jazz nightly and a secluded dance floor.				■
SPIAGGIA. Map 2 D3. $$$$ 980 N Michigan Ave, Chicago, IL 60611. 280-2750. There is not a bad seat in the house at Spiaggia. The tiered dining room and floor-to-ceiling windows afford views of Michigan Avenue, Oak Street Beach, and Lake Michigan. Perhaps the best Italian food in town.	●			
TOPOLOBAMPO. Map 1 C5. $$$$ 445 N Clark St, Chicago, IL 60610. 661-1434. Sharing the same address with Frontera Grill (see p149), Topolobampo features Mexican cuisine in a beautiful, semi-formal setting. ● Sun, Mon.	●		●	
TRU. Map 2 D4. $$$$$ 676 N St. Clair St, Chicago, IL 60611. 202-0001. A new entry on the ultra-chic dining scene. Every detail here is thoughtfully considered. The cuisine is mainly French, with frequent Italian and Asian influences. The presentation is delightful. ● Sun.	●			■

SOUTH LOOP AND NEAR SOUTH SIDE

	VEGETARIAN SPECIALTIES	GOOD WINE LIST	OUTDOOR SEATING	LIVE MUSIC
EMPEROR'S CHOICE. Map 5 C2. $ 2238 S Wentworth Ave, Chicago, IL 60616. 225-8800. The decor at this, one of Chinatown's most elegant restaurants, reflects an emperor motif. The owner is exceptionally helpful.	●			
HONG MIN. Map 5 C1. $ 221 W Cermak Rd, Chicago, IL 60616. 842-5026. This Chinatown spot may not have much atmosphere, but dip into the hot-and-sour soup and ambiance won't matter. Bring your own wine.	●			
PHOENIX. Map 5 B2. $ 2131 S Archer Ave, Chicago, IL 60616. 328-0848. The spacious and modern second-floor Chinatown restaurant draws a large crowd for *dim sum* (small brunch dishes, served from passing trolleys), especially on weekends. Ask for jasmine or chrysanthemum tea.	●			
CHICAGO FIREHOUSE RESTAURANT. Map 4 D5. $$$ 1401 S Michigan Ave, Chicago, IL 60605. 786-1401. This restaurant inside a converted firehouse offers creative American fare, such as coriander-crusted salmon, in a restrained, tasteful setting. ● Mon.	●		●	
PRAIRIE. Map 3 C3. $$$ Hyatt on Printer's Row Hotel, 500 S Dearborn St, Chicago, IL 60605. 663-1143. Prairie proves that Midwest cooking is much more than meat and potatoes. The spare, elegant dining room was inspired by Frank Lloyd Wright.	●			
PRINTER'S ROW. Map 3 C3. $$$ 550 S Dearborn St, Chicago, IL 60605. 461-0780. This restaurant is notable for its innovative American dishes, such as sage-and-mustard-rubbed pork rack served with cornbread pudding, smoked bacon greens, and bourbon-molasses sauce. ● Sun.	●			

SOUTH SIDE

	VEGETARIAN SPECIALTIES	GOOD WINE LIST	OUTDOOR SEATING	LIVE MUSIC
CAFFE FLORIAN. Map 8 D4. $ 1450 E 57th St, Chicago, IL 60637. (773) 752-4100. A café popular with university students. Though not a culinary destination, it is a good neighborhood spot for a sandwich. Bring your own wine.				

DIXIE KITCHEN AND BAIT SHOP. Map 8 D2. $
5225 S Harper Ave, Chicago, IL 60615. ☎ *(773) 363-4943.*
This roadhouse is small and busy, with decor that is a caricature of a 1930s Carolina kitchen and bait shop. Southern favorites such as the starter cornmeal johnnycakes are always superb. One of two locations *(see p152).* 🧒 💳

MEDICI. Map 8 D4. $
1327 E 57th St, Chicago, IL 60637. ☎ *(773) 667-7394.*
This café caters to university students and Hyde Park locals who appreciate items such as "Family Garbage Pizza." Bring your own wine. 🧒 💳

FARTHER AFIELD

LAKEVIEW: *Amitabul.* $
3418 N Southport Ave, Chicago, IL 60657. ☎ *(773) 472-4060.*
Amitabul is an oasis of Korean Buddhist vegetarian cuisine. The menu is vegan, and the kitchen uses no oil in the stir-fries. However, a meal here need not be monastic: beer and wine are also on the menu. 🧒 💳

LAKEVIEW: *Chicago Diner.* $
3411 N Halsted St, Chicago, IL 60657. ☎ *(773) 935-6696.*
The wooden booths and counter suggest a roadside diner rather than a vegetarian restaurant. The menu offers vegan and wheat-free items, as well as beer, wine, and cocktails. Low-energy service. Not wheelchair accessible. 🧒 💳

LAKEVIEW: *Bistrot Zinc.* $$
3443 N Southport Ave, Chicago, IL 60657. ☎ *(773) 281-3443.*
The bistro here offers a traditional French café menu, including crepes and sandwiches. For a romantic dinner, ask for a table in the salon, a small, dimly lit room with red banquettes. Or enjoy well-prepared bistro fare (grilled salmon, *bouillabaisse*) and excellent service in the dining room. ● *Mon.* 🧒 💳

LAKEVIEW: *Mia Francesca.* $$
3311 N Clark St, Chicago, IL 60657. ☎ *(773) 281-3310.*
A line for this restaurant often forms before it even opens, thanks to its no-reservations policy. Black-and-white photographs decorate the simple dining room. Large portions of good Italian food keep the place packed and noisy year after year. One of several locations. Dinner only. 🧒 💳

LINCOLN PARK: *Original Pancake House.* $
2020 N Lincoln Park West, Chicago, IL 60614. ☎ *(773) 929-8130.*
With 18 varieties of pancakes and 8 types of waffles, this restaurant is serious about breakfast, which is served until closing time, around 3pm. The wait can be daunting, but where else can you order a bacon waffle? 🧒

LINCOLN PARK: *Red Lion Pub.* $
2446 N Lincoln Ave, Chicago, IL 60614. ☎ *(773) 348-2695.*
Red Lion is a down-to-earth pub. The bar TV is more likely to be showing documentaries or old movies than sports. Cornish pasties, bangers and mash, and steak-and-kidney pie are all on the menu. 🧒 🌙 💳

LINCOLN PARK: *Café Ba-Ba-Reeba!* $$
2024 N Halsted St, Chicago, IL 60614. ☎ *(773) 935-5000.*
The *tapas* menu (offering appetizer-size portions of everything from garlic potato salad to baked goat cheese to grilled squid) is a grazer's paradise; order several and share. The Spanish cooking is good, and the vivacious staff keep things lively. The best patio in Chicago. 🧒 🌙 💳

LINCOLN PARK: *Vinci.* $$
1732 N Halsted St, Chicago, IL 60614. ☎ *266-1199.*
Rustic Italian cooking is to be found here, in a setting evocative of an Italian villa. Located in the heart of the Lincoln Park theater district, this restaurant can be very busy; reservations are recommended. ● *Mon.* 🧒 🌙 💳

LINCOLN PARK: *Aubriot.* $$$
1962 N Halsted Ave, Chicago, IL 60614. ☎ *(773) 281-4211.*
Small, bustling Aubriot serves excellent French cooking, presented with flair. Great Sunday brunch. The long, cherry-wood room is inviting. ● *Mon.* 🧒 💳

LINCOLN PARK: *North Pond Café.* $$$
2610 N Cannon Dr, Chicago, IL 60657. ☎ *(773) 477-5845.*
Both the regional American cuisine, inspired by locally grown products, and the decor reflect the philosophy of the Arts and Crafts movement: simplicity and respect for quality craftsmanship. Excellent Sunday brunch. ● *Mon.* 🧒 💳

Price categories for a three-course evening meal and a half bottle of house wine, including taxes and service:
(S) under $30
(S)(S) $30–$45
(S)(S)(S) $45–$65
(S)(S)(S)(S) $65–$90
(S)(S)(S)(S)(S) over $90

VEGETARIAN SPECIALTIES
Denotes a vegetarian restaurant, or restaurant with vegetarian selections.

GOOD WINE LIST
Denotes a wide range or specialized selection of wines.

OUTDOOR SEATING
Facilities for eating on a terrace, or in a garden or courtyard.

LIVE MUSIC
Indicates live music, usually piano or small jazz ensembles, during dinner on weekends, sometimes on weeknights.

	Price	VEGETARIAN SPECIALTIES	GOOD WINE LIST	OUTDOOR SEATING	LIVE MUSIC
LINCOLN PARK: *Ambria.* 2300 N Lincoln Park West, Chicago, IL 60614. (773) 472-5959. The kitchen at Ambria, one of the finest restaurants in the city, melds Spanish and French cooking techniques to create luxurious, intricate dishes, served in an Art Nouveau dining room. Excellent presentation and service. ● Sun. 🛉 📧	(S)(S)(S)(S)(S)	●	■		
LINCOLN PARK: *Charlie Trotter's.* 816 W Armitage Ave, Chicago, IL 60614. (773) 248-6228. A modest townhouse is home to this international culinary destination. Two tasting menus, each consisting of six to eight seasonal dishes, are offered. Impeccable service; reservations required. ● Sun, Mon. 〕 📧	(S)(S)(S)(S)(S)	●	■		
NEAR WEST SIDE: *Greek Islands.* 200 S Halsted St, Chicago, IL 60661. (312) 782-9855. This Greek restaurant, the liveliest in Greek Town, has several small dining rooms, each with its own ambiance, such as a bustling garden room. 🛉 〕 📧	(S)	●	■	●	
NEAR WEST SIDE: *Parthenon.* 314 S Halsted St, Chicago, IL 60661. 726-2407. As at any self-respecting Greek restaurant, here you'll find *moussaka, pastitsio,* and *saganaki.* Lamb slowly roasts by the front window. The plush atmosphere sets Parthenon apart from other Greek Town eateries. 🛉 〕 📧	(S)	●			
NEAR WEST SIDE: *Francesca's on Taylor.* 1400 W Taylor St, Chicago, IL 60607. 829-2828. This Little Italy restaurant offers the same rustic Italian menu as the popular Mia Francesca *(see p151).* This location is open for both lunch and dinner and accepts reservations. One of several locations. 🛉 📧	(S)(S)				
NEAR WEST SIDE: *The Rosebud.* 1500 W Taylor St, Chicago, IL 60607. 942-1117. Associated with Rosebud on Rush *(see p149),* this Little Italy establishment is said to be the home of chicken Vesuvio, a dish that is practically mandatory on Italian menus in Chicago. Music is Frank Sinatra or Italian opera. 〕 📧	(S)(S)	●		●	
OAK PARK: *Café Winberie.* 151 N Oak Park Ave, Oak Park, IL 60301. (708) 386-2600. This tidy spot serves reliable American fare with small continental flourishes. Fondues are also on the menu. 🛉 〕 📧	(S)	●			
BEYOND CHICAGO					
EVANSTON: *Dixie Kitchen and Bait Shop.* 825 Church St, Evanston, IL 60201. (847) 733-9030. Although larger, this location is just as good as, if not better than, the South Side original *(see p151)* that helped popularize such low-country and Cajun classics as po' boy sandwiches, gumbo, and pecan pie. 🛉 📧	(S)	●		●	
EVANSTON: *Sarkis Cafe.* 2632 Gross Pointe Rd, Evanston, IL 60201. (847) 328-9703. It is an experience to eat at this old diner, which specializes in breakfasts. The flamboyant proprietor, Sarkis, is ever-present and always entertaining. Breakfast and lunch only. Not wheelchair accessible. 🛉	(S)				
EVANSTON: *Davis Street Fishmarket.* 501 Davis St, Evanston, IL 60201. (847) 869-3474. Clams and oysters can be enjoyed at the raw bar, while 20 varieties of fresh fish are available in the dining room, many prepared with a Cajun accent. 🛉 📧	(S)(S)	●			
EVANSTON: *Roxy Café.* 626 Church St, Evanston, IL 60201. (847) 864-6540. A sleek dining room and diverse Italian menu draws a varied clientele. Pastas cover all bases, and entrées run from chicken scallopini to New York strip. 📧	(S)(S)	●		●	

EVANSTON: *Va Pensiero.* $$$
1566 Oak Ave, Evanston, IL 60201. ((847) 475-7779.
The quaint dining room of this intimate, upscale Italian restaurant is on the
first floor of the Margarita European Inn *(see p140)*. Game and seafood are
highlights of the menu, though the pastas are also always good.

EVANSTON: *Trio.* $$$$$
1625 Hinman Ave, Evanston, IL 60201. ((847) 733-8746.
A flawless blend of Asian and Mediterranean flavors is uniquely presented at
Trio. A nine-course chef's degustation is offered in addition to the menu.
Located in the vintage Homestead Hotel *(see p140)*. Mon.

GALENA: *Boone's Place.* $
515 S Main St, Galena, IL 61036. ((815) 777-4488.
Boone's is known for its gourmet sandwiches, as well as its assortment of
soups, salads, and deep-dish pie. The original tin walls and ceiling of the
historic building housing the café are still intact. Not wheelchair accessible.

GALENA: *Log Cabin.* $
201 N Main St, Galena, IL 60136. ((815) 777-0393.
The oldest restaurant in Galena features Greek cuisine, in addition to steaks,
seafood, ribs, and chicken. The flaming *saganaki* and the *shish kebab* are
specialties. Prime rib is served three times a week. Mon.

GALENA: *Bubba's Seafood, Pasta and Smokehouse.* $$
300 N Main St, Galena, IL 61036. ((815) 777-8030.
Bubba's contains two dining rooms: the French Quarter is on the upper floor,
the Bourbon Street Cafe on the lower floor. Both feature slow-cooked,
hickory-smoked meats and Cajun flavors. Huge portions.

GALENA: *Vinny Vanucchi's Little Italy.* $$
201 S Main St, Galena, IL 61036. ((815) 777-8100.
The menu at Vinny's, a three-story Italian restaurant with adjoining old-style
delicatessen, is extensive. Checkered tablecloths lend a homey atmosphere to
this family-owned spot. Cappuccino is served in the garden.

GALENA: *Fried Green Tomatoes.* $$$
1301 Irish Hollow Rd, Galena, IL 60136. ((815) 777-3938.
The menu of this rustic Italian-style restaurant, in an 1850s building, features
traditional favorites such as lasagna, as well as unusual Italian fare, such as
bistecca al espresso and pork medallions rolled in pine nuts. The appetizer of
fried green tomatoes is a signature dish. Not wheelchair accessible.

LAKE GENEVA: *Popeye's.* $
811 Wrigley Dr, Lake Geneva, WI 53147. ((262) 248-4381.
Enjoy casual dining and a spectacular view of the lake at this restaurant. Chicken,
pork, and lamb are barbecued over an outdoor pit during the summer. Popeye's
is also noted for its broccoli-cheese soup and award-winning apple pie.

LAKE GENEVA: *Cactus Club.* $$
430 Broad St, Lake Geneva, WI 53147. ((262) 248-1999.
The kitchen melds regional styles of Native American, Spanish, Mexican, and
American cuisine to produce flavorful southwestern dishes. Excellent
margaritas provide refreshment after a day of shopping.

LAKE GENEVA: *Grand Geneva Resort and Spa.* $$$
7036 Grand Geneva Way, Lake Geneva, WI 53147. ((262) 248-8811.
Within the resort *(see p141)* are two fine-dining establishments. Ristorante
Brissago offers traditional Italian cuisine, including homemade pastas.
Newport Grill, with its rotisserie and grills in the open kitchen, offers fine
service in an elegant setting. Live music in the bar. dinner Sun; Mon.

LAKE GENEVA: *Kirsch's at the French Country Inn.* $$$
Highway 50, Lake Geneva, WI 53147. ((262) 245-5756.
Elegant cuisine with a Hawaiian influence is standard in this charming
restaurant overlooking Lake Como. Its signature dishes – hibachi-grilled
Chilean sea bass and Kona coffee-crusted *chateaubriand* – are highly
recommended. Authentic New Orleans-style brunch on Sunday.

LAKE GENEVA: *Grandview Restaurant and Lounge.* $$$$
N2009 State Rd 120, Lake Geneva, WI 53147. ((262) 248-5680.
Superb American and continental cuisine features fresh seafood, delicious
daily specials, and decadent desserts. Excellent service and a perfect location
highlighted by panoramic windows. Formal attire required.

SHOPS AND MARKETS

SHOPPING, rather than sports, may well be the major pastime of Chicagoans. The sheer number of shops in the small area around Michigan Avenue alone makes Chicago a world-class shopping destination. Everything from basic necessities to outrageous luxuries can be found at

Clock at Marshall Field's, a favorite meeting spot

Chicago's boutiques, specialty shops, and legendary department stores. No matter what your passion, you will find a merchant in Chicago who shares it. Many of the shops listed on pages 156–9 will take you off the beaten track into the city's many distinct and charming neighborhoods.

Ghirardelli Chocolate Shop and Soda Fountain

WHEN TO SHOP

MOST CHAIN STORES are open seven days a week, from 10am to 6pm. Some shops open an hour later and close an hour earlier on Sundays. Malls and shopping centers usually stay open evenings as well as on Sundays.

Neighborhood shops, antique dealers, vintage-clothing stores, and galleries keep more relaxed hours. Many are closed on Mondays and Tuesdays and may not open until noon on other days.

Vibrant window signs brightening a storefront in Chinatown

Shops are blissfully empty on weekday mornings, gradually becoming crowded as the evening approaches. On the weekends, downtown shops and malls are packed.

SALES

PRE-SEASON SALES, end-of-season sales, 13-hour sales, Mother's Day sales – it is easy to find some kind of sale each day of the year.

Many sales, especially when shops want to clear their racks to make way for the next season's merchandise, offer great bargains.

Be wary of "going out of business" sales – some have been going on for years. However, some are legitimate sales; ask at nearby stores.

TAXES

SALES TAX in Chicago is 8.75 percent and is added to everything except magazines and groceries. Sales tax is not refundable to visitors from overseas. However, if the shop ships your purchase to an address outside Chicago or Illinois, you can avoid city

and/or state sales tax. Foreign visitors may be required to pay duty on the purchase once they arrive home.

PAYMENT

MAJOR CREDIT CARDS are accepted in most Chicago stores, as are bank debit cards, though small businesses may have a minimum-price policy (usually a $10 minimum) for purchases paid for this way. Traveler's checks must be accompanied by identification. Personal checks are discouraged; foreign currency is never accepted. A few smaller shops are still run on a cash-only basis.

RETURNS

BE SURE YOU understand the shop's return policy before you make an important purchase. Keep your receipt as a proof of purchase.

Each store sets its own return-and-exchange policies; they are generally posted at the cash register. Some shops will give a full refund with no

Sunday morning in the busy Maxwell Street Market *(see p157)*

Water Tower Place, with seven floors of boutiques and stores

questions asked, whereas other shops maintain an all-sales-are-final policy. Some places offer an in-shop credit rather than a refund. Sale items are often not returnable.

MALLS AND SHOPPING CENTERS

CHICAGO'S MALLS come in two varieties. Suburban malls resemble small cities surrounded by vast parking lots. City malls tend to rise upward from the ground. The most notable of these vertical malls are on the Magnificent Mile *(see pp60–61).*

Water Tower Place contains major department stores and seven floors with more than 100 boutiques and specialty shops, and, for those in need of a break from shopping, a movie theater.

Across the street is **900 North Michigan Avenue Shops**, with upscale shops and boutiques. A block south of these two powerhouse malls is **Chicago Place**, home to the flagship Midwest location of Saks Fifth Avenue, among other stylish shops.

DEPARTMENT STORES

MANY DEPARTMENT stores have a prominent street location. **Marshall Field's** *(see pp50–51)* is the benchmark for luxurious department stores across the country. Don't leave Chicago without a box of its Frango mints.

In years past, critics said that Chicago's other major department store, **Carson Pirie Scott** *(see p50),* did not carry the high-end merchandise that Marshall Field's did, but this criticism has faded away in recent years.

Seattle-based **Nordstrom**, known for its quality clothing and shoes for men, women, and children, recently opened its flagship Midwest location.

Posh **Neiman Marcus** bills itself as a world-famous specialty store and prides itself on its personal service and exclusivity. The store specializes in clothing and accessories by many top fashion designers. Its epicurean shop offers delectable items, including caviar and wine.

Saks Fifth Avenue attracts a ritzy clientele with its fine selection of designer and private-label clothing.

Bloomingdale's is also stylish but less pricey. It has a great selection of fashionable clothing and shoes, and a floor devoted to housewares. Watch for its legendary sales.

The most traditional of the department stores is **Lord and Taylor**, which carries conservative clothing at very reasonable prices.

PARKING

DOWNTOWN PARKING lots are expensive, street parking almost nonexistent *(see p181).* Many department stores offer discounted parking in their lots, but the few dollars saved are rarely worth the time spent in the parking maze. The CTA offers convenient public transit *(see p181).*

An interior-furnishings shop on the street level of the historic Santa Fe Building *(see p43)*

DIRECTORY

MALLS AND SHOPPING CENTERS

Chicago Place
700 N Michigan Ave.
Map 2 D4.
(266-7710.

900 North Michigan Avenue Shops
Map 2 D3.
(915-3916.

Water Tower Place
835 N Michigan Ave.
Map 2 D4.
(440-3165.

DEPARTMENT STORES

Bloomingdale's
900 North Michigan Avenue Shops.
Map 2 D4.
(440-4460.

Carson Pirie Scott
1 S State St.
Map 3 C2.
(641-7000.

Lord and Taylor
Water Tower Place,
835 N Michigan Ave.
Map 2 D4.
(787-7400.

Marshall Field's
111 N State St.
Map 4 D1.
(781-1000.
or
Water Tower Place,
835 N Michigan Ave.

Map 2 D4.
(335-7700.

Neiman Marcus
737 N Michigan Ave.
Map 2 D4.
(642-5900.

Nordstrom
55 E Grand Ave. Map 2 D5.
(464-1515.

Saks Fifth Avenue
700 N Michigan Ave.
Map 2 D4.
(944-6500.

Where to Shop

CHICAGO IS a shopper's paradise. The city's many neighborhoods attract locals and tourists alike with ethnic and one-of-a-kind shops. Visitors looking for fine and unusual artwork are sure to find a treasure in the River North Gallery District. Furnishing shops are clustered at Clybourn Corridor, while Oak Street is home to top fashion boutiques. Myriad shops, including chain and department stores, line the Magnificent Mile.

ART

RIVER NORTH GALLERY District has Chicago's highest concentration of art galleries, though there are several good galleries outside its traditional boundaries. **Stephen Daiter Gallery** offers vintage 20th-century and experimental photography. **Carl Hammer Gallery** is known for its collection of "outsider art." Art with an emphasis on realism by emerging local artists is at **Lyonswier Packer Gallery**. **Zolla/Lieberman Gallery** specializes in contemporary painting, sculpture, drawings, and photographs; **Robert Henry Adams Fine Art** sells American and European paintings and prints from the 1930s and 1940s. **Mongerson Gallery** showcases Western art: paintings, sculpture, and photographs from the 18th to 20th centuries.

The collection of original European advertising posters dating from the late 1800s at **Spencer Weisz Galleries** is marvelous. **Vintage Posters** specializes in aviation, circus, food, and wine posters.

ANTIQUES

MOST OF the antique shops in the former antique district at West Belmont and North Lincoln Avenues have dispersed. Although some of the shops remaining are worth visiting, many resemble thrift shops more than antique dealers. To find genuine antiques, go to **Jay Robert's Antique Warehouse**.

Visit **Salvage One** if you're looking for an antique doorknob, mantelpiece, or leaded stained glass. **Architectural Artifacts** has a great selection of salvaged pieces, everything from desks to church pews.

ART AND CRAFT SUPPLIES

HUNDREDS OF Japanese papers are to be found at **Aiko's Art Materials**. **Pearl Art & Craft Supplies** stocks drafting, etching, and silk-screening supplies, in addition to paints, papers, and brushes. **Paper Source** sells specialized papers and the city's largest assortment of rubber stamps.

International Importing Bead & Novelty Co. is known for handmade beads, pearls, crystals, and trim. **Tom Thumb Hobby & Crafts** offers a great selection of beads and craft materials.

BOOKS

LOCAL BOOKSHOPS abound in Chicago. **Barbara's Bookstore** specializes in small- and alternative-press titles. The **Chicago Architecture Foundation Shop** has an excellent selection of books on the city's architecture.

Afrocentric Bookstore stocks books by African Americans, from mysteries to histories; **Europa Books** stocks foreign-language publications. **Transitions Bookplace** is Chicago's – some say the country's – best new-age and self-help bookshop. The top bookshop for gay and lesbian literature in Chicago is **Unabridged Books**. **57th Street Books** has a great general selection but specializes in cookbooks, mysteries, and film, computer, and children's books. **Tower Records** carries books and magazines unavailable elsewhere in the city, on subjects ranging from cooking to the occult. **Powell's Bookstore** buys and sells used books, specializing in rare, out-of-print, and scholarly titles.

BUTTONS AND FABRICS

BUTTONS FOR SEWERS and collectors alike are to be found at **Mayet Beads & Buttons**, and in the huge selection at **Tender Buttons**.

From decorator fabrics to bridal finery, the selection at **Vogue Fabrics** is dizzying. As well as silks, woolens, and cottons, **Fishman's Fabrics** carries theatrical fabrics, laces, and decorative trims.

CAMERAS AND ELECTRONICS

CAMERA BUFFS will want to visit **Central Camera**, an old-world shop crammed with cameras of every make and model. **Helix Camera & Video** carries underwater equipment and used cameras.

Visit **Bang & Olufsen** for high-quality Danish entertainment centers. **Sony Gallery** is a wonderland of high-tech gadgets and electronics, while **United Audio** has superb home and car stereo systems and knowledgeable staff.

COINS

THE FULL-SERVICE coin dealer **Harlan J. Berk** buys and sells all currencies of coins. It also deals in paper money and rare and ancient coins. Another respected dealer is **Chicago Coin Company**, located near Midway Airport.

DISCOUNT CLOTHING

DISCOUNT CLOTHING stores are plentiful in Chicago. **Marshall's, TJ Maxx**, and **Filene's Basement** all have great selections.

Many department stores *(see p155)* also have discount outlets scattered throughout the suburbs.

DESIGNER CLOTHING

FOR HIP men's and women's fashions by designers such as Gucci and Fendi, **Ultimo** is a must-visit. **Giorgio Armani** stocks the designer's entire collection, including eyewear and fragrances. Italian design house **Prada** sells its fashions from a sleek and ultra-hip

Oak Street shop. **Barneys New York** has an excellent selection of designer clothing.

For the more adventurous, there's New Yorker **Betsey Johnson**'s shop, and **Sugar Magnolia**, for fashions from European and US designers.

SHOES

STOCKING STYLISH women's shoes, purses, and accessories, **Lori's Discount Designer Shoes** is a treasure. The somewhat hectic store is self-serve. **Altman's Shoes**, a Chicago mainstay since 1932, offers current men's styles and specialty sizes.

FURS AND LEATHERS

THE MIDWEST's largest fur importer and wholesaler is **Chicago Fur Mart**. Chic furs and leathers by top designers are sold at **Elán Furs**. **Glove Me Tender** has a vast array of gloves for men, women, and children. **Alfred Dunhill** has a large selection of luggage, cases, and accessories.

JEWELRY

THE GEMS of the jewelry district are clustered along Wabash Avenue between Madison and Washington Streets. Some are open only to the trade, but several open to the public. **Harold Burland & Son** sells diamonds and other precious stones. **Tiffany & Co.** sells designer jewelry, crystal, and clocks.

FOOD AND WINE SHOPS

VISITING THE **Spice House** is an aromatic adventure. Its proprietors will gladly discuss the differences between the several varieties of cinnamon or basil they sell. **Treasure Island** carries hard-to-find imports and the city's best selection of gourmet foodstuffs. The organic food at **Whole Foods** is delicious.

For a rare Bordeaux or obscure Puerto Rican rum, visit **Sam's Wines & Spirits**. **House of Glunz** carries wines in vintages as early as 1804. It also has a tasting room and wine museum.

MARKETS

FROM JUNE to October, Midwest farmers come to sell their produce at Chicago's 30 or so markets. Some markets are on weekdays, but Saturday is the main market day. Hours are usually from 7am to 1pm. **Near North Market** is held Saturdays, as is **Lincoln Park Market**. **Evanston Farmers' Market**, on Saturday mornings, has wonderful organic produce. The fabulous **Daley Plaza Market** is alternate Thursdays.

Chicago's famous **Maxwell Street Market** has been around since 1871. Up to 400 vendors sell new and used items, from power tools to fresh delicacies. The market runs Sundays, April to October.

Be prepared to pay with cash at the markets. Prices are generally not negotiable. Call the **Farmers' Market Information Line** for details and to confirm locations.

GIFTS AND SOUVENIRS

FOR A PIECE – literally – of Chicago, visit the **City of Chicago Store**. It sells fragments of Chicago landmarks, such as bricks from the old Comiskey Park, as well as other, more commonplace, souvenirs. The **Chicago Architecture Foundation Shop** has a good selection of souvenir books, posters, and Chicago memorabilia.

Take home original arts and crafts from **Illinois Marketplace**. The **Illinois Artisans Shop** is an excellent source of affordable crafts by local artisans, while the **Gallery 37 Store** sells a wide range of artwork by teenagers enrolled in its nonprofit art program.

HOME AND GARDEN FURNISHINGS

UPSCALE reproductions of vintage furniture and fixtures are the specialties of **Restoration Hardware**. **Jayson Home & Garden** carries unusual furnishings and garden pots. **Urban Gardener** sells interesting garden decorations, pots, and garden tools.

Smith & Hawken offers pricey but alluring garden supplies and accessories. Its discount outlet is next door.

MEMORABILIA

YOU WILL FIND a fascinating, and broad, collection of political, sports, and movie memorabilia at **Yesterday**. **Metro Golden Memories** has posters, movie stills, and vintage radio-show tapes from the 1920s onward.

MUSIC

A VAST classical-music collection, as well as folk, jazz, rock, pop, and show tunes, is to be found at **Tower Records**. Its only competition is **Virgin Megastore**.

What is arguably the world's best collection of jazz recordings is found at **Jazz Record Mart**. Staff here are extremely knowledgeable. **Dr. Wax Records** is a fun place to browse through secondhand CDs.

SPORTING GOODS

EVERYTHING the company manufactures can be found at **Nike Town**, while **Vertel's Authentic Running & Fitness** is serious about athletic shoes. If outdoor equipment is an interest, an expedition to **The North Face** is worthwhile.

TOYS, GADGETS, AND SPECIALTY SHOPS

USEFUL GADGETS are stocked at **Hammacher Schlemmer** and **Sharper Image**, while **Kite Harbor** entices with an astonishing selection of kites and radio-controlled toys. Extraordinary miniature dollhouse furniture and figures are offered at **Think Small By Rosebud**. Everything from chemistry kits to telescopes is sold at **American Science and Surplus**.

For children, **F.A.O. Schwarz** is a must-see for its huge stuffed animals and electronic toys. The popular **American Girl Place** sells historic and contemporary dolls and doll accessories.

DIRECTORY

ART

Carl Hammer Gallery
740 N Wells St.
Map 1 C4.
266-8512.

Lyonswier Packer Gallery
300 W Superior St.
Map 1 B4.
654-0600.

Mongerson Gallery
704 N Wells St.
Map 1 C4.
943-2354.

Robert Henry Adams Fine Art
715 N Franklin St.
Map 1 B4.
642-8700.

Spencer Weisz Galleries
214 W Ohio St.
Map 1 C5.
527-9420.

Stephen Daiter Gallery
311 W Superior St.
Map 1 B4.
787-3350.

Vintage Posters
1551 N Wells St.
Map 1 C1.
951-6681.

Zolla/Lieberman Gallery
325 W Huron St.
Map 1 B4.
944-1990.

ANTIQUES

Architectural Artifacts
4325 N Ravenswood Ave,
North Center.
(773) 348-0622.

Jay Robert's Antique Warehouse
149 W Kinzie St.
Map 1 C5.
222-0167.

Salvage One
1840 W Hubbard St.
Wicker Park.
733-0098.

ART AND CRAFT SUPPLIES

Aiko's Art Materials
3347 N Clark St,
Lakeview.
(773) 404-5600.

International Importing Bead & Novelty Co.
111 N Wabash Ave.
Map 4 D1.
332-0061.

Paper Source
232 W Chicago Ave.
Map 1 C4.
337-0798.

Pearl Art & Craft Supplies
225 W Chicago Ave.
Map 1 C4.
915-0200.

Tom Thumb Hobby & Crafts
1026 Davis St, **Evanston**.
(847) 869-9575.

BOOKS

Afrocentric Bookstore
333 S State St.
Map 3 C2.
939-1956.

Barbara's Bookstore
233 S Wacker Dr,
Sears Tower. **Map** 3 B2.
466-0223.
One of several locations.

Chicago Architecture Foundation Shop
224 S Michigan Ave.
Map 4 D2.
922-3432.
One of two locations.

Europa Books
832 N State St.
Map 1 C3.
335-9677.

57th Street Books
1301 E 57th St.
Map 8 D4.
(773) 684-1300.

Powell's Bookstore
1501 E 57th St.
Map 8 D4.
(773) 955-7780.
One of two locations.

Tower Records
See Music, p159.

Transitions Bookplace
1000 W North Ave,
Lincoln Park.
951-7323.

Unabridged Books
3251 N Broadway,
Lakeview.
(773) 883-9119.

BUTTONS AND FABRICS

Fishman's Fabrics
1101 S Des Plaines St.
Map 3 A4.
922-7250.

Mayet Beads & Buttons
826 W Armitage Ave,
Lincoln Park.
(773) 883-9508.

Tender Buttons
946 N Rush St. **Map** 2 D3.
337-7033.

Vogue Fabrics
718 Main St, **Evanston**.
(847) 864-9600.
One of two locations.

CAMERAS AND ELECTRONICS

Bang & Olufsen
15 E Oak St. **Map** 2 D3.
787-6006.
One of two locations.

Central Camera
230 S Wabash Ave.
Map 4 D3.
427-5580.

Helix Camera & Video
70 W Madison Ave.
Map 3 C1.
444-9373.
One of several locations.

Sony Gallery
663 N Michigan Ave.
Map 2 D4.
943-3334.

United Audio
900 N Michigan Ave.
Map 2 D3.
664-3100.

COINS

Chicago Coin Company
6455 W Archer Ave,
Garfield Ridge.
(773) 586-7666.

Harlan J. Berk
31 N Clark St.
Map 3 C1.
609-0016.
One of three locations.

DISCOUNT CLOTHING

Filene's Basement
830 N Michigan Ave.
Map 2 D4.
482-8918.
One of two locations.

Marshall's
600 N Michigan Ave.
Map 2 D4.
280-7506.
One of three locations.

TJ Maxx
11 N State St.
Map 3 C1.
553-0515.
One of three locations.

DESIGNER CLOTHING

Barneys New York
25 E Oak St. **Map** 2 D3.
587-1700.

Betsey Johnson
72 E Oak St. **Map** 2 D3.
664-5901.

Giorgio Armani
113 E Oak St. **Map** 2 D3.
751-2244.

Prada
30 E Oak St. **Map** 2 D3.
951-1113.

Sugar Magnolia
34 E Oak St. **Map** 2 D3.
944-0885.

Ultimo
114 E Oak St.
Map 2 D3.
☏ 787-1171.

SHOES

Altman's Shoes
120 W Monroe St.
Map 3 C2.
☏ 332-0667.

Lori's Discount Designer Shoes
824 W Armitage Ave,
Lincoln Park.
☏ (773) 281-5655.

FURS AND LEATHERS

Alfred Dunhill
835 N Michigan Ave.
Map 2 D4.
☏ 467-4455.

Chicago Fur Mart
166 E Superior St.
Map 2 D4.
☏ 951-5000.

Elán Furs
675 N Michigan Ave.
Map 2 D4.
☏ 640-0707.

Glove Me Tender
900 N Michigan Ave.
Map 2 D3.
☏ 664-4022.

JEWELRY

Harold Burland & Son
5 S Wabash Ave,
suite 712. **Map** 4 D2.
☏ 332-5176.

Tiffany & Co.
730 N Michigan Ave.
Map 2 D4.
☏ 944-7500.

FOOD AND WINE SHOPS

House of Glunz
1206 N Wells St.
Map 1 C2.
☏ 642-3000.

Sam's Wines & Spirits
1720 N Marcey St,
Depaul.
☏ 664-4394.

Spice House
1941 Central St,
Evanston.
☏ (847) 328-3711.

Treasure Island
75 W Elm St.
Map 1 C3.
☏ 440-1144.
One of several locations.

Whole Foods
1000 W North Ave,
Lincoln Park.
☏ 587-0648.
One of several locations.

MARKETS

Daley Plaza Market
Richard J. Daley Center
Plaza, Washington &
Dearborn sts.
Map 3 C1.

Evanston Farmers' Market
☏ (847) 866-2936 for
*market times, location,
and further details.*

Farmers' Market Information Line
☏ 744-9187 for market
*times, locations, and
further details.*

Lincoln Park Market
Armitage Ave & Orchard
St, **Lincoln Park**.

Maxwell Street Market
Canal St between W
Taylor St & 15th Pl.
Map 3 B4–B5.
☏ 922-3100.

Near North Market
Division & Dearborn sts.
Map 1 C3.

GIFTS AND SOUVENIRS

Chicago Architecture Foundation Shop
See Books, p158.

City of Chicago Store
163 E Pearson St,
Chicago Water Works
Map 2 D4.
☏ 742-8811.

Gallery 37 Store
66 E Randolph St.
Map 4 D2.
☏ 744-7274.

Illinois Artisans Shop
100 W Randolph St.
Map 3 C2.
☏ 814-5321.

Illinois Marketplace
700 E Grand Ave, Navy
Pier. **Map** 2 F5.
☏ 595-5400.

HOME AND GARDEN FURNISHINGS

Jayson Home & Garden
1915 N Clybourn Ave,
Depaul.
☏ (773) 525-3100.

Restoration Hardware
938 W North Ave,
Lincoln Park.
☏ 475-9116.

Smith & Hawken
1/80 N Marcey St,
Depaul.
☏ 266-1988.

Urban Gardener
1006 W Armitage Ave,
Lincoln Park.
☏ (773) 477-2070.

MEMORABILIA

Yesterday
1143 W Addison St,
Lakeview.
☏ (773) 248-8087.

Metro Golden Memories
5425 W Addison St,
Portage Park.
☏ (773) 736-4133.

MUSIC

Dr. Wax Records
1203 N State St.
Map 1 C2.
☏ 255-0123.
One of several locations.

Jazz Record Mart
444 N Wabash Ave.
Map 2 D5.
☏ 222-1467.

Tower Records
214 S Wabash Ave.
Map 4 D2.
☏ 987-9044.
One of two locations.

Virgin Megastore
540 N Michigan Ave.
Map 2 D5.
☏ 645-9300.

SPORTING GOODS

Nike Town
669 N Michigan Ave.
Map 2 D4.
☏ 642-6363.

The North Face
875 N Michigan Ave.
Map 2 D3.
☏ 337-7200.

Vertel's Authentic Running & Fitness
24 S Michigan Ave.
Map 4 D2.
☏ 683-9600.

TOYS, GADGETS, AND SPECIALTY SHOPS

American Girl Place
111 E Chicago Ave.
Map 2 D4.
☏ 640-5895.

American Science and Surplus
5316 N Milwaukee Ave,
Norwood Park.
☏ (773) 763-0313.

F.A.O. Schwarz
840 N Michigan Ave.
Map 2 D4.
☏ 587-5000.

Hammacher Schlemmer
445 N Michigan Ave.
Map 2 D5.
☏ 527-9100.

Kite Harbor
109 N Marion St,
Oak Park.
☏ (708) 848-4907.

Sharper Image
835 N Michigan Ave.
Map 2 D4.
☏ 335-1600.

Think Small By Rosebud
3209 N Clark St,
Lakeview.
☏ (773) 477-1920.

ENTERTAINMENT IN CHICAGO

TENS OF MILLIONS OF DOLLARS have been spent in recent years by the City of Chicago to rejuvenate old theaters and build cultural attractions. Today, a portion of the money raised through the hotel tax *(see p132)* is channeled directly to the department of culture. And it shows. Chicago's world-class orchestras and opera, intimate jazz ensembles, high-profile musicals, and

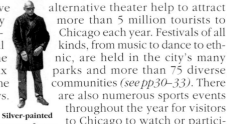

Silver-painted street performer

alternative theater help to attract more than 5 million tourists to Chicago each year. Festivals of all kinds, from music to dance to ethnic, are held in the city's many parks and more than 75 diverse communities *(see pp30–33)*. There are also numerous sports events throughout the year for visitors to Chicago to watch or participate in *(see pp162–3)*.

Chicago's listings magazine, *Reader*, published weekly

INFORMATION

THE CITY'S MOST complete entertainment listings are in the *Reader,* a free newspaper distributed Thursdays throughout Chicago. The *Reader* lists even the most obscure theatrical and musical events. *Chicago Magazine*, available at newsstands, is a glossy monthly with listings of the city's major venues. The two daily newspapers, the *Chicago Sun-Times* and the *Chicago Tribune,* publish an entertainment section in their Friday editions, with movie, music, dance, and theater reviews and listings.

Chicago's **Visitor Information Centers** sell tickets as well as providing entertainment information.

Moviephone provides recorded details of movie show times and theater locations, as well as brief descriptions of the movies.

Hot Tix, a ticket agency run by the League of Chicago Theatres, provides telephone show listings for $1 per minute. Proceeds support Chicago theaters.

Most hotels carry a wide selection of entertainment brochures, and hotel staff will help orient you and may

arrange for tickets. The **Mayor's Office of Special Events** also provides information on local events, including the numerous neighborhood festivals that take place during summer.

BUYING TICKETS

TICKETS for most major entertainment events are sold through **Ticketmaster**. You can buy tickets by phone or at one of its locations. You may be able to buy tickets for sold-out events from a ticket broker (see listings in the yellow pages of the telephone directory), but the price may be astronomical. Be wary of buying tickets from "scalpers" (ticket hawkers) on the street. Some try to sell tickets that are expired or counterfeit.

Many of the major concerts, plays, and musicals in Chicago are reviewed in the national press, which can lead to these shows selling out weeks in advance. It is best to buy tickets for such shows through a ticket agency or the

The Civic Opera House, home to the Lyric Opera of Chicago

venue's box office before arriving in Chicago.

Most people buy movie tickets at the theater. Prices range from $1.50 per ticket for second-run movies to $8.50 for first-run movies. You can buy tickets using a major credit card through **Moviephone**. This saves standing in line at the theater, but the tickets are nonrefundable and a surcharge of $1 to $2 is added to the price of each.

DISCOUNT TICKETS

HALF-PRICE TICKETS for shows on the day of performance are available from **Hot Tix**. These tickets must be purchased in person and paid for in cash or, at most locations, by credit card.

CityPass Traveler packages admissions to six of the top attractions in Chicago, saving you both time and money. The passes can be purchased through its website or at the participating venues.

TRAVELERS WITH DISABILITIES

MANY THEATERS and concert halls in Chicago are fully wheelchair accessible. Some of the smaller theaters and clubs try hard but are less than adequate when it comes to serving patrons with special needs. Even though a venue has the required seating area for persons in wheelchairs, the building may still be difficult to get around in.

Major theaters and halls provide amplifying headphones for people with hearing impairments.

The **Mayor's Office for People with Disabilities** provides details on which venues are accessible for people with disabilities.

FREE EVENTS

ACCOMPLISHED young musicians play every Wednesday as part of the Dame Myra Hess series of free noontime recitals at the **Chicago Cultural Center** *(see p52)*. Harold Washington Library Center *(see p82)* also hosts concerts, many free.

The best free seats in the city are in Grant Park and, beginning in spring 2002, in the new Millennium Park *(see p53)*. The first-rate Grant Park Symphony gives evening concerts, mid-June to mid-August, Wednesday to Sunday, in Grant Park. (See page 162 for details on other free music events.)

Grant Park is also home to many summertime festivals. The Gospel Festival kicks off the season early in June, followed by the renowned Blues Festival. A country-music festival is usually held in July. The season winds down with the Viva! Chicago Latin Music Festival at the end of August, followed by the Jazz and World Music festivals, held in September.

Throughout the summer, dozens of Chicago's neighborhoods block off streets to traffic and hold weekend festivals. Most are free or require a minimal entrance fee. Vendors sell refreshments, artists show arts and crafts, and local bands perform. You can hear great salsa, gritty rock and roll, country music, blues, or jazz

Buddy Guy, one of the world's greatest blues guitar soloists

Concert in Preston Bradley Hall at the Chicago Cultural Center

Sidewalk signs in the Loop's theater district

– sometimes all on the same day. These festivals are an excellent opportunity for visitors to experience Chicago's neighborhoods and mix with locals.

Oprah Winfrey, **Jenny Jones**, and **Jerry Springer** all tape their TV talk-shows in Chicago. Tickets to attend as part of the studio audience are free, but reserve at least one month in advance.

FREE-ADMISSION DAYS

Monday
Chicago Historical Society *(p74)*.
Shedd Aquarium *(pp96–7)*.
Tuesday
Adler Planetarium *(pp92–3)*.
Art Institute of Chicago *(pp46–9)*.
Brookfield Zoo (Oct–Mar; *p117)*.
Chicago Children's Museum (5–8pm; *p65)*.
Museum of Contemporary Art *(p65)*.
Terra Museum of American Art *(p63)*.
Wednesday
Field Museum *(pp86–9)*.
Thursday
Brookfield Zoo (Oct–Mar; *p117)*.
Museum of Science and Industry *(pp106–109)*.
Friday
Spertus Museum *(p84)*.
Sunday
DuSable Museum of African American History *(p104)*.

DIRECTORY

USEFUL NUMBERS

Chicago Cultural Center
📞 744-6630.
🌐 *www.ci.chi.il.us/Tourism/ CulturalCenter*

City Helpline
📞 *311 (event information)*.

Dance Hotline
📞 419-8383.

Mayor's Office for People with Disabilities
📞 744-6673.
🌐 *www.ci.chi.il.us/Disabilities*

Mayor's Office of Special Events
📠 744-3370.
🌐 *www.ci.chi.il.us/SpecialEvents*

Visitor Information Centers
📞 744-2400.
163 E Pearson St. **Map** 2 D4.
77 E Randolph St. **Map** 4 D1.
700 E Grand Ave. **Map** 2 F5.
🌐 *www.ci.chi.il.us/Tourism/ GeneralInfo/VisitorsInformation Centers.html*

TICKET AGENCIES

CityPass Traveler
🌐 *www.citypass.net*

Hot Tix
📠 977-1755 (hours, locations).
📠 (900) 225-2225 (show listings).
📞 902-1500 (arts line).
🌐 *www.theatrechicago.org/ hot-tix.html*

Moviephone
📠 444-3456.
🌐 *moviephone.com*

Ticketmaster
📞 559-1212.
🌐 *www.ticketmaster.com*

TV TALK-SHOWS

Jenny Jones Show
📞 836-9400.

Jerry Springer Show
📞 321-5365.

Oprah Winfrey Show
📞 591-9222.

Arts, Film, and Sports

WHEN IT COMES TO ENTERTAINMENT, Chicago is second to none. The Chicago Symphony and the Lyric Opera are both world-class, while Steppenwolf Theatre grew from its beginnings in a basement to become one of the leading theater troupes in the country. Chicago also has its share of art film houses. Many events take place at the city's 550 parks and playgrounds. Ravinia Festival, in Highland Park, showcases music and dance throughout the summer. Spectator sports, especially baseball, are also enormously popular in Chicago, the numerous teams providing year-round entertainment.

MUSIC

THE GUIDING LIGHT of classical music in Chicago is the **Chicago Symphony Orchestra**. From September through June, it performs at **Symphony Center**. During the summer, it performs at the **Ravinia Festival**.

The highly acclaimed **Lyric Opera of Chicago** presents lavish productions and brings international stars to **Civic Opera House** during its September-to-March season.

Music of the Baroque is Chicago's leading early-music ensemble. A consortium of Chicago's finest musicians, **Chicago Chamber Musicians** presents a series of free concerts throughout the year at the **Chicago Cultural Center**, held on the first Monday of each month.

Chicago's two world-class string quartets are the venerable **Vermeer String Quartet** and the **Chicago String Quartet**. Both perform frequently at the **DePaul University Concert Hall**.

Mandel Hall at University of Chicago hosts folk, jazz, and classical groups. Northwestern University presents concerts by leading touring ensembles at **Pick-Staiger Auditorium**.

DANCE

THE UNIQUE BLEND of jazz, ballet, and modern dance that **Hubbard Street Dance Chicago** offers will transport you to new places in entertainment. Performances take place at **Shubert Theatre** from September to May.

Each season, **Joffrey Ballet of Chicago** presents four performances of classical ballet with a contemporary edge, reflecting the dance company's mandate to present the works of 20th-century American artists.

THEATER

CHICAGO HAS A vibrant theater scene. **Goodman Theater**'s new home is located in the Loop's theater district. The troupe presents contemporary plays as well as the classics directed with a fresh approach. Productions often star well-known stage and screen actors.

Nearby is the restored **Ford Center for the Performing Arts Oriental Theater**, which, along with **Shubert Theatre**, brings Broadway productions to the city. The **Chicago Theatre** is a multi-purpose venue that presents concerts and theater. The **Auditorium Theatre** (*see p42*) hosts mainstream musicals such as *Les Miserables* and *Showboat*.

Since its inception in a church basement, **Steppenwolf Theatre Company** has gained a national reputation for staging avant-garde plays. Although many of the actors who started at Steppenwolf, such as John Malkovich and Laurie Metcalf, have left, they frequently return to perform with the company or direct.

Shakespeare Repertory Company stages three productions a year in **Chicago Shakespeare Theater**, its new courtyard-style theater at Navy Pier.

Performing Arts Chicago brings in cutting-edge theater, dance, music, and puppetry groups. Performances are held at various venues.

Many notable theaters are located near Lincoln Park and in Lakeview, among them the **Ivanhoe Theater** and the **Victory Gardens Theater**.

SUMMER PERFORMANCES

CHICAGO'S SUMMER HOME for the performing arts is in idyllic Highland Park, 25 miles (40 km) north of the city, at the internationally celebrated **Ravinia Festival**. Chicago Symphony Orchestra performs here, as do leading jazz ensembles, pop and folk acts, children's performers, and dance troupes, including Hubbard Street Dance and the Joffrey Ballet of Chicago.

The park's sound system is excellent. Reserved seats in the pavilion cost from $15 to $60. General admission to the park costs about $10.

Although Highland Park has several good restaurants, most people buy general-admission tickets, bring a picnic dinner (some, lavish spreads with candles, crystal, and fine wine), and sit on the lawn to enjoy the performances.

FILM

LIKE MOST CITIES, Chicago has a cinema multiplex in almost every neighborhood showing first-run movies. There are also several art film houses in the city.

The **Fine Arts Theater** shows mainstream foreign and American art films. **The Music Box** is a fully restored 1929 movie palace designed to look as though you are outdoors at night. It shows an eclectic mix of foreign, American independent, and classic films. An organist entertains with vintage popular music during intermission on weekend evenings.

The **Film Center at the School of the Art Institute of Chicago** presents a wide range of standard-setting international cinema. Panel discussion and lectures provide context for the films.

Facets Multimedia has a small screening room where current innovative films from around the world – from South America to Eastern Europe to Africa – are shown. The theater also hosts retrospectives of great directors such as Alfred Hitchcock and Jean-Luc Godard. Facets has the country's largest collection of videos for rent or sale.

SPECTATOR SPORTS

CHICAGO BOASTS several professional sports teams, including two baseball teams. The **Chicago White Sox** play for the American League at the new **Comiskey Park** on the city's South Side. The much-loved-but-often-disappointing **Chicago Cubs** of the National League play in

Wrigley Field, a marvelous inner-city stadium in the north end of Chicago (see p114).

The formerly great **Chicago Bulls** (winners of five world championships in the 1990s) play basketball at the **United Center**, as does Chicago's hockey team, the **Chicago Blackhawks**. The inimitable **Chicago Bears** play football at **Soldier Field**.

DIRECTORY

MUSIC

Chicago Chamber Musicians
[225-5226.

Chicago Cultural Center
78 E Washington St.
Map 4 D1.
[744-6630.

Chicago String Quartet
[225-5226.

Chicago Symphony Orchestra
See Symphony Center.

Civic Opera House
20 N Wacker Dr.
Map 3 B1.
[419-0033.

DePaul University Concert Hall
804 W Belden Ave,
Lincoln Park.
[(773) 325-7664.

Lyric Opera of Chicago
See Civic Opera House.

Mandel Hall
University of Chicago,
5706 S University Ave.
Map 7 C4.
[(773) 702-8787.

Music of the Baroque
[551-1415.

Pick-Staiger Auditorium
Northwestern University,
1977 S Campus Dr,
Evanston.

[(847) 467-7425.
[(847) 491-5441.

Symphony Center
220 S Michigan Ave.
Map 4 D2.
[294-3000.

Vermeer String Quartet
[(773) 722-5463.

DANCE

Hubbard Street Dance Chicago
[850-9744.

Joffrey Ballet of Chicago
[739-0120.

THEATER

Auditorium Theatre
50 E Congress Pkwy.
Map 4 D3.
[922-2110.

Chicago Shakespeare Theater
800 E Grand Ave.
Map 2 F5.
[595-5600.

Chicago Theatre
175 N State St.
Map 3 C1.
[443-1130.

Ford Center for the Performing Arts Oriental Theater
24 W Randolph St.
Map 3 C1.
[902-1500.

Goodman Theater
170 N Dearborn St.

Map 3 C1.
[443-3800.

Ivanhoe Theater
750 W Wellington Ave,
Lakeview.
[975-7171.

Performing Arts Chicago
[(773) 722-5463.

Shakespeare Repertory Company
See Chicago Shakespeare Theater.

Shubert Theatre
22 W Monroe St.
Map 3 C2.
[722-5463.

Steppenwolf Theatre Company
1650 N Halsted St,
Lincoln Park.
[335-1650.

Victory Gardens
2257 N Lincoln Ave,
Lincoln Park.
[(773) 871-3000.

SUMMER PERFORMANCES

Ravinia Festival
Green Bay & Lake Cook Rds, Highland Park.
[(847) 266-5100 or (800) 433-8819.

FILM

Facets Multimedia
1517 W Fullerton Ave,
Depaul.
[(773) 281-4114.

Film Center at the School of the Art Institute of Chicago

280 S Columbus Dr.
Map 4 D2.
[443-3737.

Fine Arts Theater
410 S Michigan Ave.
Map 4 D2.
[939-3700.

The Music Box
3733 N Southport Ave,
Lakeview.
[(773) 871-6604.

SPECTATOR SPORTS

Chicago Bears
[(847) 295-6600.

Chicago Blackhawks
[455-7000.

Chicago Bulls
[559-1212 (tickets).

Chicago Cubs
[(773) 831-2827.

Chicago White Sox
[831-1769.

Comiskey Park
333 W 35th St.
Map 5 B5–C5.
[674-1000.

Soldier Field
425 E McFetridge Dr.
Map 4 E5.
[747-1285.

United Center
1901 W Madison St,
Near West Side.
[455-4500.

Wrigley Field
1060 W Addison Ave,
Lakeview.
[(773) 404-2827.

Taverns, Nightclubs, and Live Music

CHICAGOANS HAVE A REPUTATION for working hard and playing hard. Nowhere is the latter more evident than in the city's night life. The blues are a Chicago institution, but jazz, country, folk, and rock music thrive here as well. Acts both big and small play almost nightly, and many music venues are open into the early hours of the morning. Chicago night-life establishments tend to be clustered together. Singles' bars are gathered at the corner of Division and State streets, bars frequented by the college crowd abound on Lincoln Avenue. Clark Street near Wrigley Field, in Chicago's north end, has numerous sports bars. The gay scene is concentrated in the Lakeview neighborhood; Wicker Park offers a variety of alternative-music nightclubs.

BARS AND TAVERNS

BARS AND TAVERNS are tucked into every neighborhood of Chicago. Some are rather basic drinking places, but others offer a glimpse into neighborhood life. Most bars in Chicago have limited food choices. Taverns, on the other hand, are serious about food. The American version of European pubs and bistros, taverns are relaxed places where locals go to eat, drink, and socialize.

The most venerable of the downtown taverns is **The Berghoff**. This establishment was the first in Chicago to be issued a liquor license once Prohibition ended. Some days it may seem that everyone in the Berghoff is from out of town, but locals also love this tavern. Two other notable downtown pubs are **Miller's Pub** and **Exchequer Restaurant & Pub**. Both succeed in maintaining a neighborhood atmosphere while catering to a good number of tourists.

Near the Magnificent Mile is **Boston Blackie's**, a dimly lit Art Deco-style sports bar. **Bar Louie**, a handsome bar with good drinks and large menu, is a great place to mingle with the upwardly mobile.

Butch McGuire's has a major presence on the bar-lined block of Division Street near the Gold Coast. Its atmosphere is pub-like, the food good (especially brunch).

When the city celebrates a sports victory, fans celebrate in the many singles and sports bars near Division, Dearborn, and Rush streets.

Summer in Chicago is a great time to sit outside, enjoy a drink, and people-watch. There are several good beer gardens and patios in Lincoln Park. **John Barleycorn's** and **Charlie's Ale House** are two of the best. Nearby, **Ranalli's** serves good pizza and beer. **Goose Island Brewpub** sells brews made on the premises, some of the finest in town.

NIGHTCLUBS

CHICAGO offers a variety of nightclubs: there is sure to be one to suit your taste. Expect to pay an admission charge, though some clubs may impose a drink-order minimum instead.

Excalibur is perhaps the most mainstream club in the city. Pool tables and video games fill the first floor; the dance floor is upstairs, where retrospective music is played.

If you are into tattoos and body-piercings, visit **CroBar**. With the city's largest dance floor, complete with go-go dancers, it plays a mix of hip-hop, techno, and rock music.

Liquid presents live bands Wednesday through Saturday, as well as offering swing dance lessons for beginners on weekday evenings. Salsa and merengue lessons are offered on the weekends.

For those with little time, **Party Bus Tours** offers a tour of four of the city's top night-clubs on a Saturday evening.

JAZZ

LIVE JAZZ, from salsa to swing, is played almost every night at the stylish **Green Dolphin Street**. The **Green Mill Cocktail Lounge** may not be impressive from the outside, and its Uptown neighborhood may be slightly run-down, but it is one of the city's coolest jazz clubs, presenting great local bands. The Art Deco design adds to the club's ambiance.

Jazz Showcase is the best place in Chicago to hear top jazz artists perform.

BLUES

MAJOR BLUES acts are presented at the **House of Blues**, a 1,500-seat venue with superb acoustics.

More intimate blues venues include **B.L.U.E.S.**, a small, busy bar with a friendly atmosphere that offers live music every night of the week. **Kingston Mines** also features nightly live blues on its two stages. Both stay open into the early morning hours.

Buddy Guy's Legends brings the big-name acts downtown. Guy himself plays here each January.

FOLK AND COUNTRY MUSIC

THE CITY'S LEADING venue for folk music is the **Old Town School of Folk Music**. The **Abbey Pub** features local and touring groups, favoring Irish bands. It also offers barn dancing every Monday night.

Heartland Cafe is a throwback to the 1960s. It is a healthfood restaurant that also presents poetry readings, storytelling, and live music. **Schubas** is a neighborhood gem showcasing live folk and country music.

Although most of the line-dancing and two-stepping action is in the suburbs, it surprisingly can also be found in the city, at **Charlie's**. A gay bar serious about country music, Charlie's always welcomes straight folks.

ROCK MUSIC

ROCK MUSIC is alive and well in Chicago. At **Brother Jimmy's**, bands play rock music from the 1970s onward while patrons experience authentic Southern cooking in the form of barbecued ribs.

House of Blues presents big-name rock stars. **Cubby Bear**, across from Wrigley Field (see p114), is a huge sports bar that presents local bands and touring talents, whereas **Metro**, in Lakeview

(see p114), is an independent-rock and dancing mecca. Wicker Park's (see p114) intimate **Double Door** is an excellent place to see live music. Many famous groups, such as the Smashing Pumpkins and the Rolling Stones, play here under fictitious names, to the delight of unsuspecting patrons.

The **Wild Hare** is the city's best venue for live and reggae and African music. National or international acts are presented here nightly.

COMEDY CLUBS

FOR WELL-KNOWN stand-up comedy acts, visit **Zanies**. Comedians Jerry Seinfeld and Jay Leno have entertained here.

Second City, the celebrated venue that produced many of the comedians who went on to *Saturday Night Live* fame, offers a mix of social-satire sketches and improvisation. Dinner-theater packages are available. Its offshoot, **Second City E.T.C.**, presents comedy revues next door.

DIRECTORY

BARS AND TAVERNS

Bar Louie
226 W Chicago Ave.
Map 1 C4.
☎ 337-3313.

The Berghoff
17 W Adams St.
Map 3 C2.
☎ 427-3170.

Boston Blackie's
164 E Grand Ave.
Map 2 D5.
☎ 938-8700.

Butch McGuire's
20 W Division St.
Map 1 C3.
☎ 337-9080.

Charlie's Ale House
1224 W Webster Ave,
Lincoln Park.
☎ (773) 871-1440.

Exchequer Restaurant & Pub
226 S Wabash Ave.
Map 4 D2.
☎ 939-5633.

Goose Island Brewpub
1800 N Clybourn Ave.
Map 1 A1.
☎ 915-0071.
One of two locations.

John Barleycorn's
658 W Belden Ave,
Lincoln Park.
☎ (773) 348-8899.

Miller's Pub
134 S Wabash Ave.
Map 4 D2.
☎ 263-4988.

Ranalli's
1925 N Lincoln Ave,
Lincoln Park.
☎ 642-4700.

NIGHTCLUBS

CroBar
1543 N Kingsbury St.
Map 1 A1.
☎ 413-7000.

Excalibur
632 N Dearborn St.
Map 1 C4.
☎ 266-1944.

Liquid
1997 N Clybourn Ave,
Lincoln Park.
☎ (773) 528-3400.

Party Bus Tours
☎ 266-7330.

JAZZ

Green Dolphin Street
2200 N Ashland Ave,
Bucktown.
☎ (773) 395-0066.

Green Mill Cocktail Lounge
4802 N Broadway Ave,
Uptown.
☎ (773) 878-5552.

Jazz Showcase
59 W Grand Ave.
Map 1 C5.
☎ 670-2473.

BLUES

B.L.U.E.S.
2519 N Halsted St,
Lincoln Park.
☎ 409-7090.

Buddy Guy's Legends
754 S Wabash Ave.
Map 4 D3.
☎ 427-0333.

House of Blues
329 N Dearborn St.
Map 1 C5.
☎ 527-2583 or
923-2000 (tickets).

Kingston Mines
2548 N Halsted St,
Lincoln Park.
☎ (773) 477-4646.

FOLK AND COUNTRY MUSIC

Abbey Pub
3420 W Grace St,
Northwest Side.
☎ (773) 478-4408.

Charlie's
3726 N Broadway Ave,
Lakeview.
☎ (773) 871-8887.

Heartland Cafe
7000 N Glenwood Ave,
Rogers Park.
☎ (773) 465-8005.

Old Town School of Folk Music
4544 N Lincoln Ave,
Lincoln Square.
☎ (773) 525-7793 or
(773) 728-6000.

Schubas
3159 N Southport Ave,
Lakeview.
☎ (773) 525-2508.

ROCK MUSIC

Brother Jimmy's
2909 N Sheffield Ave,
Lakeview.
☎ (773) 528-0888.

Cubby Bear
1059 W Addison Ave,
Lakeview.
☎ (773) 327-1662.

Double Door
1572 N Milwaukee Ave,
Wicker Park.
☎ (773) 489-3160.

Metro
3730 N Clark St,
Wrigleyville.
☎ (773) 549-3604.

Wild Hare
3530 N Clark St,
Lakeview.
☎ (773) 327-4273.

COMEDY CLUBS

Second City
1616 N Wells St.
Map 1 C2.
☎ 337-3992.

Second City E.T.C.
1608 N Wells St.
Map 1 C2.
☎ 337-3992.

Zanies
1548 N Wells St.
Map 1 C1.
☎ 337-4027.

SURVIVAL
GUIDE

PRACTICAL INFORMATION

CHICAGO LOVES VISITORS. Its Visitor Information Centers are an invaluable source of information, and a stop at one of them should be on every traveler's itinerary. The centers also have details of the many tours available, an excellent way to see the many different faces of Chicago. Getting around the city is both easy and

Newspaper box

safe, if you follow a few guidelines *(see pp170–71)*. The practical information that follows offers a variety of tips, from locating banks *(see pp172–3)* to making a local phone call *(see pp174–5)*. There is also a section on transit in and around Chicago, as well as details on how to get downtown upon your arrival in Chicago *(see pp176–83)*.

VISITOR INFORMATION

THE **Illinois Bureau of Tourism** will mail you information about Illinois hotels, restaurants, and attractions. The **Chicago Convention and Tourism Bureau**'s website will also help you plan your trip. Upon your arrival in Chicago, visit one of the three **Visitor Information Centers** for maps, entertainment and tour brochures, tickets, public transportation passes, and general information.

Sign for one of the city tourist offices

OPENING HOURS

MOST BUSINESSES are open from 9am to 5pm weekdays and do not close for lunch. Banks are generally open weekdays from 9am to 5pm. Some bank branches open from 9am to early afternoon on Saturdays.

Most major museums are open daily from 9am to 5pm, often with later hours on one weekday night. Smaller museums keep more limited hours; phone for details.

Banks and museums usually close on major holidays.

ETIQUETTE

SMOKING IS PROHIBITED in public buildings and airports, except in designated areas. Restaurants provide separate seating areas for smokers. Smoking is usually permitted in the bar area. Some establishments have cigar rooms, but most do not permit cigar or pipe smoking.

Tipping is integral to Chicago's service industry. For

details on restaurant tipping, see page 143. Tip $1 per coat checked; taxi drivers, hairdressers, and bartenders, from 10 to 15 percent. Tip hotel or airport porters up to $1 per bag, valet-parking attendants $1 after they bring you your car. Tip tour drivers between $2 and $3 per group member. If a concierge was especially helpful, acknowledge it by tipping between $5 and $10.

MUSEUMS

MUSEUMS either charge an admission fee or suggest a donation. Expect a separate charge to special exhibits. Smaller museums are often free. Entrance to large museums may be free either once a week or once a month *(see p161)*. Tours are often free.

Museum Campus, a park on the lakefront, is home to the Field Museum *(see pp86–9)*, Shedd Aquarium *(see pp96–7)*, and Adler Planetarium *(see pp92–3)*. Free trolleys run between these museums and public transportation stations. Call the **Museum Campus Information Line** for details.

GUIDED TOURS

EXCELLENT WALKING, bicycle, bus, and boat tours are offered by the **Chicago Architecture Foundation** (CAF). A fabulous way to discover a few of Chicago's 77 neighborhoods is to take one of the Saturday tours offered by **Chicago Neighborhood Tours**. **American Sightseeing** offers two-hour narrated tours. **Chicago Trolley Charters** sells an all-

day pass for tours aboard old-fashioned trolleys. **University of Chicago Walking Tours** *(see pp100–101)* are led by students on Saturdays.

Boat tour season is from April to October. **Wendella Sightseeing** offers evening and lakefront tours. **Mercury, Chicago's Skyline Cruiseline** has narrated 90-minute tours. **Shoreline Sightseeing** offers 30-minute narrated tours on Lake Michigan.

Many companies offer discounts when two or more tours per person are purchased; be sure to ask.

Antique Coach and Carriage will pick you up at your hotel or a restaurant in a horse-drawn buggy.

New to the city are Italianstyle gondola rides on the Chicago River, offering a unique view of downtown.

A river cruise tour offered by the Chicago Architecture Foundation

NEWSPAPERS

CHICAGO HAS TWO major dailies: *Chicago Tribune* and *Chicago Sun-Times*. The *Chicago Defender* is published weekdays, primarily for

Special-interest newspapers in Chicago

the city's African-American readership. Business news is found in the weekly *Crain's*. For details on entertainment news, see page 160. Foreign newspapers are available at Europa Books *(see p156)*.

CUSTOMS AND IMMIGRATION

HOLDERS of a valid EU passport and a return ticket do not need a visa if staying 90 days or less in the US. Canadians need only to show proof of their residence. New Zealanders and Australians need a current passport, tourist visa, and onward or return ticket. Foreign visitors may need to prove they carry sufficient funds for survival. Check current requirements and stipulations with your travel agent or the US embassy in your country.

TRAVELERS WITH DISABILITIES

ALL FACILITIES operated by the city are wheelchair accessible. Most attractions, buildings (including restaurants), and public transportation are equipped for easy access. However, small entertainment venues may not be. Parking spaces reserved for vehicles with disabled permits are marked by the handicapped symbol either on a sign or painted on the concrete.

Phone the **Mayor's Office for People with Disabilities** for information.

STUDENTS AND SENIORS

MANY businesses offer student and senior discounts. For seniors, all that is needed is picture identification with their birthdate on it.

Students will need current student photo ID. An international student ID card is widely accepted. Purchase one at your local youth travel association or

hostel organization. The card can also be purchased from **Council Travel** with proper credentials.

CONVERSION CHART

Imperial to Metric:
1 inch = 2.5 centimeters
1 foot = 30 centimeters
1 mile = 1.6 kilometers
1 ounce = 28 grams
1 pound = 454 grams
1 US pint = 0.5 liter
1 US gallon = 3.8 liters

Metric to Imperial:
1 millimeter = 0.04 inch
1 centimeter = 0.4 inch
1 meter = 3 feet 3 inches
1 kilometer = 0.6 mile
1 gram = 0.04 ounce

Bear in mind that 1 US pint (0.5 liter) is a smaller measure than 1 UK pint (0.6 liter).

ELECTRICITY

ALL US electric current flows at a standardized 110 to 120 volts AC (alternating current). You may need an adapter plug and voltage converter that fits standard US electrical outlets. US plugs have two flat prongs. Batteries are readily available.

Standard US two-pin plug

DIRECTORY

VISITOR INFORMATION

Chicago Convention and Tourism Bureau
📞 567-8500.
🌐 www.chicago.il.org

Illinois Bureau of Tourism
📞 (800) 226-66328.
🌐 www.enjoyillinois.com

Visitor Information Centers
📞 744-2400.
Chicago Cultural Center
77 E Randolph St. **Map 4**
D1. 🕐 10am–6pm Mon–Fri; 10am–5pm Sat, Sun.
⬤ major public hols.

Chicago Water Works
163 E Pearson St. **Map 2**
D4. 🕐 7:30am–7pm daily
⬤ major public hols.

Navy Pier
700 E Grand Ave. **Map 2**
F5. 🕐 10am–8pm Sun–Thu; 10am–10pm Fri, Sat.

GUIDED TOURS

American Sightseeing
📞 251-3100.

Antique Coach and Carriage
📞 787-1349.

Chicago Architecture Foundation
📞 922-8687.

224 S Michigan Ave,
Santa Fe Building.
Map 4 D2.
or
875 N Michigan Ave, John
Hancock Center.
Map 2 D3.

Chicago Neighborhood Tours
📞 742-1190.

Chicago Trolley Charters
📞 663-0260.

Mercury, Chicago's Skyline Cruiseline
📞 332-1353.

Shoreline Sightseeing
📞 222-0936.

University of Chicago Walking Tours
📞 (773) 702-9636.

Wendella Sightseeing
📞 337-1446.

USEFUL NUMBERS

Council Travel
1160 N State St.
Map 1 C3.
📞 951-0585.

Mayor's Office for People with Disabilities
📞 744-6673.

Museum Campus Information Line
📞 409-9696.

Personal Security and Health

CHICAGO IS A FRIENDLY CITY, and most visitors do not encounter any problems. However, it is always best to take common-sense precautions and be aware of your surroundings. If you don't feel safe, you probably aren't. Public transportation is generally safe during the day, but after dark, you may feel more comfortable taking a taxi to your destination. The best source of information is often your hotel concierge. Don't hesitate to ask if your destination or day's itinerary will take you into unsavory neighborhoods. Parks and the paths along the lakefront are populated during the day but are often fairly deserted at night.

Osco Drug, many locations with a 24-hour pharmacy

LAW ENFORCEMENT

THE CHICAGO Police Department has bicycle, motorcycle, car, and foot patrols day and night. There is also a police presence at major community and cultural events. Police officers are usually very helpful if approached, but be mindful: they are not tour guides.

Parking-enforcement and traffic officers make their rounds on foot or in small vehicles. Airports, stores, and hotels have uniformed and plain-clothes staff who also provide security services.

PERSONAL SAFETY

IN RECENT YEARS, violent crime has decreased in Chicago. However, petty crime is still a problem. Your best protection is common sense. Never walk in dark alleys or deserted streets. Don't leave purses or valuables unattended in public places, and don't carry a lot of cash or wear flashy jewelry. Keep one credit card in a concealed secondary

Chicago Fire Department on early-morning firefighting duty

wallet or in the hotel safe. Keep your wallet in an inconspicuous place, and have enough change handy for phone calls and bus fares. Defeat purse snatchers by carrying your bag with the clasp facing toward you and the shoulder strap across your body. Carry your passport separate from your money.

Do not allow anyone other than hotel and airport personnel to carry your belongings. Stow valuables in the room or hotel safe, keeping an inventory of items you deposit. Chicago's homeless sell the newspaper *Streetwise* for $1. Buying the paper is a help to the homeless. Otherwise, do not give money to, or make eye contact with, people asking for spare change.

Much of Chicago's West Side and South Side are inhospitable. Notable exceptions are Little Italy, Chinatown, Hyde Park, and Pullman. Some safe North Side neighborhoods are next to troubled areas. And, like most US cities, the downtown is primarily a business district: bustling during the day and quiet at night. While the Loop is becoming busier during the evenings, in part because of its theater district, caution should still be exercised.

Chicago parks are safest when crowds are present. Avoid parks after dark, unless you're attending a special event held in one. If you want to go for a jog, ask the concierge at your hotel to map out a safe route.

Finally, be sure you fully understand your hotel's fire-escape procedures.

MEDICAL MATTERS

MANY WALK-IN medical and dental clinics in Chicago are open 24-hours, and are often sufficient for minor injuries and ailments.

Without medical insurance, medical services can be expensive. Even with insurance, you may have to pay for the services yourself, then claim reimbursement from your insurance company.

Traveler's checks or cash are sometimes the only methods of payment accepted from visitors, though many practitioners take credit cards. Anyone taking a prescription drug should ask their doctor for an extra supply to take with them and a copy of the prescription in case more is needed. Both **Walgreen's** and **Osco Drug** have pharmacies open 24-hours. Call them to find the location nearest you.

EMERGENCIES

CALL 911 for emergencies requiring medical, police, or fire services. For non-emergency police situations, such as theft, dial 311, to reach the **City HelpLine**.

Hospital emergency rooms and city hospitals are listed in the Yellow Pages of the telephone directory. Most Chicago hospitals have 24-hour emergency rooms. Your hotel concierge will know the one closest to the hotel. **Northwestern Memorial Hospital** has an emergency room convenient to both

Police car

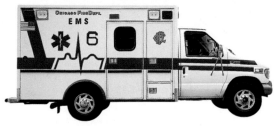

Emergency ambulance

Fire boat

downtown and North Side visitors. It also provides a **Physician Referral Service**. The **Bernard A. Mitchell Hospital**, at the University of Chicago, serves the city's South Side.

Private hospitals are listed in the Yellow Pages of the telephone directory. Or, your hotel may be able to arrange for a doctor or dentist to visit you in your room.

For dental emergencies, call the **Chicago Dental Society**, which provides referrals 24 hours a day, every day.

LOST PROPERTY

THE CHANCE of recovering stolen property is poor. Nevertheless, you should report all lost or stolen items to the police. Keep a copy of the police report if you plan to make an insurance claim.

The Chicago Police Department has a location at O'Hare Airport; call if you have misplaced something at the airport other than at a restaurant or on a plane.

Most credit card companies have toll-free numbers to call to report a loss, as do Thomas Cook and American Express (see p173) if you lose or have your traveler's checks stolen.

If you lose your passport, contact your embassy or consulate immediately.

TRAVEL INSURANCE

TRAVEL INSURANCE coverage of a minimum of $1 million is strongly recommended, mainly because of the high cost of medical care in the US. Among the most important features the policy should cover are accidental death, dismemberment, emergency medical and dental care, trip cancellation, and lost or stolen baggage coverage. Your travel agent or insurance company should be able to recommend a suitable policy, but it is worth shopping around for the best deal.

Rush - Presbyterian - St. Luke's Medical Center

Sign outside a Chicago medical center

DIRECTORY

CRISIS INFORMATION

All Emergencies
911 for police, fire, and medical services.

City HelpLine
311 for nonemergency police situations and City services.

Illinois Poison Center
(800) 942-5969.

Emergency Rooms
Bernard A. Mitchell Hospital, 901 E 58th St. **Map** 7 B4.
(773) 702-6250.

Northwestern Memorial Hospital, 250 E Superior St. **Map** 2 D4.
908-5222.

Medical Referrals
Chicago Dental Society Referrals
726-7290 or (630) 978-5745.

Physician Referral Service at Northwestern Memorial Hospital
(877) 926-4664 (toll free).

24-Hour Pharmacies
Osco Drug
(800) 654-6726.

Walgreen's Drugstore
(800) 925-4733.

LOST PROPERTY

Midway Airport
(773) 838-3003.

O'Hare Airport Police
(773) 686-2385.

Public Transit
Chicago Transit Authority
664-7200.

Metra at Union Station
322-4269.

Regional Transit Authority (RTA)
917-0734.

Lost or Stolen Credit Cards

American Express
(800) 327-2177.

MasterCard
(800) 307-7309.

VISA
(800) 847-2911.

Banking and Local Currency

MOST NATIONAL AND INTERNATIONAL banks have branches in Chicago. The cheapest exchange, though, may be offered on your credit or debit card, which can be used at most ATMs (automated teller machines). It is a good idea to arrive in Chicago with about $100 cash in US currency, including a few dollars in coins, to cover incidental costs until you are able to exchange your money.

BANKING

BANKS ARE GENERALLY open Monday to Friday from 9am to 5pm; 9am to early or mid-afternoon on Saturday.

Many banks charge fees to use a teller for routine matters

Logos of two major Chicago banks

such as withdrawing money. Always ask if any fees apply before making a transaction with a bank teller.

The major consumer banks in Chicago include **Bank One, LaSalle Bank**, and **Harris Trust and Savings**. Credit unions will usually serve only their members.

AUTOMATED TELLER MACHINES

THERE IS NO NEED to carry large amounts of cash in Chicago. Hundreds of automated teller machines (ATMs) can be found throughout the city. They are almost always in bank lobbies or on an outside wall near the bank's entrance, as well as in many convenience and grocery stores. Some bars and fast-food outlets also have ATMs on their premises.

US currency, usually in $20 bills, can be electronically withdrawn from your bank or credit-card account through an ATM. Ask your bank at home which American ATM network your card can access in Chicago, and what transaction fees will apply.

Cirrus and **Plus** are common networks in Chicago. You can also do transactions with some credit cards at ATMs.

Use ATMs only in secure conditions, daylight hours, or when there are plenty of people nearby in order to deter robbers.

CREDIT CARDS

CREDIT CARDS allow you to carry minimal cash and may offer merchandise guarantees or other benefits. American Express, Diners Club, MasterCard, and VISA are widely accepted.

Most hotels ask for a credit-card number to guarantee a reservation, taking an imprint of the card when you check in. Car rental agencies insist on a credit-card guarantee even if you are paying for the rental in cash (see p183).

Credit cards are very helpful in emergencies, should you have to fly home on short notice or need medical treatment during your stay. Many hospitals will accept a major credit card as a method of payment.

EXCHANGING MONEY

EXCHANGE RATES are printed in the daily newspapers and posted in banks where exchange services are offered, usually at the main branches of large banks. Some banks have designated tellers for foreign exchange.

Foreign exchange brokers in Chicago are few. Among the solidly established is **Thomas Cook**. **World's Money Exchange** also deals in foreign currency. Two

exchanges are located at O'Hare Airport, in terminals 3 and 5 (open daily); there are no currency exchanges at Midway Airport. Keep in mind, however, that an ATM may provide a better exchange rate and charge a lower transaction fee than a bank or exchange bureau.

Chicago has hundreds of state-regulated "currency exchanges." Most do not exchange foreign currency but instead cash checks, sell money orders, and offer notary services.

CASHING TRAVELER'S CHECKS

TRAVELER'S CHECKS issued by American Express and **Thomas Cook** in US dollars are widely accepted without a fee by most shops, hotels, and restaurants, if accompanied by a recognized form of photographic identification, such as a passport, driver's license, or international student card (see p169).

US-dollar traveler's checks can be cashed at most banks. Checks in foreign currency can be cashed at a bank branch offering foreign-currency exchange, usually the banks' main locations.

American Express and Thomas Cook will cash their own checks at no fee.

Automated teller machine (ATM)

Coins

*American coins (actual size shown)
come in 1-, 5- , 10-, and 25-cent, as
well as $1, denominations; 50-cent
pieces are minted but rarely used.
Each value of coin has a popular
name: 1-cent coins are known as
pennies, 5-cent coins as nickels, 10-
cent coins as dimes, 25-cent coins as
quarters, and 1-dollar coins (and
bills) as bucks.*

**25-cent coin
(a quarter)**

**10-cent coin
(a dime)**

**5-cent coin
(a nickel)**

**1-cent coin
(a penny)**

**1-dollar coin
(a buck)**

Bank Notes

*Units of currency in the US are dollars
and cents, with 100 cents to a dollar.
Notes, or "bills," come in $1, $2, $5,
$10, $20, $50, and $100 denomina-
tions. The $2 bills are rarely seen. The
US mint plans to gradually replace the
$1 bill with the new "golden dollar"
coin. New versions of the $20, $50, and
$100 bills are the same color as the old
versions, but the presidential portraits
are larger and positioned off center.*

1-dollar bill ($1)

5-dollar bill ($5)

20-dollar bill ($20)

50-dollar bill ($50)

100-dollar bill ($100)

Communications

Express Mail box

CHICAGO'S COMMUNICATION systems are, for the most part, both efficient and reasonably priced. Public pay phones are located throughout the city, and at gas stations and tourist centers along the interstates. Ameritech is the major player in the Chicago telecommunications field, though it has been seeing healthy competition recently. Regular letter service offered by the US postal system is reliable, if slow; two express services and independent courier services are also available. Visitors will find that Internet, e-mail, and fax services are readily available in Chicago at business centers and Internet cafés, as well as at many hotels.

CHICAGO TIME

Chicago is on Central Standard Time (CST). It is one hour behind Eastern Standard Time (EST) and six hours behind Greenwich Mean Time (GMT). Daylight saving time begins on the first Sunday in April, when clocks are set ahead one hour. It ends on the last Sunday in October, when clocks are set back one hour.

PHONE NUMBERS AND PREFIXES

MOST US phone numbers have seven digits. Some emergency and public-service numbers have only three. US prefixes (area codes) are always three digits.

Chicago and its environs use five prefixes: 312 for the Downtown Core, 773 for the city surrounding downtown, 847 for the north and northwestern suburbs, 708 for the near western and southern suburbs, and 630 for the far western suburbs.

PUBLIC PAY PHONES

CHICAGO'S PAY PHONES are found throughout the city, particularly in restaurants, gas stations, and department stores. All are coin operated, though you can use a calling-card number to charge calls to your account. Some also accept credit cards.

Most pay phones are operated by Ameritech. Some may belong to a company other than Ameritech, though the phones often look similar. Phone companies set their own rates, so prices vary. Use only public phones that have details of the charges posted.

PAY PHONE CHARGES

CALLING A NUMBER with the same prefix as the one from which you are calling is considered a local call. The minimum charge for a local

call made from a pay phone is 35 cents and will buy from three to five minutes. When it is time to insert more money, a recording will interrupt to tell you how much to deposit.

When calling within the same area code, simply dial the phone number. When calling another area code, first dial 1 and the prefix.

Phone books are now rare at pay phones. Dial 411 to connect to national directory assistance. The minimum charge is 35 cents.

Rates for long-distance calls vary, depending on the time

of day, the distance called, and the long-distance carrier. Be sure to have plenty of coins or a calling card before placing the call from a pay phone. If billing the call to a calling-card number, follow the instructions on the card or those on the phone. Dialing instructions are in the white pages of the phone directory.

Long-distance calls are less expensive when dialed without the help of an operator. Savings on calls within the US are available during the night and weekends. Discounts for calls to locations outside the US vary; ask the international operator for details. A list of country codes is in the Yellow Pages of the phone directory.

USING A COIN-OPERATED PHONE

1 Lift the receiver and listen for the tone.

3 Press the number.

Coins
Make sure you have the correct coins available before you dial and a sufficient quantity of them.

25 cents

5 cents   **10 cents**

2 Insert the required coin or coins. The coin drops as soon as you insert it.

4 If you do not want to complete your call or the call does not connect, press the coin-release lever and take the coins from the coin return located at the bottom left-hand corner of the phone.

5 If the call is answered and you talk longer than the allotted time, a recorded message will interrupt and tell you how much more money to deposit. Pay phones do not give change but will return unused coins to the coin return.

CELL PHONES

IT IS POSSIBLE to rent a cell phone in Chicago. **International Sound** offers free downtown delivery. AT&T, Nextel, and Sprint are the largest mobile service providers. Chicago's cell phone network is not GSM-compatible. Check with your carrier before leaving home as to whether you will be able to tune your own phone to local Chicago networks.

TV AND RADIO

FIVE MAJOR TV networks are broadcast in Chicago: CBS on channel 2, NBC on channel 5, ABC on channel 7, WGN on channel 9, and FOX on channel 32.

AM radio stations include WBBM news (780Hz) and WGN talk/sports (720Hz). FM radio stations include WBEZ news and jazz (91.5M).

See pages 168–9 for details on Chicago newspapers.

USEFUL DIALING CODES

- Long-distance direct-dial call outside your local area code, but within the US and Canada: dial **1**.
- International direct-dial call: dial **011**, followed by country code (Australia: 61; New Zealand: 64; UK: 44; Ireland: 353), then the city or area code, then the local telephone number.
- International call via the operator: dial **01**, followed by the country code, then the city code (minus the first 0), then the local telephone number.
- International directory inquiries: dial **00**.
- International operator assistance: dial **01**.
- An **800**, **888**, or **877** prefix indicates that the call is toll-free. Dial **1** before the prefix.
- Directory assistance for toll-free numbers: dial **1-800-555-1212**.
- Local operator assistance: dial **0**.
- Local directory inquiries: dial **411**.

Entrance to Oak Park's post office

POSTAL SERVICES

APART FROM post offices, letters can be mailed at most hotel concierge desks (which usually also sell stamps); at letter slots in the lobbies of office buildings; at air, rail, and bus terminals; and at a street mailbox, though these can be few and far between. Collection times are printed on the inside of the pull-down door of each mailbox, which are always painted blue, or red, white, and blue. Stamps can be bought at the **Chicago Main Post Office** or branch offices located throughout the city.

All letters are delivered on first-class service. The delivery time can sometimes be as long as five business days.

The US Postal Service offers two special delivery services. **Priority Mail** guarantees the delivery in two to three business days; **Express Mail** guarantees delivery on the next business day. If using either Express Mail or Priority Mail, first weigh your letters at a post office to determine the postage required.

Two other companies offer mail services. **FedEx** offers a variety of overnight mail services. **UPS** delivers parcels and packages. FedEx and UPS services are usually available through mailing businesses such as **Mail Boxes Etc**.

Letters and parcels will be held for 30 days for collection at the Main Post Office. Address mail with: Name, General Delivery, Chicago Main Post Office, 433 West Harrison Street, Chicago, IL 60607. You will need to show photo ID to collect mail.

E-MAIL AND FAXES

VISITORS TO CHICAGO can use e-mail and the Internet, as well as fax machines, in the larger hotels and those with business facilities, or at one of the Internet cafés now beginning to dot the Loop and North Side. However, these businesses tend to close down as quickly as they open, so it is best to ask your hotel concierge or at a visitor center about current businesses. One popular Internet café in Chicago is **Screenz**, part of a national chain.

Online time at cafés may be charged by the minute (from 8 cents to 20 cents) or by the hour (from $4 to $10).

DIRECTORY

MOBILE PHONE RENTALS

International Sound
311 W Superior St. **Map** 1B4.
☎ (800) 353-2100.

US POSTAL SERVICE

Chicago Main Post Office
433 W Harrison St. **Map** 3 B3.
☎ 654-3895. ⏱ 24 hrs. ● Sun.

Express and Priority Mail
☎ (800) 222-1811.

PRIVATE EXPRESS MAIL

FedEx
☎ (800) 463-3339.

UPS
☎ (800) 742-5877.

INTERNET CAFÉS

Screenz
2717 N Clark St, **Lincoln Park**.
☎ (773) 348-9300.

Mail Boxes Etc., a national mailbox-service business

GETTING TO CHICAGO

CHICAGO IS ONE of the US's most important transportation hubs. All major airlines fly into one of its two airports: O'Hare or Midway. The major carriers often have similar fares, though you can sometimes find savings by flying into Midway. Discount ticket services, travel companies on the Internet, and charter

Star Alliance passenger jet

airlines may also offer very substantial savings. Amtrak trains from across the US and from Canada arrive in Chicago daily, and several interstate highways run through Chicago *(see pp182–3)*, making the city easily accessible by train, car, or bus. Long-distance bus travel is generally both comfortable and convenient.

ARRIVING BY AIR

ASIDE FROM DRIVING into the city, the easiest way to get to Chicago is by air. Flights from the East Coast of the US take about two hours; from the West Coast about four hours.

All major airlines fly into Chicago, among them Air Canada, Continental, British Airways, Lufthansa, American Airlines, and United Airlines.

Chicago is served by two airports. The largest and busiest is O'Hare, located 17 miles (27 km) northwest of the city. Midway Airport is much smaller and located about 8 miles (13 km) southwest of downtown.

AIR FARES

IT PAYS TO SHOP around for fares, especially if you are booking a departure flight less than 14 days in advance. Many major airlines offer discounts for tickets purchased at least 14 days before departure. These tickets usually carry restrictions and penalties for changes to your itinerary; ask before paying.

Investigate smaller carriers, especially if you are making last-minute plans; their fares are often less than half those of the major airlines. You may also find flights into Midway Airport to be less expensive than those into O'Hare.

For inexpensive consolidated tickets (those bought from a travel agent), contact **Travel City** or **Priceline.com** online. An extensive list of consolidators can be ordered from **Intrepid Traveler**.

When booking a flight, bear in mind that "direct" means that the plane may make one or two stops along the way, but you won't need to change planes. "Nonstop" means you fly directly to your destination.

O'HARE AIRPORT (ORD)

CHICAGO'S O'HARE Airport is one of the world's busiest airports, servicing up to 70 million passengers each year. Three terminals are used for domestic flights, one for international flights.

O'Hare has been extensively remodeled in recent years. Today it is clean and spacious. The food at most of its restaurants is good, prices aren't grossly inflated, and the atmosphere is pleasing. There are also many upscale stores and kiosks throughout the airport. A branch of the Chicago Children's Museum *(see p65)* is in Terminal 2.

Rental carts are available for use within the airport. Skycaps (porters) will also transport your luggage to a taxi or shuttle; they should be tipped from 50 cents to $1 per bag.

Terminal 1 is dominated by United Express, United Airlines, and Lufthansa. Terminal 2 serves Continental, Air Canada, American Trans Air, Northwest Airlines, TWA, and US Airways. Terminal 3 serves American, American Eagle, Delta, Reno Air, and Singapore Air. Terminal 5 is for international flights. There is no Terminal 4.

To get between domestic terminals, the international terminal, and the long-term parking lot, take the free Automated Train System (ATS). There is also free shuttle service between parking lot F and the ATS terminal at parking lot E.

O'Hare has several Airport Information counters on the lower level of each domestic terminal, and on the lower and upper levels of the international terminal. The counters are open daily from 8:15am to 8pm. Multilingual specialists are on hand to provide directions and translation assistance.

Teletext phones for the hearing impaired are located next to the airport information booths as well as at phone banks located throughout the airport.

Automatic bank teller machines are located on the upper levels of all terminals. See page 173 for locations of foreign currency exchanges.

AIRPORT	✆ INFORMATION	DISTANCE TO CHICAGO	TAXI FARE (OFF-PEAK HOURS)	CONTINENTAL EXPRESS TO DOWNTOWN	OMEGA SHUTTLE TO SOUTH SIDE
O'Hare	(733) 686-2200	17 miles (27 km)	$25–$30	$17.50	$17
Midway	(733) 838-0600	8 miles (13 km)	$20–$23	$12.50	$12

MIDWAY AIRPORT (MDW)

MIDWAY IS everything O'Hare isn't. It is small, laid out on one level only, and relatively uncongested. It services about 13 million passengers each year. Although it is a bit worn around the edges, this is a small price to pay for the airport's advantages.

Terminals A, B, and C are within the airport's one building. The Airport Information counter is in the lobby by the main entrance.

A $761-million development project, to be completed in 2004, will triple the size of the existing building, expanding the concourse from 28 to 41 gates, and improve road links to and from the airport. New parking facilities and concessions are also planned.

Midway currently has no foreign currency exchange.

GETTING INTO THE CITY

A CONVENIENT, inexpensive way to get into the city from either airport is via CTA train (see p180).

Blue-line trains run directly to and from O'Hare Airport, 24 hours a day. The ride to the downtown Dearborn Street station takes about 45 minutes. Orange-line trains run between Midway Airport and downtown, stopping at all orange-line Loop stations, from early morning to late evening. Allow 35 minutes for the ride. Trains on both lines depart frequently. One-way train fare is about $1.50.

Continental Airport Express operates a shuttle service between each airport and downtown Chicago. Shuttles operate daily, beginning at 6am. Continental also provides service between both airports and McCormick Place Convention Center.

Omega Airport Shuttle operates shuttle service between O'Hare and Midway airports between 7am and 10pm daily. Omega also offers shuttle service to Hyde Park on Chicago's South Side.

It is possible to share a taxi ride from either airport to downtown. Airport curbside dispatchers will help get you a taxi or put you with other

Blue line trains
54/Cermak-Forest Park-O'Hare

Sign for CTA blue-line trains

Concourse of the international terminal at O'Hare Airport

persons going to the same area; it will cost you about $15 for the shared taxi ride.

Information counters of limousine and rental car agencies (see p183) are in the baggage claim areas of both Midway and O'Hare airports.

Driving time from O'Hare to downtown Chicago is about 45 minutes, and 30 minutes from Midway, but allow up to twice this during rush hour (from 6am to 9am; 3pm to 7pm). Taxis are not immune to traffic jams. During rush hour, it is much faster to use public transportation to and from either of the airports.

DIRECTORY

AIRPORTS

Midway Airport
☎ (773) 838-0600.
🔲 www.ci.chi.il.us/
Aviation/Midway

O'Hare International Airport
☎ (773) 686-2200.
🔲 www.ci.chi.il.us/
Aviation/O'Hare

AIRLINE NUMBERS

Air Canada
☎ (800) 776-3000.

American Airlines
☎ (800) 443-7300.

British Airways
☎ (800) 247-9297.

British Midland
☎ (800) 788-0555.

Continental Airlines
☎ (800) 525-0280.

Lufthansa
☎ (800) 645-3880.

United Airlines
☎ (800) 241-6522.

AIR FARES

Intrepid Traveler
☎ (212) 569-1081.
FAX (212) 942-6687.
🔲 www.
intrepidtraveler.com

Priceline.com
🔲 www.priceline.com

Travel City
🔲 www.travelcity.com

AIRPORT SHUTTLES

Continental Airport Express
☎ 454-7800 or
(800) 654-7871.

Omega Airport Shuttle
☎ (773) 483-6634.

AIRPORT HOTELS

At O'Hare Airport
Holiday Inn O'Hare
5440 N River Rd,
Rosemont, IL.
☎ (847) 671-6350 or
(888) 642-7344.

Hyatt Regency O'Hare,
9300 W Bryn Mawr Ave,
Rosemont, IL.
☎ (847) 696-1234 or
(800) 233-1234.

Rosemont Suites Hotel
O'Hare
5500 N River Rd,
Rosemont, IL.
☎ (847) 678-4000 or
(888) 476-7366.

Westin O'Hare
6100 N River Rd,
Rosemont, IL.
☎ (847) 698-6000 or
(800) 228-3000.

At Midway Airport
Holiday Inn
7353 S Cicero Ave,
Bedford Park, IL.
☎ (773) 581-5300 or
(800) 465-4329.

Courtyard Chicago
Midway Airport
6610 S Cicero Ave,
Bedford Park, IL.
☎ (708) 563-0200 or
(800) 321-2211.

ARRIVING BY CAR

IF YOU ARRIVE in Chicago from the south, on I-55 (Stevenson Expressway), follow the freeway to its end, to Lake Shore Drive, then follow Lake Shore Drive north. Shortly you will pass the city center, and have one of the best views of Chicago's skyline. Several exits lead off Lake Shore Drive into downtown or the North Side, including the Wacker Drive exit. Taking Lake Shore Drive is a good way to traverse the city.

Historic Route 66 running from Los Angeles joins I-55 on the outskirts of Chicago.

I-90 East (Northwest Tollway to Kennedy Expressway) running from the north, from O'Hare Airport, will bring you into the city. Take the Ohio Street exit for downtown.

Arriving by car from the west, I-290 East (Eisenhower Expressway) will become Congress Parkway at the southwest edge of Chicago's downtown Loop. From the parkway, drive north for destinations downtown or beyond.

I-90 and I-94 converge in the city. For destinations in the Loop, there are a number of options. The Washington Street or Monroe Street exits will put you on one-way streets that run into the Loop. For destinations just north of the Loop, such as the Magnificent Mile, take the Ohio Street exit east.

The **Illinois Department of Transportation** has a useful website, which details driving directions to Chicago and throughout Illinois, providing information on interstate rest areas, welcome centers, road and weather conditions, as well as how to obtain state highway maps. See pages 182–3 for more details on driving in Illinois.

ARRIVING BY LONG-DISTANCE BUS

THE MAIN TERMINAL in Chicago for **Greyhound Bus Line**, the bus line that services almost all parts of the US, is in the Downtown Core. However, it is not within easy walking distance to hotels in the Loop, so plan on taking a taxi or public transportation to your final destination.

Greyhound also stops near O'Hare Airport at the CTA Cumberland station and on the city's South Side at 95th and Dan Ryan Expressway.

Greyhound buses are clean and modern. Ask when purchasing tickets about any discounts. They are usually offered to children, seniors, students, members of the military, and US veterans. Ask also about any promotional packages that may be available.

Greyhound's Ameripass allows up to 60 consecutive days of unlimited travel anywhere in the continental US. Tickets may be less expensive if you buy them in advance, though walk-up, or unrestricted, fares are also readily available.

Greyhound provides assistance to travelers with disabilities with 48 hours' notice, including priority seating. In some cases, a personal care assistant may travel for free. Call the Greyhound **ADA Assist Line** for details.

Sign for historic Route 66

Amtrak train in train yard near Union Station

ARRIVING BY TRAIN

CHICAGO IS the national rail hub of **Amtrak**, the US's passenger rail line. Fifty trains linking to hundreds of US destinations, as well as those from Canada, arrive at or depart from Chicago's **Union Station** daily. Amtrak also services 35 destinations in Illinois, either through trains or connecting buses.

Its commuter trains have refreshment cars. Long-distance routes have both dining cars and sleeping cars.

Amtrak offers discounts to travelers with disabilities, students, seniors, and children. There are also group and convention rates. Ask too about any promotional discounts or package deals.

Reservations are necessary on many Amtrak routes and advised for all travel during peak periods: the summer months and major holidays.

The 1925 building housing Union Station was renovated in the early 1990s. Ticket agents, a food court, lounge, 10-story waiting area, storage lockers, and Metra commuter train station *(see pp182–3)* are all to be found within the building, which is wheelchair accessible. "Red cap" Amtrak porters are available to help you with your luggage.

Although Union Station is just west of the Loop and close to downtown Chicago, it is not an easy walk to hotels or CTA trains when you are carrying luggage. If arriving in Chicago by train, it is best to plan on taking a taxi to your hotel.

Long-distance Greyhound bus

A typical Chicago taxi cab

GETTING TO McCORMICK PLACE

L OCATED ONE MILE (1.5 km) south of downtown Chicago, McCormick Place Convention Center is the largest exhibition and meeting facility in North America. Even though it is close to the Loop, the walk is not a practical one. A taxi ride from the Loop to McCormick Place will cost about $5. Large conventions often provide shuttle bus service to McCormick Place from major downtown hotels, and sometimes, from the airports.

The Metra Electric line *(see pp182–3)* services the 23rd Street/McCormick Place station. Trains depart from the Randolph Street and Van Buren Street stations.

If you are arriving in Chicago at Union Station, take the No. 1, 7, or 126 east-bound CTA bus to Michigan Avenue. Transfer to either southbound bus No. 3 or 4; both will take you to the 23rd Street bus stop outside the convention center.

If driving to McCormick Place from O'Hare Airport, take I-90 (Northwest Tollway) east to I-94 (Kennedy/Dan Ryan Expressway), exiting to I-55 north (Stevenson Expressway). Follow the signs to Lake Shore Drive South (31st Street exit) and to McCormick Place.

From Midway Airport, take Cicero Avenue north to the I-55 (Stevenson Expressway), then continue north to Lake Shore Drive South, following the signs to McCormick Place.

The convention center can be reached via public transportation from O'Hare and Midway airports. However, you may find it more convenient to take a taxi or, if available, a shuttle bus, as there is no direct transit route: you will need to transfer to a CTA bus once downtown.

If using public transportation from O'Hare Airport, take the blue-line CTA train *(see p177)* downtown, transferring to the brown, green, orange, or purple line to reach Adams station. Then take the southbound CTA bus No. 3 or 4 from Michigan Avenue to 23rd Street.

From Midway Airport, take the orange-line CTA train *(see p177)* to Roosevelt Street station, then southbound CTA bus No. 3 or 4 to 23rd Street.

The **Chicago Convention and Tourism Bureau** provides information on meeting services, convention planning, and accommodations. Visit its website to view the online convention calendar.

Trade show in Hall B, North Building, McCormick Place

Getting Around Chicago

No parking from 11pm to 6am

Aʟᴛʜᴏᴜɢʜ ᴄʜɪᴄᴀɢᴏ is a sprawling Midwestern metropolis, many of the city's sights and main cultural centers are located downtown, making the city a walker's dream. The city's public transportation is inexpensive and efficient. The train system, known as the "L" for "elevated," is the easiest way to get around. Buses crisscross the city, but the system is complicated and best left to regular commuters. Taxis are affordable, convenient, and readily available.

PLANNING YOUR JOURNEY

Pᴜʙʟɪᴄ ᴛʀᴀɴsɪᴛ in Chicago is extremely busy during the rush hours, which are weekdays from 6am to 9am and 3pm to 7pm. You may wish to avoid it at these peak times. Ask your hotel concierge and check a calendar of events to avoid getting caught in the middle of a particular celebration, of which there are many (see pp30–33).

STREET LAYOUT AND NUMBERING

Cʜɪᴄᴀɢᴏ sᴛʀᴇᴇᴛs are laid out on a grid system. Most streets run north and south or east and west, though some run on the diagonal.

The zero point in the city is at Madison and State Streets, in the Loop. Street numbers ascend by 50 or 100 numbers in each block as they radiate out from Madison and State. Most streets in the Loop are one-way streets.

Typical pedestrian and vehicular traffic on busy State Street

TRAFFIC SIGNS

Aʟʟ ᴛʀᴀғғɪᴄ sɪɢɴs, including those denoting speed limits, are black and white. Informational signs, such as those indicating highway exits, are green and white. Most intersections are also marked with green-and-white signs bearing the name of the streets. These signs are posted high on utility poles.

"Caution" and "Yield" signs are yellow and black. White-and-brown signs indicate the major city sights and landmarks.

WALKING

Tʜᴇ ʙᴇsᴛ ᴡᴀʏ to explore downtown Chicago is on foot. Many of the major sights and shopping areas are only a short walk from each other. Streets are relatively flat, so you will not have to tackle hills during your outings.

Traffic lights signal drivers to stop (red), go (green), and proceed with caution (yellow). For pedestrians, electronic "Walk" signs show an illuminated human figure. A red hand indicates that pedestrians should not cross the street. Never rely solely on the traffic lights; look both ways before crossing the street, and watch for cars making right turns or racing through yellow lights.

In the Loop, an extensive system of pubic underground pedestrian walkways, or pedways, links train stations with major buildings.

Walkway sign

Cyclist taking advantage of a quiet spell on Chicago's lakefront path

BICYCLING

Cʜɪᴄᴀɢᴏ ɪs ɴᴏᴛ a bike-friendly city: traffic can be heavy and snarled. Very few dedicated bike paths exist, so cyclists are forced to share the streets with drivers. It is advisable to wear a safety helmet when cycling.

The lakefront, however, offers miles of scenic path for recreational riding. **Bike Chicago** rents bicycles and in-line skates; the **Bike Stop** also rents bicycles.

Informal rules-of-the-road exist on the path, but it is still often difficult for walkers, cyclists, and in-line skaters to coexist on it. The best time to take advantage of the lakefront path is during business hours, when traffic on it is quieter.

TAXIS

Mᴏsᴛ ᴄʜɪᴄᴀɢᴏ taxi drivers are good drivers. But, as in any city, there are exceptions. For a serious complaint, note the name of the taxi company and the car number (on the side of the taxi) and call **Consumer Services**.

You likely will be able to flag a vacant taxi on a busy street, or find one waiting outside a hotel. If the taxi's roof light is lit, it is available. To be picked up at a specific time, phone to reserve at least one hour in advance.

Taxis charge a base fare of about $1.60, plus 50 cents for each additional passenger. A $1 surcharge is added to all airport trips. Fare information is posted inside each taxi.

DRIVING

VEHICLES ARE DRIVEN on the right-hand side of the road in the US, except on one-way streets. The Illinois speed limit is 35 mph (56 km/h) on city and residential roads, 55 mph (88 km/h) on metro highways. You must wear a seatbelt.

A right turn on a red light is permitted unless a sign prohibits it. Left turns are not allowed at some intersections during peak times, or are allowed only when the green arrow signal is illuminated.

See pages 182–3 for details on interstates and renting a car.

PARKING

STREET PARKING in Chicago falls into three categories: free, metered, and restricted. Free street parking is scarce. Metered street parking is most readily available. The parking meters usually take quarters only. Depending on the area, 25 cents will buy from five minutes to one hour of parking time. The vehicle may be ticketed once the time runs out. Parking is free in some metered areas after 9pm and on Sundays.

Residential areas often have permit-only parking at night; restrictions are noted on signs. Parking tickets are expensive and tickets for a rental car will follow you home. Never park in front of a fire hydrant or driveway; your car will likely be towed.

Parking meter for street parking

The city operates a few parking lots that have low rates. Commercial lots abound; the closer the lot is to downtown, the more expensive. Some businesses offer customers validated parking (discounted or free parking if you have your ticket stamped in the store).

PENALTIES

IF YOUR CAR is towed off a downtown city street, call **City Services** to locate it. If it is towed from a privately managed parking lot, call the telephone number on the sign posted nearby.

Expect to pay at least $100 to retrieve your car. If it is a rental car, be prepared to show your rental contract.

Parking tickets and minor traffic violations may be paid by money order or credit card. For moving violations, your ticket will have information about where and how to pay or contest the ticket.

TRAVELING BY PUBLIC TRAINS AND BUSES

THE **Chicago Transit Authority** (CTA) operates an extensive system of trains and buses. They are both frequent and convenient. The train system is called the "L," for "elevated" – even when the lines run underground. There are six train lines: blue, brown, red, green, orange, and purple. Free CTA system maps *(see inside back cover)* are available at the stations. Many CTA train stations are wheelchair accessible. Buses stop about every two blocks at posted CTA signs that indicate the number and name of the route, but not the direction. Some buses do not travel the entire route; check the destination sign on the bus. To board a bus, hail the driver and remain on the curb until the bus has come to a stop.

Adult fare is about $1.50; child fare about 75 cents. Transferring between routes costs 30 cents. Change is not provided on CTA buses.

Machines in the stations will dispense cards that can be used on both CTA trains and buses. Passes for unlimited travel are available at the CTA website, Visitor Information Centers, and other locations.

Trolleys and shuttle buses provide free service to several

CTA transit card

A Chicago Transit Authority elevated train in the Loop

city sights. Visit the **Department of Transportation** website or a Visitor Center *(see pp168–9)* for details.

Traveling Outside Chicago

TRAVELING OUTSIDE CHICAGO is most convenient by car, though there is also an inexpensive and extensive public transportation system to the many suburbs and beyond. Rush hours are the only real obstacle to smooth traveling. The so-called reverse commute has vanished. At peak times during the day, city dwellers are going to work at industry headquarters located in the suburbs; at the same time, suburbanites are heading into the city to office jobs. Rush hour can start as early as 5:30am and last until 9am. The afternoon rush begins as early as 3pm and often lasts until past 7pm.

METRA

A NETWORK of 12 commuter train lines that begin in the city center and stretch out like tentacles to the suburbs is operated by **Metra**. The 495-mile (795-km) system has 230 stations in the Illinois counties of Cook, Du Page, Lake, Will, McHenry, and Kane. It also services some cities in Indiana and Wisconsin. Trains run on a published schedule, frequently during rush hour and every one to three hours at other times. The trains are more comfortable than CTA trains (see p181). They do not have baggage check.

On weekends and holidays, youngsters ages 12 to 17 ride for half fare. Kids under 12 may ride free when accompanied by a fare-paying adult. Weekend passes are also available for unlimited travel on all Metra lines.

Metra trains depart from five stations surrounding the Loop: Union Station, Ogilvie Transportation Center, Randolph Street Station, Van Buren Street Station, and LaSalle Street Station.

Union Station, at Adams and Canal streets, is the main Metra station. The Electric Main Line, which runs to McCormick Place, stops at three stations along Michigan Avenue: at Randolph Road and at Van Buren and Roosevelt Streets. The Union Pacific North Line runs to Highland Park, stopping just outside the Ravinia Festival gate.

Metra has wheelchair-accessible cars; phone for details or visit the **Metra Passenger Services** center.

PACE

THE SUBURBAN BUS system, **Pace**, is a division of the Regional Transportation Authority (RTA), which also oversees Metra and the CTA. Pace provides fixed bus routes, Dial-a-Ride services for travelers with disabilities, vanpools, and special-event buses throughout Chicago's six-county suburban region. Pace buses also provide good connections between Metra stations and shopping malls.

Much of the Pace system is wheelchair accessible; phone for details, or visit the **RTA Customer Service Center** for information, along with free maps and timetables.

INTERSTATES

THE SEVERAL highways running through and around Chicago are of two types: freeways and tollways. Freeways are tollfree public highways. The charge for driving on a state tollway ranges from 15 cents to $2, which will be collected at a tollbooth. Generally, lanes at the tollbooths are designated as exact change (automatic), needing change (manual), and I-Pass (an electronic system that allows specially equipped cars to drive through, automatically deducting the toll from the vehicle's account). Getting on or off a tollway usually also involves a fee, and because those booths are unattended, exact change is necessary.

Interstates are divided multilane highways and are the main routes between cities. Most swell to six or more lanes as they near large cities. Interstate numbers are posted on red, white, and blue shield-shaped signs.

Main interstate routes have two-digit numbers, with those with even numbers generally running east-west and those with odd numbers generally running north-south. There are exceptions, however. While I-94 runs east-west across the US, it runs north-south in Illinois.

Interstates with three digits are loops (if the first digit is 2, 4, 6, or 8) or spurs (first digit

CTA bus No. 56, serving
Chicago's northeastern suburbs

Stairs to main concourse at Chicago's historic Union Station

View from scenic US Route 20, running northwest through Illinois

of 1, 3, 5, 7, or 9) of the main interstate route.

I-55 (Stevenson Expressway) runs from US-41 (Lake Shore Drive) in Chicago to St. Louis, then to New Orleans via Memphis.

I-90 runs from Boston to Seattle, and in Illinois from the Indiana line on the Chicago Skyway through Chicago on the Dan Ryan and Kennedy Expressways, and to Rockford and the WI line on the Northwest Tollway. The Chicago Skyway, however is no longer designated as I-90, but rather, as TO I-90.

I-190 is the spur from I-90 to O'Hare Airport.

I-94 runs from Montana to Michigan. In Illinois, it is called Edens Expressway and merges with I-90, the main highway through Chicago.

NAMED HIGHWAYS

M ANY ILLINOIS highways are commonly referred to by name rather than by number. The stretch of I-90/94 that runs from the city center south to 95th Street is called the Dan Ryan Expressway.

The stretch that runs from the city center northwest to O'Hare Airport is known as the Kennedy Expressway.

I-290 is also known as the Eisenhower Expressway, and as Congress Parkway within the city center. I-55 is called the Stevenson Expressway.

SPEED LIMITS AND FINES

T HE SPEED LIMIT for cars on Illinois' open highways is 65 mph (105 km/h) and 55 mph (88 km/h) on metro highways. Speeding tickets

carry heavy fines. A minimum speed regulation in Illinois means you also could be ticketed for driving so slowly that you impede traffic.

Speed limit (in mph) | Rest area, indicated off an interstate

Roadside tests and fines for drinking and driving are increasingly common.

RENTAL CARS

T O RENT A CAR, you must be at least 25 years old, with a valid driver's license (for foreign visitors, an international driver's license) and a major credit card in your name.

Before leaving home, check your insurance policy to see if you are covered in a rental car. If not, you should buy damage and liability insurance when renting the car.

Most agencies offer a range of vehicles, from "economy" models to convertibles. All rental cars are automatic and have power steering.

Refill the car with gasoline before returning it or you will pay a service charge.

Two car rental agencies in Chicago

STREET FINDER

MAP REFERENCES given in this guide for sights, hotels, restaurants, shops, and entertainment venues refer to the Street Finder maps on the following pages (*see* How the Map References Work *below*). A complete index of the street names and places of interest marked on the maps can also be found on the pages that follow. The map opposite shows the area of Chicago the eight *Street Finder* maps cover. This includes the sightseeing areas (which are color-coded) as well as the whole of central Chicago. The symbols used to represent sights and useful information on the *Street Finder* maps are listed below in the key.

How the Map References Work

The first figure tells you which *Street Finder* map to turn to.

Sears Tower ❶

233 S Wacker Dr. **Map** 3 B2
█ 875-9696. Ⓜ *Quincy.*
◯ Mar–Sep: 9am–11pm daily;
Oct–Feb: 9am–10pm daily; last
adm 30 min before closing.

The letter and number are a grid reference. You will find the letters at the top and bottom of the map and the numbers at the sides.

The map continues on map 5 of the *Street Finder.*

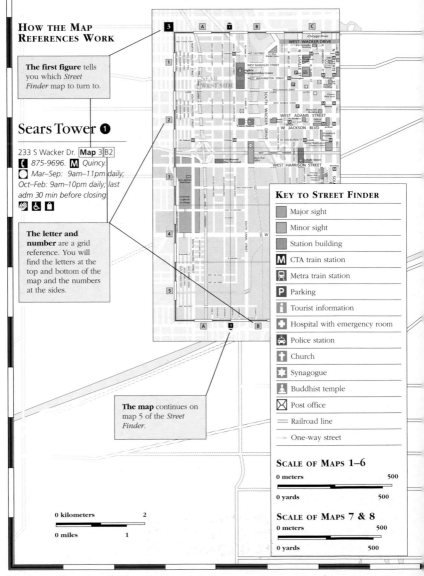

Key to Street Finder

■	Major sight
■	Minor sight
■	Station building
Ⓜ	CTA train station
🚆	Metra train station
Ⓟ	Parking
ⓘ	Tourist information
✚	Hospital with emergency room
🚓	Police station
✝	Church
✡	Synagogue
卍	Buddhist temple
⊠	Post office
═	Railroad line
→	One-way street

Scale of Maps 1–6

0 meters	500
0 yards	500

Scale of Maps 7 & 8

0 meters	500
0 yards	500

0 kilometers	2
0 miles	1

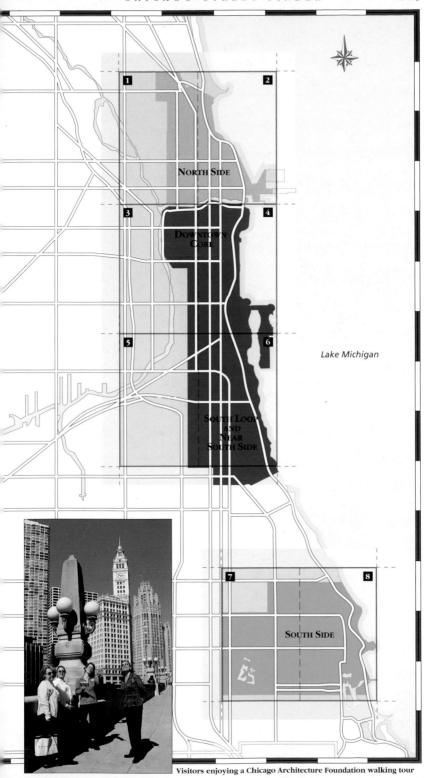

NORTH SIDE

DOWNTOWN CORE

Lake Michigan

SOUTH LOOP AND NEAR SOUTH SIDE

SOUTH SIDE

Visitors enjoying a Chicago Architecture Foundation walking tour

Street Finder Index

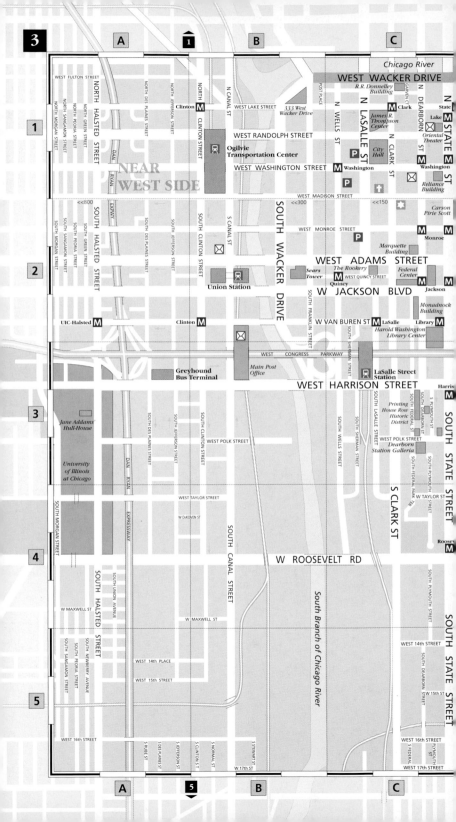

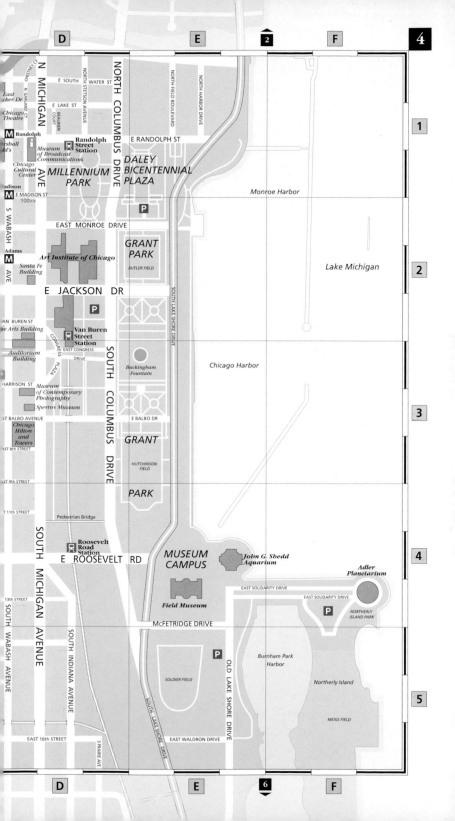

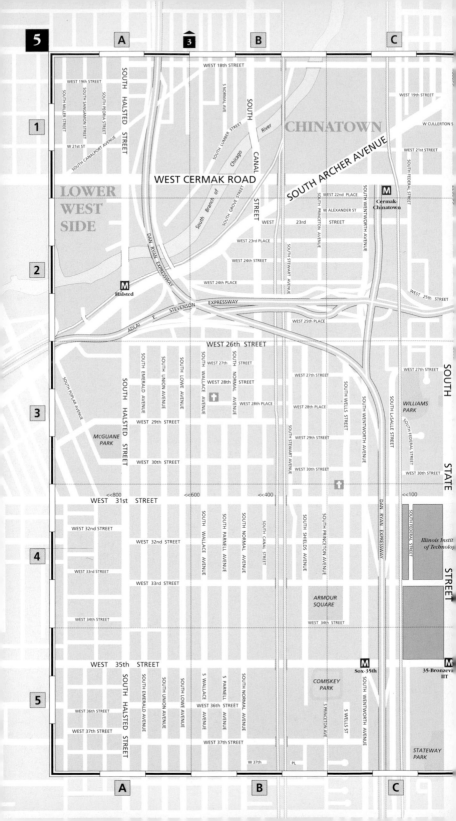

7

A B C

1

EAST 47th STREET
EAST 47th STREET
MARTIN
LUTHER
KING
JR.
DRIVE
SOUTH VINCENNES AVENUE
SOUTH FORRESTVILLE AVENUE
SOUTH ST. LAWRENCE AVENUE
SOUTH CHAMPLAIN AVENUE
SOUTH LANGLEY AVENUE
SOUTH EVANS AVENUE
SOUTH COTTAGE GROVE AVENUE
E 47th PL
SOUTH DREXEL BOULEVARD
KENWOOD
EAST 48th STREET
EAST 48th STREET
4800>>
EAST 49th STREET
EAST 49th STREET
SOUTH ELLIS AVENUE
SOUTH GREENWOOD AVENUE
SOUTH WOODLAWN AVENUE
S WASHINGTON
PARK COURT
EAST 50th STREET
EAST 50th STREET
PARK NO.278
EAST 50th PLACE
800>>
1200>>
400>>
EAST 51st STREET
EAST HYDE PARK BOULEVARD

2

BOWEN DR
P
EAST 52nd STREET
S BERKELEY AVE
5200>>
ELLSWORTH DRIVE
PAYNE DRIVE
EAST 53rd STREET
SOUTH INGLESIDE AVENUE
SOUTH DREXEL
SOUTH ELLIS AVENUE
SOUTH GREENWOOD AVENUE
SOUTH UNIVERSITY AVENUE
EAST 54th STREET

3

WASHINGTON
PARK
EAST 54th STREET
BLVD
WILLOW PLAYLOT PARK
PARK NO.291
EAST 54th STREET
SOUTH WOODLAWN AVENUE
EAST 55th STREET
SOUTH COTTAGE GROVE AVENUE
P
MORGAN DRIVE
RAINEY DRIVE
P
Smart Museum of Art
EAST 56th STREET
DuSable Museum of
African American History
SOUTH MARYLAND AVENUE
SOUTH DREXEL BOULEVARD
SOUTH ELLIS AVENUE
SOUTH UNIVERSITY AVENUE
5600>>

4

NESSET DRIVE
P
Lagoon
PAYNE DRIVE
EAST 57th STREET
University of
Chicago
EAST 58th STREET
EAST 58th STR
Oriental
Institute Museum
P
Rockefeller
Memorial Chapel
EAST 59th STREET
NORTH PLAISANCE
Midway Plaisance
BEST DRIVE
SOUTH PLAISANCE
EAST 60th STREET
EAST 60th STREET

5

EAST 60th STREET
SOUTH VERNON AVENUE
SOUTH EBERHART AVENUE
SOUTH RHODES AVENUE
SOUTH ST. LAWRENCE AVENUE
SOUTH CHAMPLAIN AVENUE
SOUTH LANGLEY AVENUE
SOUTH EVANS AVENUE
SOUTH COTTAGE GROVE AVENUE
SOUTH INGLESIDE AVENUE
SOUTH ELLIS AVENUE
SOUTH UNIVERSITY AVENUE
6000>>
EAST 61st STREET
STREET
EAST 61st STREET

A B C

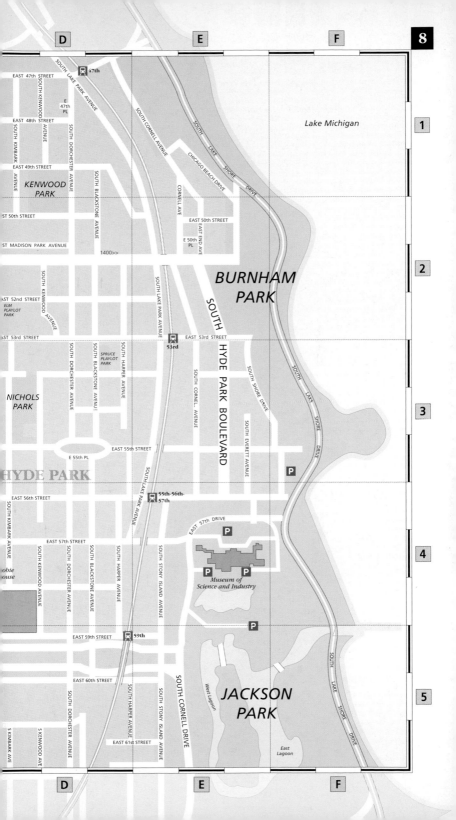

General Index

Acknowledgments

Dorling Kindersley and International Book Productions would like to thank the following people whose contributions and assistance have made the book possible:

AT DORLING KINDERSLEY:
Managing Art Editor: Jane Ewart
Managing Editor: Helen Townsend
Senior Publishing Manager: Louise Lang
Production Controllers: Marie Ingledew, Michelle Thomas
Cartographers: Casper Morris, Dave Pugh

MAIN CONTRIBUTORS
LORRAINE JOHNSON is a freelance writer living in Toronto who has a lifelong fascination with Chicago. She is the author of six books and contributes articles and book reviews regularly to magazines and newspapers.

JOHN RYAN lives in Chicago. A professional musician and former chef, he manages the Elgin Symphony Orchestra in addition to writing regular food columns for America Online.

ADDITIONAL CONTRIBUTOR
Penney Kome

SPECIAL RESEARCH
Dana Joy Altman
Deanna Cates

PROOFREADER
Maraya Raduha

INDEXER
Barbara Sale Schon

CARTOGRAPHY
Visutronx, Ajax, Ontario, Canada

SPECIAL ASSISTANCE
Particular thanks go to Vanetta Anderson, Chicago Office of Tourism
Norah Zboril, City of Chicago, Mayor's Office, Special Events
Daniel J. Curtin, City of Chicago, Department of Aviation
Jeff Stern, Chicago Transit Authority
Diana Holic and Dawn Kappel, Adler Planetarium and Astronomy Museum
Brigid Murphy, Newberry Library
Mily Anzo, Museum of Science and Industry
Patricia Kremer, Field Museum
Corey Tovian and Gwen Biassi, John G. Shedd Aquarium
Rosemary Haack, City of Lake Forest
Janice Klein, Mitchell Museum of the American Indian
Ms. Chase Ruppert, McCormick Place Convention Center
Stephen Majsak, Chicago Architectural Foundation
Lois Berger, Chicago Public Library, Harold Washington Library Center
Jennifer Swanson, Lincoln Park Zoo
Adam Davies, Chicago Place
Angela Sweeney, Water Tower Place
Kelly Boggs and Michael Rilley, Chicago Theatre
Sarah Hamilton Hadley, Terra Museum of American Art
Karen Irvine, Museum of Contemporary Photography
Zarine Weil, Robie House
Ken Price, Palmer House Hilton Hotel
Michilla Johnson, Buddy Guy's Legends
Jennifer Kocolowski, Goose Island Beer Co.
Jan Berghoff, Berghoff Restaurant
Janet Femarek and David Caruso, Ed Debevic's Restaurant

PHOTOGRAPHY PERMISSION
Dorling Kindersley and International Book Productions would like to thank everyone for their assistance and kind permission to photograph at their establishments.

PICTURE CREDITS
KEY: t=top; tl=top left; tlc=top left center; tc=top center; trc=top right center; tr=top right; cla=center left above; ca=center above; cra=center right above; cl=center left; c=center; cr=center right; clb=center left below; cb=center below; crb=center right below; bl=bottom left; b=bottom; br=bottom right; bcl=bottom center left; bc=bottom center; bcr=bottom center right.

Every effort has been made to trace the copyright holders. Dorling Kindersley apologizes for any unintentional omissions and would be pleased, in such cases, to add an acknowledgment in future editions.

The Publishers are grateful to the following museums, companies, and picture libraries for permission to reproduce their photographs:

© ADLER PLANETARIUM AND ASTRONOMY MUSEUM: 19bl, 92tr, 93tc.

THE ART INSTITUTE OF CHICAGO: All rights reserved – Mary Cassatt, American, 1844–1926, *The Child's Bath*, oil on canvas, 1893, 39 1/2 x 26 inches, Robert A. Waller Fund, 1910.2 – 47tl; Marc Chagall, French, born Russia, 1887–1985, *American Windows*, glass, 1977, Gift of the City of Chicago and the Auxiliary Board of The Art Institute of Chicago commemorating the American Bicentennial in memory of Mayor Richard J. Daley, 1977.938, © 2000 – 46cl; Rembrandt Harmenszoon van Rijn, Dutch, 1606–1669, *Old Man with a Gold Chain*, oil on panel, c.1631, 83.1 x 75.7 cm, Mr. and Mrs. W.W. Kimball Collection, 1922.4467 – 47bc.

BUDDY GUY'S LEGENDS: 161bl.

THE CANADIAN PRESS/ASSOCIATED PRESS AP: 29ca; AP/Wide World Photos Inc. Charles Bennett 170bl.

CHICAGO ARCHITECTURE FOUNDATION: Bill Richert 168br, 185bl.

CHICAGO HISTORICAL SOCIETY: 74bl; ICHi-2212 – 8–9; ICHi-08732 – 13bl; ICHi-30084 – 15cb; ICHi-31412 – 17tl; ICHi-31413 – 29tr; ICHi-31411 – 71br; ICHi-09440 – 72cla; ICHi-31414 – 72c; ICHi-14063 Currier & Ives 14crb; ICHi-05630 Inger & Bodtker 167 (inset); ICHi-10889 Edward Kemeys 13c; ICHi-05769 Louis Kurz 9 (inset), 35 (inset); ICHi-05836 Leslie's Weekly 15bc; ICHi-06291 Scribner's Magazine 131 (inset); ICHi-13946 US Treasury Department 121 (inset); ICHi-27363 Paris Raoul Varin 13bc.

CHICAGO PUBLIC LIBRARY, HAROLD WASHINGTON LIBRARY CENTER: 82tl; *Events in the Life of Harold Washington* ceramic tile mosaic by Jacob Lawrence 22br; *Sleeping Beauty* sculpture by Alison Saar 80tr.

CHICAGO TRANSIT AUTHORITY: 182c.

CITY OF CHICAGO, DEPARTMENT OF AVIATION: 16cb, 177tr.

CITY OF CHICAGO, OFFICE OF TOURISM: © Willy Schmidt 33bl, 60bc; © Peter J. Schultz 19tr, 31bt, 180bl; Chicago Air and Water Show 31cr.

COLUMBUS ASSOCIATION FOR THE PERFORMING ARTS: 54b.

CORBIS: © Corbis 16cra, 109cra; © Sandy Felsenthal 26cl, 30cl; © Mitchell Gerber 28br; © Robert Holmes 48br; © Layne Kennedy 46tr, 48cl; © Francis G. Mayer, *The Basket of Apples* by Paul Cézanne 49tr, *The Gourmet* by Pablo Picasso 49cl, *On the Seine at Bennecourt* by Claude Monet 49br; © Derick A. Thomas, Dat's Jazz 28tr; © AFP/Corbis 17crb, 29clb; © Bettmann/Corbis 15tl, 27cla, 28cl, 29bc, *A Sunday on La Grande Jatte* by Georges Seurat 47cr, *American Gothic* by Grant Wood 47br, 77crb, 77br; © Hulton-Deutsch Collection/Corbis 16tl; © UPI/Corbis-Bettmann 16bc.

THE DAVID AND ALFRED SMART MUSEUM OF ART, THE UNIVERSITY OF CHICAGO: reproduced with permission 101tc; University Transfer – Dining Table and Six Side Chairs, Frank Lloyd Wright 102cr.

FIELD MUSEUM: Courtesy of the Field Museum, 86cl, 89bl; John Weinstein © 1998 – 21ca, © 1994 – 87ca; George Papadakis © 1998 – 86tr; Ron Testa 87crb.

GOOSE ISLAND BEER COMPANY: © Daniel J. Wigg 143br.

THE GRANGER COLLECTION, NEW YORK: 12.

HENRY MOORE FOUNDATION: *Sundial* 1965–66 (LH 528) on the title page and *Nuclear Energy* sculpture illustrated on pages 4tr and 103tc are reproduced by permission of the Henry Moore Foundation.

INTERNATIONAL MUSEUM OF SURGICAL SCIENCE, CHICAGO: 20clb; *Hope and Help* sculpture by Edouard Chaissing reproduced with permission 75c.

JANE ADDAMS' HULL-HOUSE: Jane Addams' Hull-House Museum, University of Illinois at Chicago 116tl.

JOHN G. SHEDD AQUARIUM: © Edward G. Lines 96tr, 96cl, 96bc, 97tl, 97ca, 97c, 97cb.

KIMPTON GROUP: 132cl, 133tl, 133bc.

LINCOLN PARK ZOO, CHICAGO: © Grant Kessler 19crb; © Todd Rosenberg 113tc.

McCORMICK PLACE CONVENTION CENTER: 179bl.

MILLENNIUM PARK PROJECT: Skidmore, Owings & Merrill LLP 53b.

MITCHELL MUSEUM OF THE AMERICAN INDIAN: 125tl.

MUSEUM OF CONTEMPORARY PHOTOGRAPHY, COLUMBIA COLLEGE CHICAGO: Tom Nowak 81tl, 84tr.

MUSEUM OF SCIENCE AND INDUSTRY: 106tr; © 2000 Dirk Fletcher 21br, 107tl, 108bl, 109tl.

THE NEWBERRY LIBRARY: 67br.

PALMER HOUSE HILTON HOTEL: 5tr, 132br.

SOCIETY FOR REPRODUCTION RIGHTS OF AUTHORS, COMPOSERS AND PUBLISHERS IN CANADA (SODRAC) INC: SODRAC (Montreal) © Estate of Pablo Picasso (Paris)/SODRAC (Montreal) 2000 – 37 (inset); SODRAC (Montreal) © Estate of Joan Miró/ADAGP (Paris)/SODRAC (Montreal) 2000 – 44tr; SODRAC (Montreal) © Estate of Marc Chagall/ADAGP (Paris)/SODRAC (Montreal) 2000 – 44bl.

SPERTUS MUSEUM: *Flame of Hope* by Leonardo Nierman, 1995. Collection of Spertus Museum 81tc.

WATER TOWER PLACE: 155tl.

FRANK LLOYD WRIGHT HOME AND STUDIO FOUNDATION: Courtesy of Henrich Blessing and the Frank Lloyd Wright Home and Studio Foundation, 23br.

WRIGLEY BUILDING: The Wrigley Building and design are registered trademarks of the Wm. Wrigley Jr. Company, used by permission 60br, 62tl.

Jacket: All special photography except; ALLSPORT: © Matthew Stockman front cover left; © CORBIS: front cover cra; © Sandy Felsenthal front cover crb and br, spine top and bottom, back cover br; © EYE UBIQUITOUS: David Forman back cover bl; © DAVID NOBLE: front cover top, back cover tl; © MAJOR LEAGUE BASEBALL PROPERTIES: spine center.

DORLING KINDERSLEY SPECIAL EDITIONS

Dorling Kindersley books can be purchased in bulk quantities at discounted prices for use in promotions or as premiums. We are also able to offer special editions and personalized jackets, corporate imprints, and excerpts from all of our books, tailored specifically to meet your own needs. To find out more, please contact:

(in the United Kingdom) – SPECIAL SALES, DORLING KINDERSLEY LIMITED, 80 STRAND, LONDON WC2R 0RL; (in the United States) – SPECIAL MARKETS, DEPARTMENT, DORLING KINDERSLEY PUBLISHING, INC., 95 MADISON AVENUE, NEW YORK, NY 10016; TEL. 212 213 4800.

EYEWITNESS *TRAVEL GUIDES*

COUNTRY GUIDES

AUSTRALIA • CANADA • FRANCE • GREAT BRITAIN
GREECE: ATHENS & THE MAINLAND • THE GREEK ISLANDS
IRELAND • ITALY • JAPAN • MEXICO
PORTUGAL • SCOTLAND • SINGAPORE
SOUTH AFRICA • SPAIN • THAILAND
GREAT PLACES TO STAY IN EUROPE
TASTE OF SCOTLAND

REGIONAL GUIDES

BARCELONA & CATALONIA • CALIFORNIA
FLORENCE & TUSCANY • FLORIDA • HAWAII
JERUSALEM & THE HOLY LAND • LOIRE VALLEY
MILAN & THE LAKES • NAPLES WITH POMPEII & THE
AMALFI COAST • PROVENCE & THE COTE D'AZUR • SARDINIA
SEVILLE & ANDALUSIA • SICILY • VENICE & THE VENETO

CITY GUIDES

AMSTERDAM • BERLIN • BRUSSELS • BUDAPEST
CRACOW • DELHI, AGRA & JAIPUR • DUBLIN
ISTANBUL • LISBON • LONDON • MADRID
MOSCOW • NEW YORK • PARIS • PRAGUE • ROME
SAN FRANCISCO • STOCKHOLM • ST PETERSBURG
SYDNEY • VIENNA • WARSAW • WASHINGTON, DC

NEW FOR SPRING 2001

BALI & LOMBOK • BOSTON • CHICAGO
CRUISE GUIDE TO EUROPE AND THE MEDITERRANEAN
GERMANY • NEW ENGLAND • NEW ZEALAND

FOR UPDATES TO OUR GUIDES, AND INFORMATION ON
TRAVEL PLANNERS, CITY MAPS, &
DK EYEWITNESS TRAVEL GUIDES
PHRASEBOOKS

VISIT US AT
eyewitnesstravel.dk.com

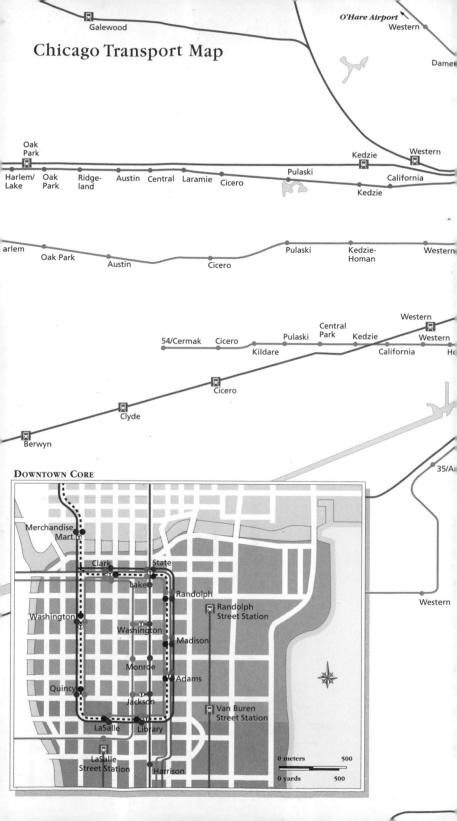

Chicago Transport Map

O'Hare Airport
Western

Damen

Galewood

Oak Park
Kedzie
Western

Harlem/Lake Oak Park Ridgeland Austin Central Laramie Cicero Pulaski California
Kedzie

arlem Oak Park Austin Cicero Pulaski Kedzie-Homan Western

Western

54/Cermak Cicero Kildare Pulaski Central Park Kedzie Western
California H

Western

Cicero

Clyde

Berwyn

35/A

DOWNTOWN CORE

Merchandise Mart

Clark State

Lake

Randolph

Randolph Street Station

Washington

Washington

Madison

Monroe

Adams

Quincy

Jackson

Van Buren Street Station

LaSalle Library

Western

LaSalle Street Station

Harrison

0 meters   500

0 yards   500